Chinese Astrology
2020
Year of the Metal Rat

D1407672

Donna Stellhorn

Published by
ETC Publishing
Carlsbad, California
WWW.ETCPUBLISHING.COM

First Edition, First Publication 2019

ISBN: 978-1-944622-29-9

Cover design by Gary Dunham and Donna Stellhorn

Concepts presented in this book derive from traditional Chinese,
European, and American metaphysical and folk lore. They are not
to be understood as directions, recommendations or prescriptions
of any kind. Nor does the author or publisher make any claim
to do more than provide information and report this lore.

Contents

Introduction 7

Celebrating Chinese New Year 14

Find Your Chinese Zodiac Sign 16

Where Are You in the 12-year cycle? 20

Rat 23

Ox 47

Tiger 70

Rabbit 94

Dragon 118

Snake 142

Horse 165

Sheep/Goat 188

Monkey 213

Rooster 236

Dog 260

Pig/Boar 284

Compatibility Between Signs 308

Chinese Zodiac Signs and Compatibility 311

Rat Compatibility 311

Ox Compatibility 313

Tiger Compatibility 315

Rabbit Compatibility 318

Dragon Compatibility 320

Snake Compatibility 323

Horse Compatibility 325

Sheep/Goat Compatibility 328

Monkey Compatibility 330

Rooster Compatibility 333

Dog Compatibility 335

Pig/Boar Compatibility..337

Eclipses..341

Mercury Retrograde...344

What Is Feng Shui and How to Use Cures....................347

Why Feng Shui Works...352

Our Reticular Activating System.................................353

Flying Star for 2020..355

The Five Elements...361

Using and Clearing Feng Shui Cures..........................368

How to Clear Gemstones and Crystals........................369

How to Identify the Wealth and Love Areas of Your House..........370

Bibliography and Recommended Reading....................372

About Donna Stellhorn...374

Introduction

On January 25, 2020, we enter the Year of the Metal Rat, the first year of the natural Chinese Zodiac 12-year cycle; it's time for a new beginning. We feel moved to discard the excess of the past and let go of everything which no longer serves us. At the same time, we look forward a brighter, more expansive future. There are so many possibilities. Surrounded by open, fertile fields, we are ready to plant the seeds of our tomorrows. We feel optimistic, happy, and excited.

Let us consider the Chinese Zodiac 12-year cycle as if it were a single year of life on a farm, where each month represents a year of the cycle. This Year of the Metal Rat would represent the very beginning of Spring. The sun is warming the frozen lands, buds are appearing on the trees, and small sprouts are coming up in the garden. This is a time when we fling open the windows and doors to let fresh air into the house. We grab our bag of seeds and head out to the fields. There's work ahead, but it's a joyful, magical process of seeing life begin to bloom before our eyes.

Now we are filled with energy, powered by so many possibilities. Each new thing we do and each new person we connect with represents a tiny seed which can grow into a sturdy plant or fruit-bearing tree. The Year of the Metal Rat is a time of high activity. We might feel a bit impatient as we stand over the field to be planted and see nothing but dirt. But the sun feels good on our backs as we get to work implementing the plans we made last year. There is a lot to do and we will get through it one step at a time, seed by seed.

If we look at the 12-year cycle as if it were the lunar cycle, this Metal Rat Year would be the New Moon period, a time when the moon reappears in the sky, at first just a sliver. It's entered the waxing period and the moon will grow. We are reminded that all things can grow and expand.

This year we'll all be busy. The year can be filled with activity, and the determination to create and build whatever you may have been dreaming of or envisioning over the past few years. You may find yourself running in multiple directions.

Rat is the first sign of the Zodiac because it's said the little rat ran quickly ahead of all the other animals of the Chinese Zodiac, arriving at Buddha's feet first. So think of the energy of this year as comprised of a series of short sprints. Take 15 minutes here or an hour there and use the time to plant a few seeds. Don't let time run through your fingers like sand. Instead, be mindful of your goals and break large-sized tasks into bite-sized pieces.

Spiritual Life and Magical Things

Beginnings are a wondrous time. Think of the magic of the seed, sprouting through the dark earth and finding the way to the sunlight. When you start something new, it's likely you don't know what direction it will take. You may not know how to find your way. You'll need to tap into your instincts and reach out to trusted others for guidance.

Even at this busy time, it will be important to stop for a few minutes each day and take time to connect with your higher self and the Universe. This can be done through meditation, prayer, lighting a candle, or taking a walk in nature. Give yourself a few minutes while you silence all the other noise around you and listen to the music of the Universe.

This can be a formal practice, with you sitting on the floor in the lotus position, or it can be an informal one where one day you walk through a park, the next you sit by a window in your bedroom, and the third you light a candle and set it on your fireplace mantle. Formal or informal, you are adding magic to your life. The Universe will open up and pour its bounty on you.

Taking Care of Yourself

In busy Metal Rat years, we can forget to take care of our physical body. During this high energy year, we feel like both working and playing hard. We may find ourselves eating healthily during the week, only to overindulge in junk food and alcohol on the weekends.

On the farm, people know the importance of taking care of the tools, the tractors, and the animals that work side by side with them. In our lives this year, we need to remind ourselves that our body is our tool, and it needs our care. Healthy eating and short bursts of intense exercise are ideal during the Metal Rat Year.

In Metal Rat Years, our health can be negatively affected by giving free rein to worry. When we focus on things we can't control or visualize a dystopian future, the pictures we create in our minds impact our health and sense of well-being. This can become a self-fulfilling prophecy as worry reduces our ability to fight illness and recover quickly. It's good to take steps to reduce anxiety by staying in the present moment and focusing on gratitude. Decide what you can do in the next hour to help you reach your goals, or to connect with friends and family. Planting seeds now leads to the abundance you seek to manifest in the future.

Another highlight of the Metal Rat Year is the urge to focus. The number of things vying for our eyeballs and our focused attention is increasing. A lack of focus now can lead to a feeling of overall dissatisfaction. The energy of the year affects us all, and Metal Rat energy can be restless and dissatisfied. One thing that seems to help is to create a peaceful home environment, free of clutter and disharmony. Also, increase your ability to focus by meditating, getting more sleep, and reducing screen time.

Business Life

Business opportunities often provide the greatest benefit during a Metal Rat Year. Even when the economy is not booming in your area, there are more opportunities and ways to make money this year than at any period of time we have recently experienced. Some options may seem daunting, as so many connections now are made through technology. You may feel you lack sufficient knowledge or the right connections to move forward.

However, this is a Metal Rat Year. Think like the little mouse— be focused and persistent. You don't have to understand everything. You only need to know how to make a meaningful connection with your potential customer, audience, or client (or even employer). You can make a lot of headway just spending 30 minutes a day learning and improving your reach if you will concentrate on the heart of what you're trying to do.

Types of Businesses

Industries likely to do well during a Metal Year are in commerce and sales, transportation and trucking, car sales, machinery and welding, tool sales, jewelry, and government. Large, traditional companies may struggle this year while new companies and new ways of doing things emerge. Small, nimble startups can eat away at the profits of larger, slower firms. A group of mice is called a "mischief," which describes how new ideas this year will disrupt old ways of doing business.

Metal Years also support businesses connected with organizing resources. This would be banking and e-commerce, any business which can facilitate your ability to move or take action more quickly, as well as businesses that help you achieve greater efficiency with timing or time management or processing information more quickly.

Student Life

The educational focus this year will be on how to acquire the greatest amount of practical knowledge quickly. Accelerated programs and online courses will be popular. People will flock to classes they can take and do from anywhere. Additionally, there will be increased interest in brain-enhancing drugs. We'll want to think faster and process information more effectively.

Metal Rat years have us watching our pocketbooks. Whether it's wise to rack up massive debt going to college or getting a college degree will become even more of a question than ever. There will be much political discussion on the topic of student debt. While a full solution may not be found this year, there will be those who propose changes in the process, making it easier to make changes in future years.

Love Life

Metal Rat years can be highly emotional and this makes for intense romantic possibilities. In general, all of us will crave feelings of rapport; we'll seek to meet others and develop deep, meaningful connections. But during a Metal Rat Year, many of us will feel the pull, the impulse to focus on career and finance, so the hard work and time needed for finding love in our busy world can get left behind. We want security this year, reassurances our hearts won't be stomped into a gooey pulp, and in Metal Rat Years we can trust our intuition. This means we need to take a little time now and again to look up from our busy schedule to make contact with someone who wants to connect with us.

As this is the beginning of the 12-year cycle, we may feel a mix of both positive and negative feelings as we mix the present up with the past. Let go of the past and move bravely forward. Focus on how to help others feel loved and accepted. You'll be showered with love and gratitude in return.

If you're looking for love, you are sure to have a lot of fun this year. Rat energy loves good food, shopping, and nightlife. You can meet new people while doing fun things like dining out, strolling through the mall, and going to the theater. And because the Metal Rat Year values career, you can also meet interesting people when you're doing business networking, and attending conferences.

If you're already in a love partnership, you can strengthen your relationship by putting down your phone and having interesting conversations with your sweetheart about things happening in your lives and in the world. Take walks together, hand in hand. Go to conferences to learn new technology or ways to make money together. Try to avoid over-analyzing the relationship and second-guessing yourself. Enjoy the simple things, good food, a great movie, and a cuddle on the sofa.

Family Life

This is a year of new beginnings, and likely some members of your family want your support for their new ideas and encouragement about the directions they want to explore. At the same time, the idea of starting something new can trigger fears.

Coming together to support each other this year can be so helpful. You may not agree with your niece's idea of becoming an Instagram star, or your son's desire to do photography for a living. But this year, consider how you can support their dream through your words and encouragement. Make it a family policy to support each other this year, and you'll welcome success knocking at your door.

Summary

There are two major challenges in the Metal Rat Year, and yet it's a year filled with possibilities. The first challenge is you may not know where to start. I often hear people tell me they don't know their path; they're not sure what they want to do. In this case, I say "Try anything!" Take a class, meet with a person in a different profession, give something new a try each week. This is the practice of planting seeds. As you plant, some will sprout and the way forward will become clear.

The other challenge shows up when you know what you want to do, but you hold back because you want to do it when you feel ready, or when you can do it perfectly. In this cycle of the Chinese Zodiac, it's springtime right now—it's time to start planting. Waiting to plant will result in a smaller harvest, or worse, no harvest at all. Think about planting right now and course-correcting as you go. The farmer may plant a few seeds then realize it will be easier to plant using this tool, or better to plant in that area. In the Metal Rat Year, take practical action, and problems will solve themselves.

In This Book

In this installment of my annual Chinese Astrology series, I offer predictions for each month of the year. There are also predictions for love, money, career, education, health, and more. There are several Feng Shui cures suggested for each Chinese Zodiac sign to help you focus and bring in positive energy. At the end of this book, you'll find sections on Feng Shui principles, the upcoming eclipses, Mercury retrograde, and the Flying Star. There is also a large section on compatibility.

This year I've added "Lucky Days." On these days, plan to take important or significant actions, make vital phone calls, and send emails. These are days when energy and luck come together for you. On these days, you may find the most significant happenings of the month will occur. The more positive action you take on these days, the better your overall results and satisfaction will be.

I hope you enjoy this book and find it useful. Please take a moment and review it so more people can find this book.

I wish you joy and prosperity in 2020.

Donna Stellhorn

Celebrating Chinese New Year

The biggest holiday of the year in China is Chinese New Year. Based on the lunar calendar, Chinese New Year falls on a different day each year—most often on the second New Moon after the Winter Solstice. The Winter Solstice is on December 21, 2019, so the 2020 Chinese New Year occurs about two months later.

Occasionally, the Chinese New Year will fall on the third New Moon after the Winter Solstice. We can next expect to experience this in the year 2033. In historical China, emperors were in charge of keeping time and telling the people when important dates would happen. Emperors marked these important dates with festivals. Chinese New Year is one such festival.

There's a legend in China, the tale of a "Nian," a fearsome creature with the head of a lion and the body of a bull. Every winter, the Nian would grow very hungry and finding nothing to eat, he would come down into the villages to snack on the villagers. But over time, the villagers learned that the Nian was afraid of loud noises, fire, and the color red.

One night, the Nian was spotted coming down from the mountains, so the villagers lit fires, waved red flags, and made lots of noise by banging gongs and setting off firecrackers. Their village was spared, and to this day, New Year's is celebrated with lots of firecrackers and red banners.

Before New Year, there is much to do. The house must be thoroughly cleaned to sweep away any of the remaining bad luck from last year. Lots of special foods are prepared. The night before New Year, it is considered "lucky" to stay up past midnight—to symbolize enjoying a long life. At midnight the firecrackers start popping.

On the first day of the New Year, everyone wears their best clothes, and everyone says only positive things to one another to secure good luck for everyone. Red envelopes are filled with money and given to children.

This begins a multi-day holiday. At Chinese New Year there is the dance of the Golden Dragon (sometimes called the Lion Dance). This dragon is decorated with representations of the five elements, lights, silver, and fur. It can take as many as a hundred people to carry the Golden Dragon through the streets. At the end of the route, the dragon is met with fire-crackers and cheers from the crowds.

On the second day of the New Year, there is a vegetarian feast, after which people go and visit relatives, bringing them oranges to wish them a prosperous new year. People eat long noodles, the longer, the better, to symbolize a long life. They indulge in Nian Gao—which is a cake made of rice flour, brown sugar, and oil—to bring prosperity.

I offer a series of videos on the subject of what to do before and during the New Year's Celebrations to bring luck.

Here's the link: *https://www.youtube.com/c/DonnaStellhorn*

Find Your Chinese Zodiac Sign

The annual Chinese Zodiac sign changes each year in January or February. If you were born in January or February of any year, check the date carefully to make sure you find your correct animal sign. Below you'll find listed the element and Yin or Yang quality for the year. If you have any difficulty determining your sign, element, and Yin or Yang quality, please email me at DONNASTELLHORN@GMAIL.COM with your birth date, and I will help you find your sign.

02/20/1920 to 02/07/1921 Yang Metal Monkey
02/08/1921 to 01/27/1922 Yin Metal Rooster (or Cock)
01/28/1922 to 2/15/1923 Yang Water Dog
02/16/1923 to 2/4/1924 Yin Water Pig (or Boar)
02/5/1924 to 1/24/1925 Yang Wood Rat
01/25/1925 to 2/12/1926 Yin Wood Ox
02/13/1926 to 2/1/1927 Yang Fire Tiger
02/2/1927 to 1/22/1928 Yin Fire Rabbit (or Hare)
01/23/1928 to 2/9/1929 Yang Earth Dragon
02/10/1929 to 1/29/1930 Yin Earth Snake
01/30/1930 to 2/16/1931 Yang Metal Horse
02/17/1931 to 2/5/1932 Yin Metal Sheep (or Goat or Ram)
02/6/1932 to 1/25/1933 Yang Water Monkey
01/26/1933 to 2/13/1934 Yin Water Rooster (or Cock)
02/14/1934 to 2/3/1935 Yang Wood Dog
02/4/1935 to 1/23/1936 Yin Wood Pig (or Boar)
01/24/1936 to 2/10/1937 Yang Fire Rat
02/11/1937 to 1/30/1938 Yin Fire Ox
01/31/1938 to 2/18/1939 Yang Earth Tiger
02/19/1939 to 2/7/1940 Yin Earth Rabbit (or Hare)
02/8/1940 to 1/26/1941 Yang Metal Dragon
01/27/1941 to 2/14/1942 Yin Metal Snake
02/15/1942 to 2/4/1943 Yang Water Horse
02/5/1943 to 1/24/1944 Yin Water Sheep (or Goat or Ram)
01/25/1944 to 2/12/1945 Yang Wood Monkey
02/13/1945 to 2/1/1946 Yin Wood Rooster (or Cock)

02/2/1946 to 1/21/1947 Yang Fire Dog
01/22/1947 to 2/9/1948 Yin Fire Pig (or Boar)
02/10/1948 to 1/28/1949 Yang Earth Rat
01/29/1949 to 2/16/1950 Yin Earth Ox
02/17/1950 to 2/5/1951 Yang Metal Tiger
02/6/1951 to 1/26/1952 Yin Metal Rabbit (or Hare)
01/27/1952 to 2/13/1953 Yang Water Dragon
02/14/1953 to 2/2/1954 Yin Water Snake
02/3/1954 to 1/23/1955 Yang Wood Horse
01/24/1955 to 2/11/1956 Yin Wood Sheep (or Goat or Ram)
02/12/1956 to 1/30/1957 Yang Fire Monkey
01/31/1957 to 2/17/1958 Yin Fire Rooster (or Cock)
02/18/1958 to 2/7/1959 Yang Earth Dog
02/8/1959 to 1/27/1960 Yin Earth Pig (or Boar)
01/28/1960 to 2/14/1961 Yang Metal Rat
02/15/1961 to 2/4/1962 Yin Metal Ox
02/5/1962 to 1/24/1963 Yang Water Tiger
01/25/1963 to 2/12/1964 Yin Water Rabbit (or Hare)
02/13/1964 to 2/1/1965 Yang Wood Dragon
02/2/1965 to 1/20/1966 Yin Wood Snake
01/21/1966 to 2/8/1967 Yang Fire Horse
02/9/1967 to 1/29/1968 Yin Fire Sheep (or Goat or Ram)
01/30/1968 to 2/16/1969 Yang Earth Monkey
02/17/1969 to 2/5/1970 Yin Earth Rooster (or Cock)
02/6/1970 to 1/26/1971 Yang Metal Dog
01/27/1971 to 2/14/1972 Yin Metal Pig (or Boar)
02/15/1972 to 2/2/1973 Yang Water Rat
02/3/1973 to 1/22/1974 Yin Water Ox
01/23/1974 to 2/10/1975 Yang Wood Tiger
02/11/1975 to 1/30/1976 Yin Wood Rabbit (or Hare)
01/31/1976 to 2/17/1977 Yang Fire Dragon
02/18/1977 to 2/6/1978 Yin Fire Snake
02/7/1978 to 1/27/1979 Yang Earth Horse
01/28/1979 to 2/15/1980 Yin Earth Sheep (or Goat or Ram)
02/16/1980 to 2/4/1981 Yang Metal Monkey
02/5/1981 to 1/24/1982 Yin Metal Rooster (or Cock)

01/25/1982 to 2/12/1983 Yang Water Dog
02/13/1983 to 2/1/1984 Yin Water Pig (or Boar)
02/2/1984 to 2/19/1985 Yang Wood Rat
02/20/1985 to 2/8/1986 Yin Wood Ox
02/9/1986 to 1/28/1987 Yang Fire Tiger
01/29/1987 to 2/16/1988 Yin Fire Rabbit (or Hare)
02/17/1988 to 2/5/1989 Yang Earth Dragon
02/6/1989 to 1/26/1990 Yang Earth Snake
01/27/1990 to 2/14/1991 Yang Metal Horse
02/15/1991 to 2/3/1992 Yin Metal Sheep (or Goat or Ram)
02/4/1992 to 1/22/1993 Yang Water Monkey
01/23/1993 to 2/9/1994 Yin Water Rooster (or Cock)
02/10/1994 to 1/30/1995 Yang Wood Dog
01/31/1995 to 2/18/1996 Yin Wood Pig (or Boar)
02/19/1996 to 2/6/1997 Yang Fire Rat
2/7/1997 to 1/27/1998 Yin Fire Ox
1/28/1998 to 2/15/1999 Yang Earth Tiger
2/16/1999 to 2/4/2000 Yin Earth Rabbit (or Hare)
2/5/2000 to 1/23/2001 Yang Metal Dragon
1/24/2001 to 2/11/2002 Yin Metal Snake
2/12/2002 to 1/31/2003 Yang Water Horse
2/1/2003 to 1/21/2004 Yin Water Sheep (or Goat or Ram)
1/22/2004 to 2/8/2005 Yang Wood Monkey
2/9/2005 to 1/28/2006 Yin Wood Rooster (or Cock)
1/29/2006 to 2/17/2007 Yang Fire Dog
2/18/2007 to 2/6/2008 Yin Fire Pig (or Boar)
2/7/2008 to 1/25/2009 Yang Earth Rat
1/26/2009 to 2/13/2010 Yin Earth Ox
2/14/2010 to 2/2/2011 Yang Metal Tiger
2/3/2011 to 1/22/2012 Yin Metal Rabbit (or Hare)
1/23/2012 to 2/09/2013 Yang Water Dragon
2/10/2013 to 1/30/2014 Yin Water Snake
1/31/2014 to 2/18/2015 Yang Wood Horse
2/19/2015 to 2/7/2016 Yin Wood Sheep (or Goat or Ram)
2/8/2016 to 1/27/2017 Yang Fire Monkey
1/28/2017 to 2/15/2018 Yin Fire Rooster (or Cock)
2/16/2018 to 2/4/2019 Yang Earth Dog

2/5/2019 to 1/24/2020 Yin Earth Pig (or Boar)
01/25/2020 to 2/11/2021 Yang Metal Rat
2/12/2021 to 1/31/2022 Yin Metal Ox
2/1/2022 to 1/21/2023 Yang Water Tiger
1/22/2023 to 2/9/2024 Yin Water Rabbit
2/10/2024 to 1/28/2025 Yang Wood Dragon
1/29/2025 to 2/16/2026 Yin Wood Snake
02/17/2026 to 02/05/2027 Yang Fire Horse
02/06/2027 to 01/25/2028 Yin Fire Sheep (or Goat or Ram)
01/26/2028 to 02/12/2029 Yang Earth Monkey
02/13/2029 to 02/02/2030 Yin Earth Rooster

Where Are You in the 12-year cycle?

In 2020, as the Year of the Metal Rat begins, we are in the first sign of the universal 12-year cycle of the Chinese zodiac. However, your personal 12-year cycle is based on your individual birth year. Here's where your sign falls in the 12-year cycle.

First, let's define the cycle itself. We can liken the 12-year cycle of the Chinese Zodiac to a single year on a farm in the following manner: three months of the year = three years of the 12-year cycle.

Therefore, the first three years of the Chinese zodiac represent the three months of spring, bringing the farmer the opportunity to plant seeds. The next three-year segment brings a similar type of energy as the three months of summer, where the farmer is busy tending the growing plants, weeding the garden, and protecting his fields.

This period is followed by the three-year segment representing the three months of autumn and harvest time. This period is marked by significant achievements, but also hard work. The cycle ends with a three-year segment representing the three months of winter, a time when the farmer finishes up tasks he didn't have time to complete during the other busy months of the year, as he plans for the future. He eats from his storehouse of food and waits for the next spring planting season to begin.

If you are born in the Year of the Rat, this year marks the beginning of your personal springtime, a time which will last for the coming three years. During this period you will want to plant lots of seeds by trying new things, meeting new people and going to new places. Anything new you do can sprout into real opportunities during this three-year period and during the three following years.

For Ox, you are in your last year of winter. You have been through some busy years, and it's time to think about what needs catching up, what to release or let go, what plans you need to put in place now to make it easier for you to plant new seeds and start new things in 2020.

Tiger natives are in your second year of winter, and it's time to take stock of what you have accomplished over the past ten years. Where are the investments of your time and energy still paying off? It's a good time to think of beginning to let go of what isn't working, and of how you can accumulate more with less effort.

Rabbit (or Hare) natives are in the first year of winter. Your storehouse and pantry are as full as they will get. To accumulate more, you will have to be energetic and clever in identifying and gathering the final bits of the harvest missed by others. This is the year you begin your time of rest and recuperation. You need to take care of yourself and your body.

Dragon is in its last year of autumn, and the harvest is underway. Take everything you have learned so far and let the world know about your skills and what you have to offer. Demand to be paid what you are worth. This is a time when you can accumulate more.

Snake natives, you are in your second year of autumn, and the harvest is in full swing. Opportunities abound, but require you to be out in the world to gather them up. Think big, connect with people who can help you gather even more.

Horse, your autumn is beginning, and you must adjust to the new workload. That said, now is the period when you can easily gather what you want and need. Don't be shy. You can accumulate much with just a little effort.

Sheep (or Goat or Ram), you are in the final year of your three-year summer. It's time to focus on the aspects of your life which are working the way you want them to! Don't put effort into things in your life that are not bringing results. You also want to take steps to gather as many people around you as you can this year, people who will help you with your harvest in the coming three-year period.

Monkey natives, you are in the middle of your summer. You see the results of the effort you've made over the past few years. There's still time to make decisions and point your life in a more fruitful direction. It's good to identify and find ways to protect what's yours, as well as to weed out anything less desirable.

Rooster natives, you are at the beginning of your summer. There are sprouts taking root everywhere. Many things you have tried now begin yielding results. This is the year you need to be discerning and try not to be everything to every person; nor should you attempt to take on every project alone. A good manager knows when to delegate.

Dog, you are in your last year of spring. You have planted many new seeds over the past couple of years. Look at what is sprouting and determine if you're happy with it. You still have time to try new things, reinvent yourself, and make progress on your goals.

Pig natives, you are entering your second year of spring. You are creating new options for yourself, but may not yet see much in the way of results. This is an excellent time to study and improve your skills. Follow your heart and plant seeds for what you want to do with your life. The sprouts are coming soon.

Rat

January 31, 1900 -- February 18, 1901: Yang Metal Rat
February 18, 1912 -- February 5, 1913: Yang Water Rat
February 5, 1924 -- January 24, 1925: Yang Wood Rat
January 24, 1936 -- February 10, 1937: Yang Fire Rat
February 10, 1948 -- January 28, 1949: Yang Earth Rat
January 28, 1960 -- February 14, 1961: Yang Metal Rat
February 15, 1972 -- February 2, 1973: Yang Water Rat
February 2, 1984 -- February 19, 1985: Yang Wood Rat
February 19, 1996 -- February 6, 1997: Yang Fire Rat
February 7, 2008 -- January 25, 2009: Yang Earth Rat
January 25, 2020 – February 11, 2021: Yang Metal Rat

Rat Personality

I am a Rat. It's hard to admit. I really wanted to be one of the cute animals. But after exploring so much about the 12 different Chinese Zodiac signs, I have come to love and appreciate being a Rat.

Rats are hardworking, ambitious, and thrifty. The Rat individual is very focused on getting ahead. Rats want to achieve success in life and aspire to reach the top first. They have a frugal reputation but are generous with loved ones. They are drawn to a bargain and are skilled at making and saving money.

In the traditional stories about the animals who make up the Chinese Zodiac, little Rat ran ahead of the other animals to be named the first of the Chinese Zodiac. This drive to move quickly is indicative of people born under this sign, and they desire to arrive first and to be noticed.

Rat natives want positive recognition for their work and to be awarded honors for their achievements. That said, they also love a challenge—but once the award is won, it's easily tossed aside as Rat focuses on taking the next step up the ladder.

Even though Rat may not be the cutest of the Chinese Zodiac menagerie, they are well-liked. Initially acting reserved, they become more social as they get comfortable with their surroundings (it's perfectly understandable to be cautious when you're a little mouse...). You'll find Rat to be more talkative when topics relating to business and money are involved.

Rat makes a loyal friend. They may not have many close friends, but those who make it to Rat's inner circle will be looked out for and supported. Those born in Rat year will gravitate to other successful people. They have trouble tolerating lazy people, and can't be bothered with anyone who wants a free ride.

Reading a Rat's feelings is easy. When upset (and they are easily irritated), they can be critical. They also tend to compare and contrast everything. This helps them identify and locate the best of everything—from bargains to close friends. Rats are adept at writing and communication. They possess excellent memories and are always asking questions.

Rats like to accumulate, although it varies from Rat to Rat what they are collecting. Some Rats accumulate money, others material things, and still others gather social or business contacts. Rat is adaptable and has acute intuition, so they can quickly determine the benefit in a situation.

Because Rat is the smallest of the animals of the Chinese Zodiac, safety and self-preservation are considered paramount. They can sense danger, but Rat finds it hard to heed the warnings if they simultaneously smell opportunity and potential success. Rat needs only to follow their gut and finish what they start, to end up the wealthiest of all the signs.

Rat: Predictions for 2020

January 2020: *There is a Lunar Eclipse on January 10. Uranus goes direct on January 11. The Lunar New Year begins on January 25. Your Lucky Days are 1, 7, 13, 19, 25, and 31. [How to use your Lucky Days: On these days, plan to take necessary actions, make vital phone calls, send emails. These are days when your energy and luck are high.]*

January marks the last few weeks of your 12-year cycle. This is the time to release any remaining old stuff so you can welcome in your new cycle with a clean slate. Besides decluttering, it's a good idea to cut cords with those people who don't support you. Remove the negative energy from your life. Focus on the things and people that enrich you and bring joy as you welcome in the new energy,

Your thoughts create your reality. This month, Rat natives should make sure the positive thoughts outnumber the negative ones.

Finances are good this month. However, some aspects of your monetary situation benefit from receiving your attention. It's a good idea to change passwords on financial accounts. See whether you can get a better deal on interest rates. Increase your automatic savings plans so more money is being transferred into savings every month. This will help you start the new year off in prosperity mode.

The Lunar Eclipse on January 10 marks a strong period for moving an intimate relationship forward. If you've wanted to take a new relationship to the next level, you can now bring up the subject.

If you're already in a love relationship, it's time to bring back the romance. Even something as simple as taking a hike to a new place will spark some romantic excitement.

February: *Mercury goes retrograde from February 16 to March 9. Your Lucky Days this month are 6, 12, 18, and 24. [How to use your Lucky Days: On these days, plan to take significant actions, make vital phone calls, send emails. These are days when your energy and luck are high.]*

Career energy is strong. You may receive an offer from a former employer. Mercury goes retrograde on February 16, and if you begin a new job after this date, you may find it's not as good a move as you thought it would be. It's beneficial to do salary negotiations this month. Remember, Rat natives tend to rise to leadership roles, and if you're going to work this hard, you should be paid accordingly.

You may be tempted to nest at home this month and binge watch through your Netflix queue. It would be better to spend a little time creating a vision board to display on a wall in your home. Enhance your intuitive ability by meditating, keeping a dream journal, or lighting candles.

You may find you are being pursued in your relationships. You are the object of interest for a special someone. You may find this very flattering; in fact, this could be an adventure.

If you're already in a love relationship, there'll be an opportunity for emotional healing this month, especially after Mercury goes retrograde on February 16. The trouble bubbling up over the past year can be forgiven and forgotten (well at least forgiven). This can lead to a better understanding between you and your partner.

This month, Rat natives may receive money from a surprising source. While this extra money is nice, this may not be proof of future income.

A friend may ask you to travel with them or to help them with their home and pets while they are away traveling.

March: *Mercury goes direct on March 9. The Sun enters Aries on March 20. Saturn enters Aquarius on March 21. Your Lucky Days are 1, 7, 13, 19, 25, and 31. [How to use your Lucky Days: On these days, plan to* *take significant actions, make vital phone calls, send emails. These are days when your energy levels and luck are high.]*

This month, you may be tempted to go back to something that worked for you before (this is not surprising—Mercury continues in retrograde motion until March 9). This could be related to a former relationship. It's understandable to want to see if things might work out differently now. But don't burn any bridges to rekindle this love affair as any changes now may not stick.

Mercury goes direct on March 9, and you find things starting to move forward again, especially regarding an important project for work or school. During the middle of the month, Rat natives find your intuition is stronger than usual. You can become aware of a friend's secret before you're told.

Some creative work is accomplished behind the scenes. This is an excellent time to produce music, art or join a theater company. The Sun enters Aries on March 20 and after that, you can display your work to the world.

Finances seem more stable this month. However, there may be some home repairs or other large purchase that throws your budget off at the end of the month. It would be a good idea to put a little extra aside, just in case you might need a cushion.

Past restrictions seem to be lifted. You want to spend time with your friends, yet at the same time, you wish for more independence.

Your powers of attraction are high. It's good to be social now. And remember, Rat native, you are at your best when you're with others. Interestingly enough, a pack of rats is called a "mischief." How fun does that sound?

April: *Pluto goes retrograde on April 25. Your Lucky Days are 6, 12, 18, 24, and 30. [How to use your Lucky Days: On these days, plan to take significant actions, make vital phone calls, send emails. These are days when your energy and luck are high.]*

Your financial picture improves and you have your eye on some bling or a special piece of equipment to add to your collection. Rat natives do love the good things in life. Try to pay for this with cash rather than racking up debt for this indulgence.

What starts as a challenging month turns into a favorable relationship period. You may be surprised to find your sweetheart going out of their way to make you happy. There can be an agreement now about household chores, or a money matter that was a sticking point in the past.

If you're looking for love, you can meet interesting people in neighborhood places like gyms and health food stores. Also, consider going to sites like Meetup.com to find where single people gather to eat or do activities together. Interesting people are attracted to you now. They may seem to be quite straight-laced, but they do have a quirky side to their personality which can spark your interest.

Toward the end of the month, you begin a period of power in your career marked by Pluto turning retrograde. If you work contract jobs, this is a good time to let competing companies know when you will become available. If you own a company, look for opportunities to collaborate, or to do cooperative advertising.

Look at health habits and shift them back into line. Rat natives can worry and have trouble sleeping. You are often calm on the outside and yet have inner stress. Look into remedies for anxiety, such as hypnotherapy, tapping, or journaling. Consider exercises such as yoga before bed.

May: *Saturn goes retrograde on May 10. Venus goes retrograde on May 12. Jupiter goes retrograde on May 14. Your Lucky Days are 6, 12, 18, 24, and 30. [How to use your Lucky Days: On these days, plan to take significant actions, make vital phone calls, send emails. These are days when your energy and luck are high.]*

During this month, as Venus goes retrograde on May 12, you'll experience some holdups or delays. Really exercise patience this month—not just with other people, but with the process you're going through as well.

If you need to study for exams, try not to cram everything in at the last minute. Stick to a schedule of daily study time instead.

You feel a strong desire to take a risk this month, especially with both Jupiter and Saturn in retrograde motion. You may have a business idea, or want to spend money on a course of instruction which promises you success. While this may prove to be a good investment, remember Rat natives don't take unnecessary risks. Do your research and see if you can implement this idea, or whether it's possible to obtain the information for less money elsewhere.

A friendship can turn into a romance. If you're looking for love, you may find it within your circle of friends. Or, perhaps when meeting the friends of your friends, you see your future partner among them.

If you're already in a love relationship, there is a great deal of positive energy for moving this relationship forward to the next level. You can make plans to be an exclusive couple, move in together, or even get married. It's good to talk about the future now.

Your finances are improving. You are making some solid gains. It's good to review your investments now and see what changes are needed.

June: *There is a Lunar Eclipse on June 5. Mercury is retrograde from June 17 to July 12. Solar Eclipse on June 20. Venus goes direct June 24. Your Lucky Days are 5, 11, 17, 23, and 29. [How to use your Lucky Days: On these days, plan to take significant actions, make vital phone calls, send emails. These are days when your energy and luck are high.]*

The month begins with a Lunar Eclipse on June 5. This can bring a strong desire for a getaway, even if it's just a long weekend. There's a desire to be out of the house, perhaps even out of the country. A change of scene is what you need. This will bring new ideas and inspiration.

Mercury goes retrograde on June 17 and brings a family matter to the forefront. This is something you intuitively knew was going to surface again. You're ready to handle this head-on. Gather the family and discuss what needs to be done or changed.

Solar Eclipse on June 20 marks a period of change, one that will unfold over the next few months. An epiphany causes you to see things in a different light, and suddenly whatever seemed to be blocking your path seems to melt away. You can see opportunities where there was empty space before. You can move forward now.

Towards the end of the month when Venus goes direct on June 24, communication between Rat natives and a loved one improves considerably. There is an opportunity now to form a deeper connection and time to build some real trust.

You and a business partner need to make or discuss adjustments in your business agreement to achieve clarity about the terms of this agreement. During Metal Rat years, it's especially useful to put agreements in writing before moving forward. The two of you have a similar vision, but different ways of expressing it. Find common ground by drawing a picture through words for each other.

July: *Retrograde Saturn backs up into Capricorn. There is a Lunar Eclipse is on July 4. Mercury goes direct on July 12. Your Lucky Days are 5, 11, 17, 23, and 29. [How to use your Lucky Days: On these days, plan to take significant actions, make vital phone calls, send emails. These are days when your energy and luck are high.]*

There is a Lunar Eclipse on July 4 which unearths a desire to move or change the house in some way. If you're thinking of making a real estate transaction, use caution as Mercury continues to move retrograde for another week or so. In Metal Rat years, you may want to move quickly, but it's wise to be patient during Mercury retrograde periods.

This is a high energy month for you. You may be feeling as if you can take on the world. But there may also be days when this extra energy makes you feel restless and frustrated. This is a sign the only thing blocking you from what you want in your life is believing in yourself. Once you realize this, Rat native, you will sail right through it.

Rat natives value companionship and you can be a very attentive partner. However, in a Metal Rat year, the accelerated energy can make your schedule very tight and can cause you to forget to connect. This month, you'll be so busy, your partner is left wondering where you are. This is a good time to leave little love notes or send regular texts professing your love.

Mercury goes direct on July 12 and everything moves forward once again, especially a home project or repair you've been planning to do.

An issue is resolved with a sibling or a neighbor.

Finances improve, and you may receive a small windfall. Also, you have an opportunity for income from sales this month, especially selling books, information, or perhaps a vehicle. Work on your sales skills. You might travel a short distance to a conference where the focus is on methods of making money.

August: *Uranus goes retrograde on August 15. Your Lucky Days are 4, 10, 16, 22, and 28. [How to use your Lucky Days: On these days, plan to take significant actions, make vital phone calls, send emails. These are days when your energy and luck are high.]*

Your keen powers of observation are on overdrive this month. You can boost sales in your business. If you're looking for a job, you may receive an offer of an interview with a company you've had your eye on.

At work, you may be tempted to unleash some criticism towards one or more of the people you work with or come in contact with daily. This may not be the best move—especially if you're thinking of posting this opinion on social media. Your words and actions are very noticeable during this period.

Now is the time to make real progress on your goal of turning in a project, submitting a proposal, or publishing a manuscript. (This may be related to a creative project other than your job.) Success is at hand. Try to bring this project to a close.

You may find a recent purchase needs to be returned because you'd really like to have something entirely different. For the rest of this month, think twice before hitting the buy button on anything.

Romance energy is in the spotlight. If you're looking for love, it's a good idea to post your profile on dating sites or update your existing profile. Make an announcement to friends and family that you're looking for love and let them be your ambassadors.

If you've been planning to expand the family either through pregnancy or adoption (even adopting a pet counts in this instance), you have a lot of energy to work with. Rat native, there is fertility energy around you now.

September: *Mars goes retrograde on September 9. Jupiter goes direct on September 12. The Sun goes into Libra on September 22. Saturn goes direct on September 28. Your Lucky Days are 3, 9, 15, 21, and 27. [How to use your Lucky Days: On these days, plan to take significant actions, make vital phone calls, send emails. These are days when your energy and luck are high.]*

Mars goes retrograde on Sept 9, encouraging self-care now. You must treat yourself with love and kindness. Building your self-esteem will strengthen you for the opportunities coming your way.

You may travel to a place you've visited before. This is an opportune time to visit ancestral lands or distant relatives. Rat natives may also visit a place where you've lived before.

You are focused on income now, and you are able to put a lot of energy behind your call for cash as Jupiter goes direct around Sept 12. Consider refreshing any Feng Shui cures you've placed in the house to draw money, especially those located by the front door.

The Sun goes into Libra on Sept 22, shining a light on your health and well-being. Adjustments in medication, practitioners, or health routines can be quite beneficial now. Look at new ways of eating to nourish your body. It would be a good idea to clear the kitchen of foods that are not helpful to your health goals.

Late in the month, you may feel the things you want to achieve are blocked by others. You can face some challenges from an older family member or a supervisor at your job. In Metal Rat years, this type of situation can be made worse by focusing on how things "should be" rather than the current reality of the situation. You may have a notion to try to force the issue, but this month creative thinking can help you to find another way.

October: *Pluto goes direct on October 4. Mercury goes retrograde from October 13 to November 3. Your Lucky Days are 3, 9, 15, 21, and 27. [How to use your Lucky Days: On these days, plan to take significant actions, make vital phone calls, send emails. These are days when your energy and luck are high.]*

The energy of Pluto starting to move forward has you focused on issues regarding your career; you may even be worried about the industry you work for. You see the career landscape changing, yet you may not be willing or able to jump into anything else.

Rat natives can spend a lot of time obsessively weighing the risks around change. Many people come to you for career advice yet you may not feel so confident about your own path. Now, during this Metal Rat year where there are so many opportunities for Rat natives, ask yourself, what advice would you give a friend in your situation?

Love is in the air. If you're already in a love relationship, you can find some happiness and enjoy some very satisfying evenings together. Rat natives who are looking for love can have good luck this month finding someone who is quite compatible.

Your guardian angel is active now and can help lead you to what you want. Put your list of goals at the forefront of your mind by reading them aloud nightly.

Mercury goes retrograde on Oct 13 possibly disrupting a financial transaction you were considering. But understand this delay is to your benefit. This will give you a chance to look over everything one more time and do some further negotiations. Try to relax and go with the flow on this. You will see the guiding hand of the Universe in this matter towards the end of the month.

November: *Mercury goes direct on November 3. Mars goes direct on November 13. Neptune goes direct on November 28. There is a Lunar Eclipse on November 30. Your Lucky Days are 2, 8, 14, 20, and 26. [How to use your Lucky Days: On these days, plan to take significant actions, make vital phone calls, send emails. These are days when your energy and luck are high.]*

Finally, Mercury goes direct on Nov 3 and suddenly the people you were waiting for are now lining up at your door eager for your attention. Everyone is in a hurry to meet with you now. This can bring a spike in business, especially if you're in sales or in a profession where you take on clients.

A payment finally shows up, but it may not be all you hoped for; however, contacting the parties involved can help you rectify the situation. Don't be shy about talking to someone about this. Rat natives can be quite persistent when you know you're owed something.

You may have been struggling to get a project moving, but now that Mars is direct on Nov 13, you can make some headway. If this is a construction project, things can go very well. Whatever the project, if you find you are procrastinating after Mars is direct, then there is something you don't like about the plan. Time to reformulate the plan.

At the end of the month, you have an opportunity to sleep better and awaken feeling more rested. This may involve your relationship partner and their sleep issues as well.

The end of November brings the Lunar Eclipse. This can trigger an epiphany about how you communicate with others. You are a channel now, receiving information from the Universe. Dreams may reveal particulars; even watching TV can trigger awareness. You might open a book to a random page and find it's speaking directly to you. Use this information to adjust how you see yourself in a situation with a lover or a close family member.

December: *Solar Eclipse on December 14. Saturn goes into Aquarius on December 16. Jupiter goes into Aquarius on December 19. Sun goes into Capricorn on December 21. Your Lucky Days are 2, 8, 14, 20, and 26. [How to use your Lucky Days: On these days, plan to take significant actions, make vital phone calls, send emails. These are days when your energy and luck are high.]*

The Solar Eclipse on Dec 14 may bring a great desire to go back to school to get a degree. You may want to become a teacher or change something about the educational system in your country. You may just be focused on learning some new skills to improve career prospects.

Eclipse energy can bring big changes, and making a dramatic shift in a new direction is to be expected and beneficial at this time. However, this is not a great time to incur a lot of debt, even if it's for educational purposes. Rat natives should look for funding sources through people you know, the government, and professional organizations.

There is a focus on friendships for you. This energy will last some time and it suggests finding ways to add new friends into your life on a more regular basis. There are lots of possibilities for Rat natives at this time. You may have a person you know ask to live with you. You may want to take a vacation with friends. You may start a meetup group to find more friends, especially if you live in a new area.

The Sun goes into Capricorn on Dec 21, shining its light on your reputation. This is a fine time to be quite positive when you post on social media. There may be some sort of status change now. Perhaps you are promoted at work, or recognized for your contributions to an organization you belong to.

January 2021: *Uranus goes direct on January 14. Mercury goes retrograde from January 30 to February 20. Your Lucky Days are 1, 7, 13, 19, 25, and 31. [How to use your Lucky Days: On these days, plan to take significant actions, make vital phone calls, send emails. These are days when your energy and luck are high.]*

Your year of seed planting comes to a close. It has been an eventful year and you have planted many seeds by trying new things and making lots of changes. You will see many of these seeds sprout. As you get results, use them as signs to put more energy into these projects and possibilities. Specifically for business, put energy into products and services that are bringing profits. Put time and effort into those relationships bringing you happiness.

Children or younger relatives want more of your attention now than usual. Changes may be going on in their lives and they are reaching out to you for support. You may have to ask them to change, even though they have made it clear to you they don't want to change. Once this process is started, things will go better for all involved. Be open to discussion, knowing that good results are on their way.

In the middle of the month, the energy shifts as Uranus moves forward again, clearing the way for new technology in the home or at your job. You may be asked to learn a new computer system, or perhaps you bought a new game console for you and the kids. Get purchases and installations done before the end of the month. Mercury will go retrograde soon.

Mercury goes retrograde on Jan 30 and you may have to spend some extra time in the office. A team member may not be doing their fair share, or perhaps one or more people are on holiday. Either way, your desk is piled high. This is par for the course during a Metal Rat year and Rat natives have no trouble blazing through the list of things to do.

February 2021: *Lunar New Year begins on February 12. Happy Year of the Metal Ox.*

Attract New Love

If you're looking for love, know that your circle of friends and the friends of your friends can provide you with the connections you're looking for. It's good to be open to meeting people outside your regular circles. Opposites can attract. The new person coming may be very different than anyone you have ever dated before.

Rat natives can also meet potential relationships through social groups and charitable organizations. Plan to attend meetings regularly, or volunteer to take on a leadership role. One of these groups may lead you to find a compatible companion. August is an especially good month for being out there looking for love.

Rat natives are especially sensitive to scent. Perfumes and smell, in general, are known to influence your emotions and behaviors. Scent triggers memories in your brain and associations with those memories. This can cause you to take action even if you're not fully conscious of the reason why. Those small actions add up, bringing you closer to your goals.

The scent of vanilla is wonderful for attracting new love. Vanilla extract can be found in most grocery stores. Place a drop or two on cotton balls and place these in your bedroom. These scented cotton balls can be placed behind a picture, or on a small dish on your bedside table.

You can also spray vanilla-scented air fresheners—however, choosing a natural scent is best. You can also place a small amount of vanilla in a pot of boiling water on the stove and allow the aroma of the vanilla to fill the whole house. At the same time, visualize the love relationship you want coming to you easily.

Enhance Existing Love

This is a year when you and your partner are often drawn much closer to each other. At times this can make the relationship stronger, yet at other times cause you to irritate one another. It's like walking up a sandy hill, a few steps forward and then a slide back. Fortunately, Rat natives are light on their feet and able to navigate even when the earth under their feet shifts and slides.

You are loved by many, especially your partner. And everyone is pulling you in the direction they want you to go. So many options and choices, there is not enough time in the day to please everyone. This can make your partner a little testy when you show up late for dinner, especially if it happens to be your anniversary. But just minutes later, everything is harmonious once again and you're back on solid ground.

A trip together, or studying something with your partner is a good idea. These types of activities bring you closer together. If your partner is also a Rat native, you are both experiencing the seed planting energy of the Metal Rat year. You need to be patient with each other. May and June can be especially challenging if you're not listening to your partner.

You can enhance relationship energy by bringing a bit of art and beauty into your home. Place a figurine or statue of a couple in love in your living room, family room, or bedroom. Place this figurine in a prominent place, so it is easily seen. This will help pull the love energy into your space and your life all year long.

One additional tip is to hang a small bag of cardamom seeds from the love figurine. Cardamom has been used in passion/ lust potions for centuries. To make a bag, take a small piece of cotton cloth about four inches square and lay it out on the table. Place about a teaspoon of cardamom seeds in the center cloth. Gather the corners of the fabric and tie it together with thread or embroidery floss, leaving a bit of extra string for hanging the bag. Adding the scent of this magical spice will help bring the romance into your space and into your life.

Looking to Conceive?

For those born in the year of the Rat, it's a year to deepen your existing love relationship. You are independent, but everything is easier with someone who cares about you. This year find some pearls to bring into the bedroom. It can be a strand of pearls or a single pearl. Pearls have been worn by people in many countries to increase happiness in marriage. Pearls are said to increase loving vibrations in the people around them.

(From Donna Stellhorn's book, *A Path to Pregnancy: Ancient Secrets for the Modern Woman*)

Family and Kids

This year you are torn between wanting to be at home nesting with your dear ones and being out in the world. In a Metal Rat year, the call to be in the world usually will be the stronger.

This is your big year, a seed planting year. This means being out in the world, making new contacts and doing new things. You most likely want to pursue the countless opportunities (many money-making ones) which will be made known to you. However, this means you'll need to leave your warm, safe nest, and venture out.

Your kids may also want to be out in the world rather than at home. You may have a child who wants to leave home, but you wonder whether they are really ready. Or, maybe you are ready for them to leave home, but they are holding onto the comfortable nest you've provided. Whatever happens, know there will be a false start this year. The child who leaves the house may be back and have to try again at a later date.

Gain additional protection energy for your home by placing a pair of Foo Dogs (also spelled Fu Dogs) by your front door. These "guard dogs" come in pairs; one male with his paw on the world and one female with her paw gently on the baby. There are some Foo Dog pairs where all four of their paws are on the ground. This is fine too. In this case, you may not be able to tell which of the dogs is male or female.

Place one dog on either side of the door. You can do this inside the house or outside the house, depending on the size and material the Foo Dogs are made from. Some pairs are so large they must be outside. You can find finely decorated and painted Foo Dogs made from the most delicate porcelain and these should be placed inside.

Display the dogs with their raised foot closest to the door. So the male dog who often has his left paw on the world would be placed by the door to his left. The female dog, who holds the baby with her right paw, would be placed by the door to her right.

Money

Rat natives are known for their ambition and their ability to make money. This year is your year, your seed planting year. It's like you're a talented, hardworking farmer who's been dropped onto a lush piece of property, and in your hands, you have a large bag of seeds. The only problem is you're already hungry— and Rat natives are not known to be patient.

This year many of the ways you made money in past years either don't feel as if they will be profitable enough now, or they don't hold your interest any longer. This doesn't mean you'll abandon them entirely. You may take a break from the past activities and then return to them in a year or so with fresh energy.

But this year you'll need to plant seeds. You need to try new things, break new ground, expand your comfort zone, and reach for new heights.

This year money will come from new and interesting sources. You may be doing a lot of work behind the scenes before the payment actually arrives in your account. More career opportunities are available to you than you can count, but not all of these will lead to the money you want. The problem with this is you may not be able to recognize this fact from the outset. Which opportunities would be best? You'll have to try new things to see if they will be profitable for you.

The symbol of the fruit-bearing tree is one of abundance and prosperity and is represented by the gemstone tree. This small tree is usually made from wire with each branch ending in a gemstone. There are lots of gemstones to choose from. However, the best money-drawing gemstone trees would display citrine or clear quartz gemstones.

Place your gemstone tree on your entryway table, or on a table in your home office. Dust the tree monthly to re-energize this Feng Shui cure. You can also place a list of goals or wishes beneath the tree. Add a bit of paper currency with your list under the tree to complete the Feng Shui cure.

Job or Career

Career energy is powerful for Rat natives this year. Keep in mind this is the beginning of your 12-year cycle, and many new things will be coming into your life. So if you're thinking about changing jobs, or completely changing your career, you are in harmony with the energy of this time.

Despite what you might think, your qualifications may not be as important as who you know and how well you can blend in with the team. Apply for jobs through contacts you have made. Make sure you have a strong profile on business sites like Linkedin. Because the energy favors a change, you will be able to get a great position if you point yourself in that direction.

If you're thinking of retiring, this is another direction you can go which is in harmony with the new energy available to you at this time. Retiring constitutes a major lifestyle shift. You may also start a process towards retirement by downsizing the house this year, or doing a deep declutter in preparation. This may be enough change energy to keep you in your job.

However, if rumblings and threats of layoffs or forced retirement reverberate in your workplace—and you are at the beginning of your cycle—recognize that you may be in the crosshairs of change. Make sure your supervisor is aware of your many contributions to the company and that you want to keep your position.

You may also find changes in management seem problematic. This type of situation can be difficult at first, but the energy will improve over the course of the year. New managers may be very enthusiastic about changes, but then settle in and become more supportive after a few months.

If you own your own business, you may expand at the beginning of the year, but then see sales fall off towards the middle of the year. This will be a good time to focus on customer service and sales. By the end of the year, your expansion is paying off. You are running a more efficient and profitable business.

In Feng Shui, birds symbolize the ability to see far and anticipate market trends. The hawk, being a bird of prey, can identify it's next meal from high up in the sky. It dives and retrieves it's dinner effortlessly. This is a good symbol for your career this year to remind you to have a goal and to take action towards that goal. This is not a year for extended plans and hesitations. See what you want and dive for it.

Place a picture or figurine of a hawk in your home office, work office, or in your family room. Clean and dust it regularly to bring new fresh energy into your home or office. As you walk by this image in the course of your day, ask yourself, "What is my goal today?" This can help you focus your energy on results.

Education

As this is the first year of your 12-year cycle, you may feel like starting all over again by going back to school. If you plan to work and go to school at the same time, you are going to be very busy—which is in line with the energy of the Metal Rat year. There are opportunities for the industrious Rat native to find funding for education, enough so you don't have to burn the candle at both ends. Look into programs focused on turning your experience into credits to get you through to the diploma quickly.

If you're already in school, you may be thinking about switching gears. This year you're curious about finding new energy, so completing old stuff can be a pain. If you're in the home stretch, make a disciplined effort to sprint towards the finish line. But if you have a couple of years to go, you may want to take a break, for at least long enough to see whether the direction you're heading in is still the track you want to be on.

Legal Matters

You usually are pretty lucky when it comes to legal matters. However, this year you want to exercise some caution. There is an irritating energy surrounding contracts, agreements, and lawsuits. Things may not go as smoothly as you expect. Take extra care when putting together legal documents. Double-check for typos and missed signatures. And this year, don't sue anyone unless you really have to.

Health and Well-Being

Rat natives enjoy good health this year. You have a lot of energy, especially for friends and the projects you want to do. There may be more than a few late nights when you are working on things for your job, or just staying out too late with friends. That said, much of your general health and well-being is hinged on your own attitudes and thinking process. If you are generally optimistic—and it is your year, so why wouldn't

you be?—you can fight off most fatigue, colds, and other mala-
dies. It's also a good idea to adopt, or at least consider some
of the newer trends in diet and exercise. If you find one that
captures your interest, give it a try.

If you hope to lose weight, pay attention to what you're drink-
ing rather than what you're eating. Making a shift may make a
big difference in how you're consuming your calories. Staying
hydrated will help this year. Sleeping more or getting restful
sleep will also aid in weight loss. Consider heading to bed ear-
lier this year whenever you can.

To attract positive health energy this year, add seashells to
your home. Place seashells on your bedroom window sill or in
your bathroom. Seashells represent protection, a comfortable
home, and a sense that everything will work out just fine. This
will attract positive energy for health and vitality.

Ox

February 19, 1901 -- February 7, 1902: Yin Metal Ox
February 6, 1913 -- January 25, 1914: Yin Water Ox
January 25, 1925 -- February 12, 1926: Yin Wood Ox
February 11, 1937 -- January 30, 1938: Yin Fire Ox
January 29, 1949 -- February 16, 1950: Yin Earth Ox
February 15, 1961 -- February 4, 1962: Yin Metal Ox
February 3, 1973 -- January 22, 1974: Yin Water Ox
February 20, 1985 -- February 8, 1986: Yin Wood Ox
February 7, 1997 -- January 27, 1998: Yin Fire Ox
January 26, 2009 -- February 13, 2010: Yin Earth Ox
February 12, 2021 – January 31, 2022: Yin Metal Ox

Ox Personality

Slow and steady, the Ox is always making progress towards success and prosperity. Ox is the hardest working of all the signs of the Chinese Zodiac. Once they accept a task, they toil and toil until it's done. They like to finish one thing before starting another. Often, new projects will sit and gather dust while Ox completes any previous obligations—no matter how exciting, or how potentially profitable or beneficial the new project may be.

Those born in the year of the Ox are highly intelligent and resourceful, although these qualities may not be apparent. Ox native is often introverted and shy. The truth is, they're shy until the need arises—then they will stand up in front of a group and take on a leadership role. As one of the largest and strongest animals of the Chinese Zodiac, Ox is never intimidated and rarely at a loss for words.

Ox individuals like a routine. They will stick to a particular way of doing things and may find it extremely difficult to make a change. In some ways, this is the key to Ox's success. They use tried-and-true methods and hard work to create the outcomes they want to manifest.

Ox never jumps in, or relies on "luck" to succeed in their endeavors (or worse, "wings it"). Their tenacity and dedication to a specific outcome bring Ox the most satisfaction and the most success.

Those born in Ox year have patience and understanding with others. They take pride in being a good and loyal friend. However, they are not particularly good at being a romantic partner. It wouldn't occur to them to fly you off to Paris at a moment's notice to enjoy a weekend vacation. However, once Ox does fall in love and marries, they are in it for the long haul. They are faithful and prove to be good partners.

Ox, like buffalo, cannot be stopped once they begin moving. If an Ox person gets angry, expect to be run over. But, the Ox native can get stuck. They can walk the same path, doing the same things for so long they wear a rut so deep they can't climb out of it.

This can occur in the course of their career or their daily work, but the same pattern can also show up in their personal or intimate relationships. An Ox can hold on to grievances far longer than any other sign. You can easily identify an unhappy Ox: they work all the time.

Because Ox is so self-disciplined, they expect similar behavior from other people in their lives. Ox will patiently instruct others, but should someone refuse to listen or pay attention to their excellent advice, Ox will turn away, head out, and never look back.

Ox doesn't believe in shortcuts, not for others and definitely not for themselves. They build things that last, designs copied around the world. Everything Ox receives, he or she has earned, and no one can say otherwise.

Ox natives do not like to be in debt. They want to settle accounts as soon as possible, preferably never get into debt in the first place! When they receive something as a gift, their gratitude overflows. That being said, Ox is also likely to remember an injustice for a very, very long, long, long time.

Ox: Predictions for 2020

January 2020: *There is a Lunar Eclipse on January 10. Uranus moves direct again on January 11. The Lunar New Year begins on January 25. Your Lucky Days are 2, 8, 14, 20, and 26. [How to use your Lucky Days: On these days, plan to take significant actions, make vital phone calls, send emails. These are days when your energy and luck are high.]*

Your reputation precedes you this month and helps open the doors to new acquaintances, some who wield considerable power. Accomplished individuals can assist you with your goals this month, especially after the Lunar Eclipse on January 10.

For Ox natives, there is a lot of energy around education this month. You may be asked to teach a class, or to take one (perhaps as part of continuing education at work.) You feel motivated to jump right in. This can lead to meeting interesting people and/or adding to your skills, especially around new technology. This is marked by the forward motion of Uranus after January 11.

An attractive person with wild wisps of hair gives you information to help move you forward in a business or legal matter. Make a mental note of the advice they offer.

Even though you both sit on the same sofa, you don't feel as connected as usual to your partner. Something is on their mind, something they're not willing to talk about...yet. Just hold the space for them until they're ready. Once they start communicating their thoughts, things will improve.

If you're looking for love, you're projecting a lot of charisma! Go, be in places where you can be noticed.

February: *Mercury goes retrograde from February 16 to March 9. Your Lucky Days this month are 1, 7, 13, 19, and 25. [How to use your Lucky Days: On these days, plan to take significant actions, make vital phone calls, send emails. These are days when your energy and luck are high.]*

This month something is reaching the point of completion. This may be the last few months of school, with your graduation and degree now in sight. Or perhaps you're getting ready to enter a new profession, or to take on a new role at your current job—either of which will be starting soon. You are leaving one world behind and moving into a new phase in your life. This process will take more than one month, and will alert you that where you are now is changing.

Mercury will go retrograde towards the middle of the month, bringing a career or home project to a standstill. You may have been rushing to try to get it all done before Mercury changed directions but, alas, it's hard to fight the shifting tides. Sit back and allow for the delay. You will find this slower energy actually in harmony with your personal time table.

Ox natives, you have a lot of energy focused on children this month. If you have kids, you may be thinking, "When is my energy *not* focused on them?" but this could be the time they ask for your attention and advice more insistently. If you've wanted to expand the family, there is positive energy for fertility and adoption all throughout this Metal Rat year. Specifically, this month is a good time for you to get the help you need.

Some happy news in the area of finances comes to you. This may pertain to a loan or a possible boost in income.

March: *Mercury goes direct on March 9. The Sun enters Aries on March 20. Saturn enters Aquarius on March 21. Your Lucky Days are 2, 8, 14, 20, and 26. [How to use your Lucky Days: On these days, plan to take significant actions, make vital phone calls, send emails. These are days when your energy and luck are high.]*

This is a high energy month for you, Ox native. This can really feed into your natural workaholic tendency. It would be a good idea to schedule some fun time for yourself so you don't forget the importance of maintaining work/life balance.

You can feel inspired by a school or writing project. Light an orange candle, call in a Muse for creative inspiration. You can plow right through this task and finish before the deadline— especially if it falls after Mercury goes direct on March 9.

If you own your own business, you may find a collaboration or connection with another business really pays off this month, especially as Saturn changes signs around March 21. This is the time to reach out to professional groups. Look at B2B transactions, even if you don't normally do business with other businesses. You can make strides towards expanding your reach, especially towards the end of the month.

Much contact with family and perhaps extended family is possible now. You may be planning or attending a big family get-together. Ox natives are often tireless workers, the last to sit down at dinner because they are making sure everyone else has everything they need. However, this month, you might be missing out on the best part of spending time with others if you're toiling away in the kitchen, or working away in front of your computer while the rest of the family is socializing.

An investment opportunity presents itself. You may learn about it from either a knowledgeable woman or from a media source hosted by a woman. The time for action is now. Ox natives are often convinced that prosperity comes as a result of hard work, so you may not feel very comfortable when passive income sources show up. But this is a Metal Rat year and it's good to take calculated risks.

April: *Pluto goes retrograde on April 25. Your Lucky Days are 1, 7, 13, 19, and 25. [How to use your Lucky Days: On these days, plan to take significant actions, make vital phone calls, send emails. These are days when your energy and luck are high.]*

Changes at work can affect your daily routine or job description. There may be discussions of a merger, or a switch in management personnel or style. Your team may be changing as well. A new computer system may be coming in, or some other technological innovation may be introduced. It's a good thing to take a step back and really take a look at your company and the industry itself in general, to see where it's heading.

Ox natives often prefer to stay in the same place and keep plugging along in a familiar way. But if you see smoke up ahead, it's not a good idea to walk into the forest fire. The Universe will make opportunities known to you—you just need to begin to look.

Your powers of attraction are high now and if you're looking for love, this is an auspicious time for you. If you've not chosen well in the past, try going out with someone entirely different from your "usual" type. Ox natives can be wholly devoted to their partner. You need someone worthy of the tender love you have to share.

You may be traveling this month, or making plans and buying tickets for a future trip. There is luck for you in relation to travel/trips now. This includes trips for business, attending a conferences, or traveling to see clients in other cities.

Meditation or other spiritual practices are beneficial this month as powerful Pluto goes retrograde around April 25. Find a friend and perhaps take a class, or just sit together for your mindfulness sessions.

May: *Saturn goes retrograde on May 10. Venus goes retrograde on May 12. Jupiter goes retrograde on May 14. Your Lucky Days are 1, 7, 13, 19, 25, and 31. [How to use your Lucky Days: On these days, plan to take significant actions, make vital phone calls, send emails. These are days when your energy and luck are high.]*

You are a Star this month! The spotlight is on you—not something Ox natives are generally that happy with. You may be giving a speech for work or at a wedding. You might be asked to host a party. There could be a social or humanitarian organization where you're asked to give a short presentation. Embrace this offer even if you're nervous about it. You will benefit more from doing this than you think.

Money can come in from a couple of sources this month. You may be selling something of value, or perhaps you have a side business that makes a noticeable profit. This is not a "quit your day job" moment, but it shows you there are other ways to earn income if you bravely follow the path of possibility.

You and your sweetheart may not be seeing eye to eye this month as Saturn, Venus, and Jupiter start moving backward. This is likely to be more of a political or ideological difference, rather than something key to the relationship. Ox natives have strong opinions and can express them in rather authoritative terms. But this may not be the time to stubbornly hold onto an opinion. The energy smooths out when you put yourself in the other person's shoes. The conversations will lighten and be happier.

If you're looking for love, check out places where people focus on money, perhaps having lunch in the banking district of your town.

June: *Lunar Eclipse on June 5. Mercury is retrograde from June 17 to July 12. There is a Solar Eclipse on June 20. Venus goes direct June 24. Your Lucky Days are 6, 12, 18, 24, and 30. How to use your Lucky Days: On these days, plan to take significant actions, make vital phone calls, send emails. These are days when your energy and luck are high.]*

You and your partner can share a lot of happiness between you this month. A few kind words from you and compliments will come your way, especially after Venus goes direct in late June. Consider working together on a project side-by-side and make some great memories.

Your financial area is lit up this month. Extra money is flowing into your coffers. There can be money coming in from several sources and someone who has owed you for a long time may come to finally pay you. But the Lunar Eclipse energy can make you uncomfortable overall with this situation. It's a good idea to acknowledge and accept the uncomfortable energy. This will encourage greater monetary flow in your life.

That said, changes may happen in connection with investments, insurance, or banking. Things you thought were secure may turn out to be less so as Mercury turns retrograde around June 17. It may be necessary to move funds, change passwords, or shift accounts. Do not let this wait too long. You benefit during a Metal Rat year if you take action when notifications begin to appear.

The Solar Eclipse can bring a surprise compliment or honor from a supervisor or person you admire.

If you're having trouble sleeping, try shifting your nighttime routine. Do some online research to learn what sleep experts say. Consider adjusting your patterns and habits and you will be rewarded with some great results.

July: *Retrograde Saturn backs up into Capricorn. There is a Lunar Eclipse is on July 4. Mercury goes direct on July 12. Your Lucky Days are 6, 12, 18, 24, and 30. [How to use your Lucky Days: On these days, plan to take significant actions, make vital phone calls, send emails. These are days when your energy and luck are high.]*

The Lunar Eclipse signals a time when you may need to have a conversation with a neighbor or sibling about the changes going on in your life. They may offer you help and advice. You can entrust them with a secret.

Financial matters improve once Mercury goes direct on July 12. You have more ideas than time. It would be good to make a list, or better still, create a vision board with some of the things you want to do displayed in pictures. This is a time where you want to channel your inner curiosity. Try not to assess what will work from a distance. You learn much by moving forward and pushing the boundaries.

Activities after dark heat up. If you're in a love relationship, consider planning a steamy date night. If you're looking for love, consider going dancing, to a club, or the bar in an upscale hotel for a drink and an appetizer. Take a friend if you must, but try to be social and meet new people.

An educational opportunity presents itself for Ox natives. You may be asked to speak at a conference or teach a class. Or, you may meet a teacher who can become instrumental in your quest to grow.

You may crave a change in your physical self, perhaps a new hairstyle, wardrobe, or tattoo. The Metal Rat year is one where speed and efficiency are valued. You may find a style requiring less maintenance and care. Consider making the alteration after Mercury goes direct so you don't risk changing your mind.

August: *Uranus goes retrograde on August 15. Your Lucky Days are. 5, 11, 17, 23, and 29. [How to use your Lucky Days: On these days, plan to take significant actions, make vital phone calls, send emails. These are days when your energy and luck are high.]*

This month you may receive a job offer for something you don't want to do, or find a client you don't want to work with. It may take courage to turn this job down as you don't like to leave money on the table. However, Uranus is going retrograde around August 15, and it is likely best to choose a different path than your normally well-worn trail. There are more job offers and/or more clients coming. You don't need to settle now, as settling doesn't create a sense of security. Money options improve for Ox natives towards the end of the month.

You've been busy and may find it hard to unwind. Or perhaps you find reasons to stay up really late? This is throwing off your sleep cycle. See if you can get back into your good bedtime habits.

There's positive energy around investments, and you may have a flash of insight about where to invest your money. You can meet helpful professionals during this Metal Rat year, people to assist you in making both traditional investments, as well as explain the investment programs available through your job.

Happy energy surrounds your family now. You may throw a party or host a barbeque. It's good to cook up something you like to eat and share it with others.

Travel plans may need some adjustments, or there may be issues with your vehicle. Road construction or other city delays can create havoc with your timetable, especially as Uranus goes retrograde this month. Your intuition alerted you about this before you set out, and you may be wondering if you should go at all. But once you're on your way, things go better.

September: *Mars goes retrograde on September 9. Jupiter goes direct on September 12. The Sun goes into Libra on September 22. Saturn goes direct on September 28. Your Lucky Days are 4, 10, 16, 22, and 28. [How to use your Lucky Days: On these days, plan to take significant actions, make vital phone calls, send emails. These are days when your energy and luck are high.]*

This is a beneficial month for education. Even if you're not formally enrolled, it would be a good idea to do something to expand your mind and learn some new things, especially after Jupiter goes direct in mid-September. It would be advantageous to learn anything new related to technology. Ox natives can shy away from the new-fangled gadgets of the current age, but you can actually benefit from learning more about the devices you use every day. Focus on what you specifically want to do. Answer the question of "How?" rather than attempting to learn all about the nuts and bolts.

You have more energy this month. You can be quite productive. It's possible to finish a large project, especially one dealing with writing or your career. On the other hand, with Mars going retrograde on September 9, a project you've been working on at home is not up to your standards. You may want to take a step back and see where it's gone off the rails.

You may be tapped for a leadership position this month in your church, professional group, or a charitable organization you're associated with. This is an honor, but adds a list of things to do to your hectic schedule. If you want to gain more power socially and professionally, then say "Yes." However, if you're doing this just because Ox natives can shoulder the largest burdens, consider passing the torch on to someone else.

A child or younger relative brings you news and a reason to celebrate. Additionally, a new pet may come into your life.

October: *Pluto goes direct on October 4. Mercury goes retrograde from October 13 to November 3. Your Lucky Days are 4, 10, 16, 22, and 28. [How to use your Lucky Days: On these days, plan to take significant actions, make vital phone calls, send emails. These are days when your energy and luck are high.]*

You are quite spiritually connected this month and your angels/ guides are active. You have more intuitive ability and can receive answers to questions you are pondering. This is a prime month to take risks since you have additional protection. If you want to visit a new place, meet new people and try new things, go with confidence as the Universe is watching over you.

A family matter has a happy resolution as one or more people in the extended family come around to your point of view after Pluto goes direct around October 4. Your legendary patience has paid off.

If you're looking for love, you may have the opportunity to reconnect with someone from the past, especially after Mercury goes retrograde on October 13. Ox natives tend to be idealistic and devoted, so you may give this one more try, but keep your boundaries in place and allow the other person to prove their devotion to you.

A legal matter can come to a happy conclusion if you do your homework. Ask for help if you feel you are in over your head.

Career energy is humming along. You are a valued member of the team and you may hear positive words from a supervisor or higher up. Even though Metal Rat years are career-focused, it's okay to take some time off if you need it. If you have been feeling tired or frustrated with the job, ask to work at home, or just take a few days for yourself.

November: *Mercury goes direct on November 3. Mars goes direct on November 13. Neptune goes direct on November 28. There is a Lunar Eclipse on November 30. Your Lucky Days are 3, 9, 15, 21, and 27. [How to use your Lucky Days: On these days, plan to take significant actions, make vital phone calls, send emails. These are days when your energy and luck are high.]*

There are changes in your financial picture now. You have most likely been anticipating this—Ox natives are very good at handling their money. You may receive an increase in your paycheck or additional money from a side business. But you may also experience a wake-up call around the time Mars goes direct on November 13. If you haven't been keeping up with the finances or bookkeeping, keeping track of funds, or your credit card expenditures, you will find it necessary to pay attention. Keeping an eye on your money will help it grow.

A loved one wants to have a serious conversation with you after Mercury goes direct around November 3. They may be looking for your support because of a change they want to make. You can be asked to support them even if the family, in general, would prefer things go in a different way. If you believe this person is heading in the right direction, it can benefit you to offer your support and pronounce it to the family.

If you are an Ox native looking for love, you may find someone of interest at your job, or somewhere you go on a regular basis. You often feel more comfortable with those who are part of your routine. Notice who's paying you attention these days.

Towards the end of the month, especially around the time of the Lunar Eclipse, there is a lot of forward movement on projects. These are things you have likely been working on behind the scenes. Your desire to perfect things may slow you down. Instead, lift off the cover and show your work to the world.

December: *Solar Eclipse on December 14. Saturn goes into Aquarius on December 16. Jupiter goes into Aquarius on December 19. Sun goes into Capricorn on December 21. Your Lucky Days are 3, 9, 15, 21, and 27] [How to use your Lucky Days: On these days, plan to take significant actions, make vital phone calls, send emails. These are days when your energy and luck are high.]*

You're a very hard worker and never shy away from a long list of tasks. In December, this particular Ox native quality can be to your benefit as you find the extra work gives you a boost financially. There may be a large ticket item you want to buy, an annual bill coming due, or perhaps you want to make a contribution to your retirement savings.

The attention you pay to your finances helps you make the right decisions. It's also a good idea to do spiritual things to attract more money, time for some Feng Shui, lighting candles, prayer, meditation, and affirmations. By combining the spiritual with the practical activity, especially after the Solar Eclipse on December 14, you can achieve amazing results.

As Jupiter and Saturn move into a new sign, your relationship improves. There is a feeling of harmony between the two of you. You are ready to take this relationship to the next level. This may mean you commit to living together or getting engaged. If you're already married, you may want to plan a big anniversary party for the coming year.

There may be another shift in management at your current job. If you like the new manager, it's a good idea to stay where you are for now. But many changes can occur in business during a Metal Rat year. If you are unhappy with the changes, then Ox native, you would do well to look for another position. Update your resume and get ready for the new energy coming in February with the Year of the Metal Ox. There will be several outstanding opportunities for you in the next few months.

January 2021: *Uranus goes direct on January 14. Mercury goes retrograde from January 30 to February 20. Your Lucky Days are 2, 8, 14, 20, and 26. [How to use your Lucky Days: On these days, plan to take* *significant actions, make vital phone calls, send emails. These are days when your energy and luck are high.]*

The Year of the Metal Rat comes to a close and for Ox natives, it is the end of your personal 12-year cycle. Next month, you will begin a brand new 12-year cycle, which will feel like springtime.

This month you may look around and decide to start releasing any remaining old stuff. This is a perfect time to do a deep declutter. Really get into the rafters and to the back of the garage, getting rid of stuff you may not have used for years. Selling off stuff can be a source of income for you now, but don't let that get you bogged down. It's better to release excess and open up your space for the new energy that is coming.

A shift in eating habits is beneficial now. Ox natives may be attracted to a new diet or style of eating. You don't often make a change like this, so when you feel inspired to do so, don't let anyone talk you out of it. Your intuition is speaking to you. Healthy eating can help your body heal in so many ways.

As Uranus moves direct on January 14, you may be planning to change your appearance. Consider a new hairstyle, new clothes, or add jewelry that sparkles.

Your experience at work improves as the changes in management settle down.

If you own your own business, it's a good time to automate some of your procedures or processes. Plan to outsource some of the tasks rather than to hire new people. Start your hunt by asking the question, "How can this be done automated?" or "What would be a way I could avoid doing this task at all?" You will receive some helpful answers and information from the Universe when you are aware you are looking for it. Try to implement changes before Mercury goes retrograde on January 20

February 2021: *Lunar New Year begins on February 12. Happy Year of the Metal Ox.*

Attract New Love

You've been patiently waiting for love to knock on your door. This is the year for Ox natives who are looking for a partner. Your work or a hobby brings you attention. This year you are more visible to the people you admire, and to those who admire you. In short, love can find you this year.

Very uncharacteristically, you may want to be intimate with this new person quickly. The energy of the Metal Rat year is quick and decisive, but take advantage of your signature Ox patience to wait until the time is right. A new relationship may also bring a new hobby or interest to you. It's good to try new things. Take a cooking class, go parasailing, join hot yoga, or take up bowling. Any new activity can bring you closer to love.

This year there are many reasons you may want to add the essence of joy to your home to help attract love. You can attract joyful energy by adding floral scents to your home either by burning floral incense or using a scented floral spray. A floral-scented incense like Nag Champa works very well. Or, pick up a bouquet of floral-scented incense and fill the house with the sweet scent of flowers. Add floral scent or flowers to your home weekly to keep the energy of love and joy all around you.

Enhance Existing Love

Your love relationship is going better than ever. You seem to be finishing each other's sentences. Your schedules are in sync. There's trust between the two of you. If things are not in harmony in the bedroom, this is just the last hurdle. You may want something different in this part of your life, or your partner may want something they've been too shy to mention. Time for a little playful love-talk.

As the two of you talk, discuss your feelings openly and share your vision of the future. This will help both of you find a deeper, more meaningful connection with your sweetheart. As you convey love and respect to the other, you build an even stronger union.

There may be an issue with friends or friendships this year. Perhaps a friend is monopolizing your time, keeping you from your partner. You need to find a gentle way to detach yourself. Or, maybe you don't really like your partner's friends, but they've been together since childhood, so what can you do? This is another matter that needs to be discussed quite frankly, possibly some sacrifice on someone's part needs to happen for the good of the relationship.

To strengthen the bond in your love relationship, find a heart-shaped bowl to display in your home. The bowl can be made out of wood, stone, or fabric. Choose red or hot pink. (Avoid pastel colors as this can cause your partner to be passive.) Write your wishes for your love relationship on a small piece of paper and place it inside the bowl. Then place this bowl on your bedside table to bring more romance to the bedroom.

Looking to Conceive?

The mighty oak tree may provide help for those wanting to conceive. In Feng Shui, an oak tree in your back yard is a symbol of fertility and success of children. In fact, any oak tree on your property is good energy for conception. Hang a small chime or bell from the tree to call in the fertility energy. If you don't have a tree, find and plant an acorn. And if you don't have a yard, plant it in a flowerpot, or better still, take a trip to a forest and plant several.

(From Donna Stellhorn's book, *A Path to Pregnancy: Ancient Secrets for the Modern Woman*)

Family and Kids

During Metal Rat years, Ox natives will need to make some decisions about living arrangements. A relative comes to live with you. Or you may be expected to take part in a family argument about a living situation, and asked to take a side. Neither of these scenarios is one you would place on your wish list. It will all work out in the end, so if you can, try to go with the flow while it's happening.

Expect is some activity in connection to your home as well. There may be a change of neighbors, or the neighborhood itself may be altered through building or construction. Parking may become an issue. There may be a need to have a discussion with a neighbor about boundaries, or perhaps you need an actual fence.

Your children are doing well. Be proud of their accomplishments. There may be recognition received from a school. If you have adult children, one or more of them may receive a promotion or a boost in their business. You may be asked to lend your skills to their career. This is fine, just don't overextend yourself energetically or financially.

Amber is not a stone, but a fossilized resin from pine trees. Its warm honey color reminds of hearth and home. Because pieces of amber are truly ancient, the energy is about longevity and strength. It's a symbol of the love of a relationship stretching back to the beginning of time and going forward for all time.

Find a specimen of amber to display in your family room or bedroom. It doesn't have to be large, but if it's small it should be in a place of honor such as next to a family portrait or on the fireplace mantle. Clear the stone when you get it (see the section at the end of this book on clearing crystals) and then clear it again every few months to renew the energy. This year, Ox natives can also wear amber to bring positive relationship energy.

Money

You are in the last year of your 12-year cycle. This is the year to take all your skills and accumulated experience and parlay them into your biggest paychecks. Income can come from several sources for you. You may receive money from a side business or a source of passive income as well as from your full-time job. This may sound like a lot of work, but Ox natives are the hardest working sign of the zodiac, so this isn't difficult for you.

One key to receiving or having more money will be asking for it. This is not a time to be shy or modest. You have a long list of accomplishments and this year, and you should let everyone know your full CV. The sooner you ask for more money, the sooner you are likely to get it. And if you get a hard "No!" response to your request, then you know you'll need to start looking around for a door that opens to something better.

In a Metal Rat year, you can make money from many sources, but one of the best will be creating passive income. You may not be comfortable with investing, but this is a good year to find trusted people to help you. Ox natives tend to swing from the frugal to the super-frugal. You don't have trouble saving money. Your problem may be more that you don't feel comfortable receiving money you haven't worked for (passive income would be included here). It's a skill worth practicing.

To help attract money this year, consider placing a Lucky Money Frog by your front door. The Lucky Money Frog sits on a pile of coins and has a coin in his mouth. If you place him by your front door, he will collect money as a result of the energy that comes in. Place him on the floor by the front door or on a table nearby. If he's sitting inside the house (most people do place him inside the house), he should be facing the door, like your personal, butler. If he's sitting outside the door, his back should be to the door, like your personal bouncer.

Job or Career

You are in the last year of your 12-year cycle, making this an accumulation year. It is time to use your accumulated knowledge and experience acquired over the previous 12 years. Package it up in a way to bring you the job or the clients who can make you some serious money. Strive to move up in your current company. Or, if you must make a move this year, consider moving to a competitor (or within your same industry). This can be a very profitable year for you if you focus on capitalizing on what you already know.

If you work for someone else or you work a contract position, you will discover management will turn out to be rather helpful this year. In your dealings with one particularly difficult supervisor, you may see them switch to being supportive of you. At the same time, one you've trusted for a long time and have had a good relationship with may be leaving the company. They will no longer be in a position to help you as they once did.

With all that said, it's a good time for you to look at the industry you currently are familiar with. Ask yourself what are the long term prospects for a company like yours. If you see your industry in decline, it's the right time to start looking at what you'd like to do in the future. Consider reaching out to people who work in a job you think would be interesting; find out how they got started in their current work. Consider classes and vocational programs, as well. If you are thinking of starting your own business, this is the time to do it; start it as a side project. Build it slowly during the year and get ready for a big launch in 2021.

Maps are both practical and can serve as a symbol for finding your way. Some people are naturally drawn to maps and decorate their space with city plans and country charts. Ox natives are in the planning year of the 12-year cycle, so a map is a suitable symbol to express the energy of how you will get from where you are, to the goal you have for your future.

Choose any map or globe to display in your home. Hang or place it in a spot near the front door, but don't let it block the door in any way. Every once in a while, look at the map and trace how to get from one point to another. Ask the Universe for your own intuitive map for your goals. With an internal, personal map, you'll know how to get to where you want to go and the kind of obstacles you may encounter along the path.

Education

You may feel as if it's time to study something new. This would be a good year for you to get some additional education, especially if your goal is a career transition in 2021 or 2022. Carefully consider the industry you think would be a possible alternative to your current work. Check to see if any current jobs are about to be displaced by technology. You can find your niche. It's better to study something you're genuinely interested in than go for the latest "hot" job.

If you're already in school and plugging along as Ox natives do, you'll be happy to know you are well-liked by teachers and staff. Your work is a credit to you, even if you look at it with your usual modesty. If you stand up and feel proud of the work you do, you will find others willing to support you. You can find mentors and guides who are happy to help you with your next career steps.

Legal Matters

You have luck and protection this year when it comes to legal matters. This doesn't mean your year will be free of legal issues, but you will likely come out on top no matter how dire it may look in the first place. It can be a busy year concerning contracts and negotiations. It's a good idea to have a clear vision of what you want before you sit down at the table. Ox natives can be stubborn, especially when you're right, but don't throw the baby out with the bathwater. Stand your ground when you must, but be ready to negotiate when necessary.

Health and Well-Being

Ox natives will enjoy increased powers of healing this year. Visualization can be key to speeding this along. If you stay positive and clear away negative thoughts, you can even amaze your doctors with the progress you make physically. This is an excellent year to choose healthy friends to hang out with. At this time, you are likely to mirror those you spend a lot of time with, so make sure they are making good choices, and thus their positive energy can rub off on you.

This year you would benefit from some kind of meditation. You can use one of those popular meditation apps, or you can find a quiet place in the house to sit and practice on your own. Your intuition and overall sense of spiritual well-being improve when you do this.

You may experience the joy of having friends around and also interacting with their kids or pets. This can bring you a lot of happiness, which in turn helps your physical self.

The leaves of the eucalyptus tree have long been recognized for their healing qualities. Even smelling the leaves is said to help. Branches of eucalyptus are available in craft and florist shops. Find six to nine cuttings from a eucalyptus tree and bring these into your home. Place them in a vase (vases represent peace in Feng Shui). Display your eucalyptus near where you cook or eat. This may be in the kitchen or dining room. About once a month, gather the leave and branches and go outside to give them a good shake. Remove excess dust throughout the month. Keeping your eucalyptus plant looking beautiful will help attract positive energy to your home.

Tiger

February 8, 1902 -- January 28, 1903: Yang Water Tiger
January 26, 1914 -- February 13, 1915: Yang Wood Tiger
February 13, 1926 -- February 1, 1927: Yang Fire Tiger
January 31, 1938 -- February 18, 1939: Yang Earth Tiger
February 17, 1950 -- February 5, 1951: Yang Metal Tiger
February 5, 1962 -- January 24, 1963: Yang Water Tiger
January 23, 1974 -- February 10, 1975: Yang Wood Tiger
February 9, 1986 -- January 28, 1987: Yang Fire Tiger
January 28, 1998 -- February 15, 1999: Yang Earth Tiger
February 14, 2010 -- February 2, 2011: Yang Metal Tiger
February 1, 2022 – January 21, 2023: Yang Water Tiger

Tiger Personality

There are two ways to think about Tiger. First and most obvious, consider the beautiful beast in its jungle habitat, hiding in the tall grass, patiently waiting for his prey. A herd of antelope comes loping into view, pausing at the local waterhole. The Tiger watches and waits until one not too bright antelope wanders away from the herd. Lunchtime!

But that's only one aspect of the Tiger. There is also an impatient side, the "bounce-bounce-bounce energy" we saw in Tigger, the Tiger of Winnie the Pooh fame. This Tiger is the impulsive, leap-before-you-look energy.

Those born during the year of the Tiger have a personality with a combination of these two aspects. They are both patient and spontaneous. For instance, they can be very patient when they are stalking something they want. But when they find it, they jump in, completely committing themselves to having it, with no thought to the consequences.

The Tiger is a powerful sign, the second most powerful (and second most popular) of all the Chinese Zodiac. People born under this sign are rebellious and unpredictable, but they command our respect. They are ready for anything. Overall, they love life, and they want to experience it fully. Sometimes this sits well with those around them, and sometimes it doesn't.

Those born in the Year of the Tiger are suspicious. They don't trust easily. When their suspicions are confirmed, they are quick-tempered and will say whatever is on their mind. Be cautious of a Tiger's temper—after all, they have sharp claws.

There is also a gentle side to the Tiger. Tigers are very affectionate and devote themselves to those they care about. They can hug, snuggle and purr, just like a soft, little kitten.

Tigers are dreamers and artists at heart. At the mere suggestion of it, they are ready to fly off to Bali with you. They will join your band. They will audition when the reality show comes to town looking for contestants. Everything is possible!

Tiger people may spend their whole lives running after exciting adventures, or they may have short periods of rebellion when they quit their job, leave their relationship, and throw caution to the wind. The rest of us watch quietly and hope the Tiger succeeds.

Tigers are emotional; their highs are really high, and their lows are very low. When the low periods happen, Tiger needs a shoulder to cry on. It will tempt others to offer advice, but Tigers won't listen. As a Tiger, you've learned it's better to stick with who you are, and know that tomorrow is another day.

Tigers can be very charismatic and easily influence others when they put their mind to it. They make compelling speakers, teachers, and politicians. Tigers are charming; potential lovers fall for their flattery. The passion will burn hot—at least for a while.

But when the initial excitement is over, Tiger can fall out of love just as quickly as they fell into it, and just drift away. If, on the other hand, the object of their attention starts to stray away from them, Tiger is quickly back on the hunt, eager to renew the chase.

Tiger: Predictions for 2020

January 2020: *There is a Lunar Eclipse on January 10. Uranus moves forward in direct motion once again on January 11. The Lunar New Year begins on January 25. Your Lucky Days are 3, 9, 15, 21, and 27. [How to use your Lucky Days: On these days, plan to take significant actions, make vital phone calls, send emails. These are days when your energy and luck are high.]*

This is the last month of the Lunar Year, and the importance of resources is highlighted in your chart. Over the last year, you have learned new skills and sharpened your abilities. You have met some supportive people who are able and willing to help you. You have a list of innovative ideas to implement. Now it's time to put it all together. The future may feel uncertain, but that's what Tigers love, a sense of liberation, adventure, and racing towards the goal. Don't let the hesitation and caution of others hold you back.

The song that keeps playing over and over in your mind is a message. Time to decipher it. In fact, fascinating signs show up in your life now. Some of these are multiples of numbers or lines from movies that have a special meaning or message for you now. Your psychic ability is robust now.

If you're in a long-term relationship, you may be feeling intimately connected to that person to a greater extent than you have in many months. Take hold of the person's hand. This relationship is growing closer.

If you're looking for love, you need to consider what's been blocking you. There are no obstacles but the ones you keep constructing. The love you want is waiting on the other side of the wall you've built. Tear down this wall. Be your rebellious, captivating self, and welcome love into your life.

February: *Mercury goes retrograde from February 16 to March 9. Your Lucky Days this month are 2, 8, 14, 20, and 26. [How to use your Lucky Days: On these days, plan to take significant actions, make vital phone calls, send emails. These are days when your energy and luck are high.]*

The Metal Rat year begins with others offering you multiple opportunities. This is a great month to be asking for help. It may not be a Tiger native's favorite thing to ask for assistance, you tend to prefer moving quickly while others move more slowly. You may find it quite irritating to wait for other people to come through for you, but this month you are able to multiply the best results of your abilities as a result of enlisting the aid of those who want to help you.

Income from a business, side job, or partnership can be quite impressive —especially at the beginning of the month. When Mercury goes retrograde, you may find that clients and customers from long ago once again seek you out to do business with you. If you work a contract job, try to sign new contracts before or after the retrograde period to keep from finding yourself in a situation you'll want to get out of quickly.

When it comes to romance, there are several opportunities for an intimate encounter. If you're already in a love relationship, you and your partner can have some fun times this month behind closed doors. Tigers who are not yet in a relationship could find themselves falling into bed with someone you've only recently met. Consider what's going on in this new relationship, and whether your new lover gives as much of themselves to you as you give to them before starting to spend all of your time with this new lover.

You may be having trouble sleeping. Too much nightlife or just too much TV could be taking time away from sleep. Your temper won't be as sharp if you are well-rested.

March: *Mercury goes direct on March 9. The Sun enters Aries on March 20. Saturn enters Aquarius on March 21. Your Lucky Days are 3, 9, 15, 21, and 27. [How to use your Lucky Days: On these days, plan to take significant actions, make vital phone calls, send emails. These are days when your energy and luck are high.]*

Tiger native, you are usually confident to the point of daring, yet this month you seem to be a little unsure of yourself when it comes to a new relationship. You are capable of passionate love, but if you find yourself walking on eggshells, this is not the right love for you. Step back and regain your balance.

You may be tapped on the shoulder for a new set of responsibilities at work as Saturn, the planet of career, enters a new sign. You may be given a larger team to lead, or you may get a project you've had your eye on. Tiger natives who own a business are now likely ready to launch an innovative design. This is best done towards the end of the month.

This is a favorable time to set goals, especially financial ones. In past years, you may have let money run through your fingers. But now is the time to accumulate money towards payment of debt, or use it to increase your retirement accounts. In Metal Rat years, calculated risks are best. Tiger's love risks, but are not fond of the calculating part. This month, think about the downside before you leap off a financial cliff.

A compelling dream you may remember has you thinking about a special someone from a romantic perspective. Can a dream become a reality? Reach out to this person and ask them to coffee. Start by being a friend and see what direction things take.

A child or younger relative makes a declaration to the family. You see yourself in this bold young person.

April: *Pluto goes retrograde on April 25. Your Lucky Days are 2, 8, 14, 20, and 26. [How to use your Lucky Days: On these days, plan to take significant actions, make vital phone calls, send emails. These are days when your energy and luck are high.]*

Your powers of attraction are high. You are likely to be on the receiving end of compliments and looks from many interesting and interested people. They may be attracted to you physically, but they can also find you intellectually compelling because Tiger natives can have an audacious sense of humor. Expand your circle of friends. Be aware of who is showing their admiration for you. If you are interested in knowing more about why, you may want to meet for coffee and conversation to learn more about them, and what a potential connection might lead to.

As Pluto turns retrograde towards the end of April, you have the opportunity to say "Yes." to something on your bucket list. This could be a quick trip, or an experience you've been waiting for, but couldn't get tickets for. This adventure may shake up the budget, but it's worth it.

Your current job may not be measuring up to your vision of the ideal career. It's time to close the gap. Take one aspect of your current job and see if you can change it. Maybe you'd like more flexible hours or a work-at-home option. Or perhaps adding commission for sales you make would add some challenge you'd enjoy. Take your ideas to your supervisors or those above them. See if you can make some changes for yourself from within the organization. Don't underestimate Tiger power.

You've always been an early adopter. Some new technology or gadget may be captivating your attention now; in fact, you're feeling inspired. This may lead to you creating something quite useful in connection with this development, or you may have one or more really creative ideas about new, related possibilities.

Finances improve now as a result of receiving several streams of income flowing in from multiple sources. Keep exploring new streams of potential income.

May: *Saturn goes retrograde on May 10. Venus goes retrograde on May 12. Jupiter goes retrograde on May 14. Your Lucky Days are 2, 8, 14, 20, and 26. [How to use your Lucky Days: On these days, plan to take significant actions, make vital phone calls, send emails. These are days when your energy and luck are high.]*

If you are in a relationship and want to take it to the next level, this is an opportune time to pop the question (this can include marriage proposals or a commitment to move in and live together). You are emotionally sensitive and very affectionate. But note, if your partner is also a Tiger, there may be some arguments as you try to stabilize this relationship.

A work or school project deadline is looming, and you may not feel ready—especially as several planets go retrograde this month. However, after a few late nights, and putting some extra hours into the project, your confidence soars. Your audience is more receptive than you expected they would be (not that you cared; you just wanted it done).

If you're considering going back to school or are looking for the right school for your kids, you can find a way to afford the expense now. Look into the options available to you, and get help navigating the enrollment process. Ask a close friend what they would do in your circumstances.

Your health is usually tip-top, but you may feel a little run down towards the middle of the month, especially when Venus goes retrograde on May 12. You could use a break, and a change of scene will inspire you. See if you can manage to arrange a weekend out of town. You will come back refreshed and full of creative ideas.

A new source of income becomes available to you. You can capture this income without spending money upfront. Trust yourself. If someone else is asking you to invest up-front, this is not the right direction for you at this time.

June: *There is a Lunar Eclipse on June 5. Mercury is retrograde from June 17 to July 12. There is a Solar Eclipse on June 20. Venus goes direct June 24. Your Lucky Days are 1, 7, 13, 19, and 25. [How to use your Lucky*

Days: On these days, plan to take significant actions, make vital phone calls, send emails. These are days when your energy and luck are high.]

The world is your oyster this month! Confidence and your rebellious nature can take you far. The Lunar Eclipse signals a time to focus on your desire to reach your goals. This is not a month for talk, but one for taking action. It's time to contact others, step up to the stage, and show the world what you can do. This is a suitable month to find funding for a business venture, or to raise capital through crowdfunding. If you need to file official paperwork, try to get it done before Mercury goes retrograde towards the middle of the month.

Real estate transactions may be delayed after Mercury goes retrograde; additionally, the Solar Eclipse energy may disrupt plans as well. For an impulsive, impatient Tiger native, it's good to have more than one option, so you have the ability to focus on something else entirely while you're waiting for others to catch up.

A new relationship may go from zero to 60 in the blink of an eye. Suddenly you could be a couple, at least in the eyes of your friends and family. On the other hand, if you're in an existing love relationship, step cautiously. Venus is still retrograde for most of the month, and this can destabilize whatever you thought was unshakable.

You may receive a spiritual message as the result of a vision, dream, or via the media. It seems like your eyes are opened—you have so many new ideas now. There is something you want to explore in-depth, and now is an excellent time to bring in new information and meet people who can help you.

July: *Retrograde Saturn backs up into Capricorn. There is a Lunar Eclipse is on July 4. Mercury goes direct on July 12. Your Lucky Days are 1, 7, 13, 19, 25, and 31. [How to use your Lucky Days: On these days, plan to take significant actions, make vital phone calls, send emails. These are days when your energy and luck are high.]*

Invest some time and energy in your appearance. You may have found a new exercise regimen that is fun and invigorating. Consider updating your wardrobe or adding a new tattoo. Exploring options for cosmetic surgery is a possibility after Mercury starts moving forward again in the middle of the month.

You have opportunities to expand your circle of friends. This may be due to a new interest or hobby you've been exploring. Others are reaching out to connect with you. Make yourself available for some get-togethers or parties.

You may be feeling intuitively guided in some investment or finance choices as the Lunar Eclipse on July 4 hits the financial house of your chart. You may have a desire to jump headfirst into a new type of business where you have little experience. That's Tiger native's M.O. You love the fast-moving energy of the Metal Rat year and the abundance of business options available to you now. But you are far more successful when you think before committing. Before you say "All in!" take a breath and do a little more research.

This month you can sell off stuff you no longer need and declutter the house. Think about selling furniture, memorabilia and other items you no longer feel are important to you, but which you currently allow to simply be stored in your home. You may want to visit garage sales and estate sales to find castoffs from others to flip on sites like eBay for extra cash at the same time.

August: *Uranus goes retrograde on August 15. Your Lucky Days are 6, 12, 18, 24, 30. [How to use your Lucky Days: On these days, plan to take significant actions, make vital phone calls, send emails. These are days when your energy and luck are high.]*

There is powerful financial energy around you now. You can tap into outside support for a big project, or find funding for something you've dreamed of doing. It will take asking, but you will get more "Yes." responses than "No!" ones. If this has to do with a business venture you're considering, now is the time to complete your business plan and get it ready for presentation.

A neighbor or sibling pays you a great compliment and points out a real talent you possess. Time to take your show to a bigger audience.

If you're looking for love, focus on what you do want, rather than lamenting what you no longer have. Opportunities for Love can show up wherever people dance, sing, bike ride, or run. Consider signing up to participate in a marathon, or to take tango lessons.

Now you have an opportunity to seamlessly transition into a new position at work, or even to start a new job. There are no boundaries in your career at the moment. You can reach out to decision-makers and identify the right person to open a door for you. Give your requests a spiritual boost through meditation, journaling, or chanting affirmations.

You may find there's a bump up in your social media following. This could mean you've tapped into the interests of a larger audience. If you see value in this, think about how you can expand your reach even further.

September: *Mars goes retrograde on September 9. Jupiter goes direct on September 12. The Sun goes into Libra on September 22. Saturn goes direct on September 28. Your Lucky Days are 5. 11. 17. 23. 29. [How to use your Lucky Days: On these days, plan to take significant actions, make vital phone calls, send emails. These are days when your energy and luck are high.]*

Home and family are highlighted this month. You may be moving or making some changes to the home. There may be someone moving in or move out. Or you may be hosting a large crowd of friends and relatives over for fun and games. At the same time, you may have some water-related issues in the house, such as backed up drains or a leaking toilet. All this is keeping you quite busy, though a busy Tiger is generally a happy Tiger.

Income increases this month, perhaps due to overtime worked last month, or maybe you're receiving pay now for a one-time project you completed in the past. These types of opportunities will be abundant in the Year of the Metal Rat. The extra money comes at a great time, as you've had your eye on something you want to purchase.

A friendship/connection may take a turn as Mars goes retrograde on September 9. This person may be leaving your sphere and moving on to a better opportunity. Spend some time being introspective and think about why you're staying where you are. Consider looking around at what else is available to you and don't let moss grow under your feet if you're not happy where you are.

You are very noticeable this month. Be thoughtful when putting content out into the world. Tiger natives like to shake things up, and your words can have a polarizing effect when you voice your opinions quite loudly. Sometimes this is great and gives you a boost. But this month, you may ruffle the wrong feathers, especially with someone you love.

October: *Pluto goes direct on October 4. Mercury goes retrograde from October 13 to November 3. Your Lucky Days are 5. 11. 17. 23. 29. [How to use your Lucky Days: On these days, plan to take significant actions, make vital phone calls, send emails. These are days when your energy and luck are high.]*

You're on your path now. Your mind is clear and know what you want to do. There's no reason to wait for others to do what they may have promised—even if they have committed to show you the way or to teach you something they know. You can move forward, especially on a creative project. Let others catch up with you when they can. In the meantime, "Wagons Ho!"

Support from a family member is available to you now. This comes quite out of the blue. You didn't expect to receive this much affection from this particular person. It's a compliment to your dynamic nature.

You are quite lucky with investments, banking, and loans right now. If you need to borrow money, you can find a lender offering good terms. Any bank errors can be rectified with little trouble—especially if done before Mercury goes retrograde on October 13. And you can connect with a helpful financial planner now. Focus on paying down debts. Look for conservative investments. In Metal Rat years, it's good to focus on increasing your net worth.

As Mercury goes retrograde towards the middle of the month, you may have an encounter with someone you loved in the past. If you are already in a good and loving relationship, use your best judgment here. Or this re-connection can lead to something really fun and fulfilling?

November: *Mercury goes direct on November 3. Mars goes direct on November 13. Neptune goes direct on November 28. There is a Lunar Eclipse on November 30. Your Lucky Days are 4, 10, 16, 22, 28. [How to use your Lucky Days: On these days, plan to take significant actions, make vital phone calls, send emails. These are days when your energy and luck are high.]*

Everything starts to move forward now. In fact, it almost feels as if you've been shot out of a cannon. Whatever you've been waiting for, less than patiently, now starts to manifest, and all of this adds to your list of things to do. Now, for a change, others are waiting on you. This is not a time to be obstinate about the details. If you want something changed in an agreement or proposal, just suggest it. It could be this is all about a job offer, but there can be options opening up for you in many areas of your life right now. It's like all the things you've been asking for are now being delivered.

It's time to take care of your physical self. How you take care of your body is a sign of how you feel about yourself. Think about how much of your diet, exercise and sleep patterns are within your control. Take steps to take care of yourself, lovingly and gently.

The Lunar Eclipse energy at the end of the month has got you thinking about making a more radical change. You might be thinking about moving, perhaps even living on a sailboat for a year. You might wonder about moving out of the country, to a land where you don't know anyone. You may decide you want to learn to fly a plane. Any of these are fine, but look at the small things you are not thinking about, things like uploading videos of your music or asking someone you like to coffee. No reason to spend weeks or months planning the future when you can add so much adventure to your life today.

December: *Solar Eclipse on December 14. Saturn goes into Aquarius on December 16. Jupiter goes into Aquarius on December 19. Sun goes into Capricorn on December 21. Your Lucky Days are 4, 10, 16, 22, 28. [How to use your Lucky Days: On these days, plan to take significant actions, make vital phone calls, send emails. These are days when your energy and luck are high.]*

Tiger native, you may have jumped into something new. Perhaps you've started a new job, or you're surrounded by moving boxes, ready to load onto the truck. Loved ones see all this change in your life and feel uncertain about your direction. They need your reassurance. The Solar Eclipse on December 14 can shake things up. If you're looking for others to offer encouragement, they may have little to give. Trust yourself. Tiger natives can be fearless revolutionaries. You are blazing a new trail, and others in your family or among your friends will follow in time. You can help them now by showing your confidence and reminding them that life is an adventure.

A work project may be coming to an end as both Jupiter and Saturn change signs this month. If you work by contract, it's a good time to put feelers out there for other options. A promised renewal may be delayed, or the contract may have terms you're not happy with. Look around for other opportunities. Once you've secured an option somewhere else, you can go back to the original place to do some negotiations.

There is a possibility of new pets coming into your life. Make sure you carefully think through the obligation you're taking on. If you want a pet, but are not yet ready for the commitment, offer to take care of a friend's pets. Both people and animals will be so grateful.

Changes in your partner's career may lead to changes in your and your family member's lives. This may require a discussion where everyone in the family can discuss the situation, as the changes could be the result of a job offer requiring a move to a different city, or an offer of a job with a very different schedule.

January 2021: *Uranus goes direct on January 14. Mercury goes retrograde from January 30 to February 20. Your Lucky Days are 3, 9, 15, 21, 27. [How to use your Lucky Days: On these days, plan to take significant actions, make vital phone calls, send emails. These are days when your energy and luck are high.]*

The Year of the Metal Rat draws to a close, and you start to feel the approaching energy shift. You will soon enter the last year of your 12-year cycle, one where you'll be able to capitalize on all the experience you've collected over the last decade or so.

Accumulate money this month towards a bigger goal. It's good to have a written budget, even if you have trouble staying on track at times. Look at reducing credit card debt. See if you can get interest rates lowered or consolidate debt if possible to aid in paying down balances. Also, find other ways to make money to increase your per-hour take-home pay. Be aware you have acquired a skill set that is valuable to others. You may be able to do consulting or tutoring. Consider all possibilities without deciding ahead of time which one you're qualified for.

It's a good time to lighten the load. Consider decluttering, getting rid of storage units, and clearing out the basement or attic. Tiger natives are not often materialistic. However, you can sometimes make hasty purchases and then not know what to do with the stuff. Check in with family and friends to see if you know someone who wants the stuff before taking it to the donation center.

Love relationships are strengthened now. If you have a sweetheart, there will be some fun times ahead this month. If you're looking for love, check out places like community centers, shopping malls, and sporting events. Any place where lots of people gather will be a good venue now for meeting new people.

February 2021: *Lunar New Year begins on February 12. Happy Year of the Metal Ox.*

Attract New Love

This is an excellent year for finding love. You will have more than one someone to choose from if you want. Your charisma is high, and you are noticed by the right people. A new love awaits who is fun, quirky, and quite interested in you. A kind woman helps you connect with someone really special. All you need to do is to get out of the house to meet this person.

Your schedule is tight, and at the end of a workday you may not feel like going out and meeting new people. This is the one thing that can delay you from finding the love you seek. You can't hide behind your studies or just hang out with the same familiar people. The month of May brings someone back to you that you thought had got away.

A good Feng Shui cure this year for Tiger natives is a garnet. Garnets have powerful energy to attract a new love into your life. For centuries, this deep red gemstone has been used to attract worthy partners. You can carry a polished stone with you or choose to wear garnet jewelry—perhaps earrings or a pendant.

If you already have the garnets and you want to use them now to attract a new love, it's a good idea to clear the stone.

See the section in this book for instructions on clearing stones and crystals.

Enhance Existing Love

Most Tiger natives already in a love relationship have a good time with their beloved this year. Occasionally your partner can irritate you, mostly minor irritations, but still, when they occur, it feels as if your partner were scratching their claws on the chalkboard of your life. These irritants are preventable for the aware and thoughtful Tiger, but they may require mutual discussion and understanding.

The aspects are lined up in a row for you this year, meaning one thing triggers the next and the next, and before you know it, you're back in an old pattern. What you need is a pattern interrupt. Some radical honestly may do the trick. However, both parties would need to agree to make an effort. It needs to be done in the spirit of love and respect, and the outcome can be you both take this love union to the next level.

June through September are the months when you can experience the greatest amount of growth in this relationship. You will then sail through the rest of the year as a happy couple who now love and trust each other even more.

Not all Feng Shui cures have to be traditionally Chinese in origin. There are many symbols broadly used in many cultures. The wedding ring quilt is such a symbol, in this case, a symbol of love and fidelity. To enhance your existing love relationship, place a wedding ring quilt on your bed. You can also hang a small lap quilt or quilted wall hanging in the same design on your bedroom wall to help enhance the energy of your partnership.

Looking to Conceive?

In many parts of China, women who want to conceive place a bowl of uncooked rice under their bed. If you would like to test this traditional approach to becoming pregnant, take a decorative bowl made of porcelain or china, and fill it about two-thirds full of uncooked rice (white rice is traditional). Place the bowl in the center, underneath the bed. Do not disturb the bowl until the baby is born.

(From Donna Stellhorn's book, *A Path to Pregnancy: Ancient Secrets for the Modern Woman*)

Family and Kids

Home and the well-being of your family is at the top of your priority list this year. You have your priorities in order, and you are receiving more support from the Universe for your goals. You may hit a big family milestone this year. This took some hard work, but climbing to the top of this particular mountain is definitely worth it.

This may be the year you buy or build your dream home. You may be renovating to bring your current residence closer to matching your dream home. There are a lot of crazy things that can happen along the way. It's good to have back up plans and to be flexible during the process.

Adult children are doing well though they may need help with managing some expected bills. Do not lend more than you can afford. Instead, do some brainstorming and creative problem solving with your kids. Younger children need extra help with important projects or tests. Your time is squeezed, but you come through with all that's needed.

Lavender is a wonderfully scented herb, popular and easy to find. It is known to clear energy, to promote healing, and to bring positive feelings into a space. Here are several ways you can use lavender this year. Plant lavender in the garden as it is said that brings longevity energy to a property and its owners. You may fill bowls with lavender buds and place them on the entryway table, the dining table, or on the kitchen island. And, of course, you can use a lavender-scented room spray to attract peaceful, harmonious energy for the family to enjoy.

Money

You have a reason to be optimistic this year when it comes to your financial circumstances. This is good news for Tiger natives, who are probably the most optimistic of all members of the entire Chinese zodiac. That said, your optimism needs to be grounded in reality. Keep track of those occasional expenditures (like biannual insurance or tax bills), so you don't have to blow your savings just to stay afloat.

You can make lots of money this year if you promote yourself and tell others of your talents. Expand your circle of business contacts. Online contacts are fine, but there's no substitute for taking someone to lunch, you may pick up several money-making tips you would never have found out about otherwise.

It's good to have insurance this year to cover yourself in case of a mishap. Also, having emergency savings, and you'll do great all year. Money may come in unexpectedly, or from seemingly impossible sources. To maximize this energy, try many new things and meet many new people. Even a friend who owes you money may need to be asked to return the funds, or perhaps the friendship may need to end.

You are probably familiar with lucky bamboo, i.e., sticks of bamboo growing in water, or small pots with bamboo growing in stones and water. There are about 10 species of bamboo grown in China, some of them grow to be as large as trees, measuring three feet in diameter and reaching a height of 40 feet.

Bamboo has many uses; it's been used for food, in the manufacture of paper, for making buckets and furniture; the leaves have been used to thatch roofs; the seeds and sap are used for medicinal purposes. This versatile plant serves as a perfect Feng Shui cure, a symbol of attracting money and benefit of all kinds this year. Place a lucky bamboo plant in your living room—within sight of your front door—to attract easy money opportunities.

Job or Career

This can be quite a lucrative year for you in your job. You may receive stock options, participate in profit sharing, bonuses, or if you own your own business, there is energy to support a general expansion of the business. Likely you will need to fill out all appropriate paperwork in order to receive company perks. If you're unsure how to do this, ask someone in personnel or your financial planner to go over it with you. That said, if you're thinking of leaving your current employer, trust your gut and don't wait around in hopes of a bonus. Instead, make the leap, and you'll find the windfall through other means.

The energy around your job shows you getting along quite well with management. However, you may have some issues with the members of your team. Most of these issues can be discussed and dealt with, but as an impulsive Tiger native, you can just as easily jump on people when you're provoked. This would not be a helpful response at this time.

Additionally, if you own your business with a partner, you may experience some struggles this year. Minor irritations are building up, and it's causing a rift in the business. The two of you think you're heading in the same direction, but any shade of a different approach at any level of the business you and your partner are unclear about can make a huge difference between you during this year. Have a talk and get back on track.

The great news for you during the Metal Rat Year is you can find ways to get additional career training at very little cost to yourself. You can find individuals and institutions that will help you with whatever questions you have, especially around technology.

Bank loans and government assistance is available for business owners who are Tiger natives. Even if the world seems to be tightening financially, you have the energy to find the resources you need. If you get a "No." this year, just move on to the next door. You will get the "Yes!" you want to hear before you know it.

When you want to attract more prosperity energy for your home and family, a good Feng Shui cure is to combine the money-attracting symbol of coins with the decisive power of a sword. By displaying a coin sword, either on a shelf or hanging on the wall, you call in prosperity energy. The coin sword does not need to be large though you'll find large ones are available. Place the coin sword in your home office, living room, or family room. Have the tip of the sword point in the direction of the front door.

Education

You can be top of your class this year, or at least voted class president with all of the positive energy you have this year. You are noticed by teachers and other faculty members, but if you're planning mischief, that too will be noticed. This is a good year to finish up studies, grab your degree and go. This may mean you need to take an extra class or two, but you can handle it. Try to focus on your studies rather than weekend parties and you'll soar.

If you're thinking of starting school, you are going to need some help to secure funding or to be accepted by the school you prefer. Enlist parents, siblings, friends, and colleagues to help you scour the internet for ways to stay out of debt. While college is important, there are often ways you can fund your education without putting yourself in the poor house. This is a challenge for impatient, impetuous Tiger. Wading through paperwork and waiting just isn't your style.

Legal Matters

While you have good fortune in relation to legal matters in general, this year something could sneak up on you. And anything that can sneak up on the Tiger does indeed require your attention. Perhaps you forgot to pay a bill, or you hit your golf ball through the neighbor's window one too many times, but you may be in for a surprise. Of course, you're still a Tiger, so keep your head, do your homework, and you will be fine. Or better yet, be friendly and happy with the people surrounding you and avoid trouble altogether.

Health and Well-Being

Tiger natives most certainly have an "On/Off" switch. This year it's more pronounced than usual. You seem to have endless energy when you are working on your business, your favorite hobby, or educational goals. But your energy can drop off sharply when others start dictating what they think you should or shouldn't do with your time. In fact, if you don't learn to say "No." (or at least "Not now!"), this year, you may find yourself not sleeping well. This robs you of the rest you need. You are generous with your time and resources, but this year you must prioritize so you can make a lot of progress on your goals.

If weight loss is your goal, consider joining a program with others who want to lose weight, too. Or consider hitting the gym with some friends from work.

Your intuition comes in spurts, and at times this year, you'll feel quite connected to the Universe. You may have unusual dreams, some that defy conventional interpretation. You are more easily hypnotized this year. You may want to take advantage of this fact if you want to quit smoking or rid yourself of some other habit.

Try not to spend too much time consuming the news and sensational headlines this year. It's okay to stay informed, but don't let it take over your life, especially if the news you're watching is very negative.

One Feng Shui cure I recommend for Tiger natives this year is the mirror; mirrors have many uses in Feng Shui. A particular kind of mirror is recognized as a potent symbol of protection, stronger than an ordinary mirror. It's known as the "Bagua mirror." This cure most commonly consists of an octagon-shaped wood frame with a small circular mirror in the center.

Symbols designed to attract the energy of protection and harmony are carved into or painted on the wooden frame. This type of mirror is never used facing into the house; it is always used pointing out of the house. Place or hang the mirror in a window facing outward. If you specifically need extra help protecting your health, hang a Bagua mirror in your bedroom or bathroom window. This will keep negative energy at bay.

Rabbit

January 29, 1903 -- February 15, 1904: Yin Water Rabbit
February 14, 1915 -- February 2, 1916: Yin Wood Rabbit
February 2, 1927 -- January 22, 1928: Yin Fire Rabbit
February 19, 1939 -- February 7, 1940: Yin Earth Rabbit
February 6, 1951 -- January 26, 1952: Yin Metal Rabbit
January 25, 1963 -- February 12, 1964: Yin Water Rabbit
February 11, 1975 -- January 30, 1976: Yin Wood Rabbit
January 29, 1987 -- February 16, 1988: Yin Fire Rabbit
February 16, 1999 -- February 4, 2000: Yin Earth Rabbit
February 3, 2011 -- January 22, 2012: Yin Metal Rabbit
January 22, 2023 – February 9, 2024: Yin Water Rabbit

Rabbit Personality

It may surprise many to learn, I consider Rabbit one of the strongest Chinese Zodiac signs. Most imagine him as a fluffy bunny, an animal who cannot speak, has no claws, and short little legs to hop away with. But the Rabbit sits between the Chinese Signs of the Tiger and the Dragon in the Chinese Zodiac wheel, and he alone keeps these two powerful forces apart.

Rabbit (also called Hare in some translations) generally serves as the sign of kindness and sensitivity. People born under this sign have good manners, common sense, and the ability to soothe and comfort others in any situation. For this reason, Rabbit often winds up in a leadership position.

The Rabbit personality is neither forceful nor rash, and they have a way of bringing people together. Rabbit is the perfect arbitrator, networking expert, negotiator, or diplomat. They always have something positive to say about and to everyone.

Because of Rabbit's love of peace, they are sometimes seen as weak, or even self-indulgent. Rabbit prefers to apply brain over brawn and will avoid a confrontation whenever possible. Often perceived as thin-skinned, actually Rabbit is merely cautious—after all, they don't want to be on anyone's menu! Rabbit can be a treasured friend, adept at keeping secrets, and offering very sensible advice.

Rabbit people tend to run in the best circles. They enjoy the finer things in life—everything from the best table in the restaurant to the best parking space at the mall. Rabbit natives seek out the easy way to do things, and often this leads to the best side of town. They tend to be a little flashy at times, which helps them fit in perfectly with their A-list friends.

Rabbit is realistic, yet sympathetic. They will listen to your troubles, and while they offer great advice, they never push an agenda. As a parent, they are neither the disciplinarian, nor are they given to criticism. They are positive and rarely embarrass their children in public.

In business Rabbit's quiet, unassuming air can cause others to think they are not paying attention. But there's more to Rabbit than meets the eye. Before you know it, you have been encouraged to sign the contract or seal the deal—with Rabbit taking the lion's share of the rewards. In spite of this (and possibly because of Rabbit's impeccable manners), you come away feeling grateful Rabbit was even willing to do business with you.

Rabbit: Predictions for 2020

January 2020: *There is a Lunar Eclipse on January 10. Uranus moves forward again on January 11. The Lunar New Year begins on January 25. Your Lucky Days are 4, 10, 16, 22, and 28. [How to use your Lucky*

Days: On these days, plan to take significant actions, make vital phone calls, send emails. These are days when your energy and luck are high.]

The new year begins with a focus on your role in the world. This could be related to your career, but it can also be your reputation (how you are seen at your church, in your neighborhood, by your friends, etc.). Also, consider your online reputation based on your past social media posts. Now is the time to remove posts which may no longer represent how you want to be seen. Avoid posting in anger or when under the influence. Rabbit natives are generally prudent about these things, but this month be extra careful.

Opportunities to make money continue to show up. Now you see a direct relationship between your state of mine and the financial support you receive. This doesn't necessarily mean you need to be positive all the time. Instead, now is a good time to activate your creative self. See problems for what they are, a challenge; then look for a creative solution. There are possibly as many as six sources of income or chunks of money available for you this month. Start every morning with the thought, "What can I do to solve the money question today?"

If you're already in a love relationship, you may feel others are trying to keep you apart. This could be quite innocent—because a friend needs your help or attention, or work happens to be hectic for your partner. Sensitive Rabbit natives will pick up whether there's anything suspicious going on. This is merely external circumstances or reality, so be patient.

February: *Mercury goes retrograde from February 16 to March 9. Your Lucky Days are 3, 9, 15, 21, 27. [How to use your Lucky Days: On these days, plan to take significant actions, make vital phone calls, send emails. These are days when your energy and luck are high.]*

This month you're likely standing at the center of a storm. Everyone around you seems to be chasing something or feeling as if they are being chased. But you're in no hurry. Nothing flusters you. This new Metal Rat energy does not intimidate you. It may, however, feel as if there is an endless stream of people in your life telling you to hurry up and to run around looking for money. They will tell you how busy they are and how much money they are making or not making. But you're fine standing in the eye of the storm. Continue what you're doing, think fast, but act at your own speed.

Rabbit natives have a lot of energy for finding love this month. If you've had trouble meeting suitable people in the past, consider a match-matching service, or find new online dating sites to join. Try to do this early in the month. Once Mercury goes retrograde in mid-February, it can make signing contracts or making lasting connections problematic.

There's a focus on having money in savings or investments now. If you work for a company, make sure you are maximizing all the benefits they offer, such as stock purchase incentive plans. On the other hand, Rabbit native, if you own the company, you may see a sizable increase in your profits. This is likely the result of attracting additional clients or customers, or you may somehow be in the process of reducing expenses by a considerable degree.

You are reunited with a friend you thought you had lost track of. The initial connection may be through Facebook or some other social media outlet. Now that the connection is made, it's good to bring this person into your life. If you live close to each other, consider meeting for coffee.

March: *Mercury goes direct on March 9. The Sun enters Aries on March 20. Saturn enters Aquarius on March 21. Your Lucky Days are 4, 10, 16, 22, 28. [How to use your Lucky Days: On these days, plan to take significant actions, make vital phone calls, send emails. These are days when your energy and luck are high.]*

Friendships are highlighted for you this month. You can expand your circle by meeting friends of friends. You may receive an invitation to a party or social event. Though your schedule is busy, it's a good idea to consider attending.

You are making changes this month as Saturn moves into a new sign. You're trying new things, perhaps aiming to get yourself unstuck, but the things you're doing are still well within your comfort zone. Consider what would stretch your abilities now. Rabbit natives are creative, gifted, and often musical. Time to explore the extent of the gifts you have.

Spiritually you're in tune this month. Towards the end of the month, you may feel a connection to a church, house of worship, or a spiritual congregation. It's good to be around others while you're connecting to a higher power.

Travel is good for you now, especially after Mercury goes direct on March 9. If you don't have the opportunity for a trip this month, at least explore some of the lesser-known areas of your city. Try a new restaurant, visit a park you've never been to, or attend a cultural event, perhaps a play or a concert.

Towards the end of the month, there is a shift towards a more serious focus on finances. Take a look at your overall money picture. You may be able to find lower interest rates on debt or to consolidate loans. A profitable investment option may be revealed.

April: *Pluto goes retrograde on April 25. Your Lucky Days are 3, 9, 15, 21, 27. [How to use your Lucky Days: On these days, plan to take significant actions, make vital phone calls, send emails. These are days when your energy and luck are high.]*

Focus on yourself this month. Sometimes, Rabbit native, you are so obliging and gracious that you can spend most of your time thinking and doing for others. But even the caregiver needs care sometimes, too. It's a good idea to pamper yourself with a spa day or give yourself permission to have a day when you don't need to answer to anyone else. Consider getting yourself a treat, such as a new outfit, piece of jewelry, or better still, an afternoon at your favorite art gallery.

Career energy is in the spotlight, and you may receive recognition from a supervisor. However, you may believe there's some ulterior motive to all this praise—planet Pluto is moving retrograde, and other people may feel they can suggest you could take on additional duties you can easily handle. This is your opportunity to do some negotiating. Decide what you are willing to do and make suggestions and requests accordingly. The boss will be more amenable than you think.

If you're in school, you may find your attention wandering, and you wonder if you will be able to get through the semester. The subjects you're studying now may not feel relevant to your future career. It's also possible the courses are just too basic for you. You may want to discuss the situation with your academic counselor to see if a change next semester is needed.

There are happy times with family. A memorable event involving siblings or extended family will bring a smile to your face.

Negotiations around a contract or vehicle purchase or lease go well. If you feel uncomfortable about doing the negotiating yourself, take a friend along with you.

May: *Saturn goes retrograde on May 10. Venus goes retrograde on May 12. Jupiter goes retrograde on May 14. Your Lucky Days are 3, 9, 15, 21, 27. [How to use your Lucky Days: On these days, plan to take significant actions, make vital phone calls, send emails. These are days when your energy and luck are high.]*

You have focused your attention on your income and finances as a new source of money may show up as a good possibility. This can be a regular stream of money you receive from a side job, or a passive income source (it's actually not so passive, if you look at it objectively). It's good to put this extra money to use by creating a written budget. Rabbit natives can accumulate wealth if they don't continually give away their money to every friend and relative who asks for it.

Relationships, especially love relationships and very close friendships, improve. It's been a long time coming. There's better communication flow, and you're starting to feel appreciated for all you do.

Your intuition is strong, and you may have some interesting dreams. Rabbit natives are known for following their heart over listening to their head. You're now in harmony with the Universe, and you can receive useful information if you ask the right questions. It's a beneficial month to get back into meditation or the divinatory arts like Tarot cards.

In the area of your job or your career, changes in management or activities related to a consolidation may be going on, leaving you feeling uncertain about your future. It may not yet be the time to leave, but it doesn't hurt to reach out to colleagues who have moved on and let them know you are open to opportunities. More than one of them would welcome your call.

June: *Lunar Eclipse on June 5. Mercury is retrograde from June 17 to July 12. There is a Solar Eclipse on June 20. Venus goes direct June 24. Your Lucky Days are 2, 8, 14, 20, 26. [How to use your Lucky Days: On these days, plan to take significant actions, make vital phone calls, send emails. These are days when your energy and luck are high.]*

Things are busy at home, thanks to the energy of the Lunar Eclipse. You may have a house full of visiting friends and/or relatives. Renovations may be going on, or perhaps you just feel the house is overly cluttered. The bottom line is you need a break, and you want to have that break in a peaceful, harmonious environment. You may need to take a quick holiday as a retreat. If you can't rent a beach house, just set yourself up in your favorite coffee shop for the day or find a table and chair and set them up an relax in the garden or in your own back yard.

Your intuition remains strong this month even as Mercury turns retrograde. You sense what people around you are feeling before they express it themselves. It's a very handy gift in your love relationship, as well as with your kids. Rabbit natives can deepen these important relationships by acknowledging back to people what they are expressing to you. As you mirror what they are saying, they will feel you understand and hear them. They feel safe and cared for, and will open up to you about the things you want to know.

If you're looking for love, you find opportunities galore among the people who are involved in spiritual activities, perhaps attending church, yoga conferences, or meditation groups. Also, if you are a vegetarian or follow a vegan diet, look for like-minded people shopping at natural food stores and through meetup groups held in or near places where you go shopping.

A financial advisor or financially savvy friend has some advice for you that could help you keep more of your money this year. This is in harmony with the energy of the Metal Rat year when it's a good time to accumulate capital and keep an eye on investments.

July: *Retrograde Saturn backs up into Capricorn. There is a Lunar Eclipse is on July 4. Mercury goes direct on July 12. Your Lucky Days are 2, 8, 14, 20, 26. [How to use your Lucky Days: On these days, plan to take significant actions, make vital phone calls, send emails. These are days when your energy and luck are high.]*

You crave change and want something different than the routine of your every day. Your eccentric nature wants to come out; you might consider coloring your hair or changing your hairstyle. You may want to change up your wardrobe or acquire a new tattoo. It's good to spend some time finding ways to express your creativity. Consider learning to make jewelry, clothes, or furniture for your home. Paint a picture or paint a room. Express yourself this month.

There may be some rumblings where you work around the time of the Lunar Eclipse. If you started to see some changes last month, now the seismic activity is getting stronger. It's good to have your updated resume ready in case you don't like where management is taking the company. If you own your own business, it's time you to shake things up in your office. This may mean firing an employee or a friend. Perhaps you need to think about a job you are currently doing—one which takes up lots of your time and effort—and hire someone else to do it better.

Income improves by facing forward. It may be something as simple as having new publicity photos taken. Examine how you're branding yourself in the marketplace. Even if you work for someone else or a large company, take note of how you present yourself. Are you the precise one? Are you the one who's easy to work with? Are you the cheerful one? Are you the one who brings the donuts?

There is fertility energy around you. There may be a pregnancy or adoption announcement in the family. Or you may be considering a new pet as an addition to your household.

August: *Uranus goes retrograde on August 15. Your Lucky Days are 1, 7, 13, 19, 25, 31. [How to use your Lucky Days: On these days, plan to take significant actions, make vital phone calls, send emails. These are days when your energy and luck are high.]*

This is a lucky month for romance. If you're looking for love, you have opportunities to meet someone special. It's a good idea to update your profile on dating websites as well as set aside some time to meet for coffee with prospective others. If you've been looking for some time and haven't found the love of your life, now would be the time to seek out some help with removing blocks in this area. This can be accomplished with the help of hypnotherapy, tapping, or EMDR, just to name a few methods. You can remove deep-seated blocks—from even as far back as your childhood—and open yourself up to love.

Your ability to attract what you want is strong now. You can combine this energy with the spiritual element by creating a little love magic. Consider lighting candles, chanting, or using some Feng Shui remedies to bring in what you want.

A change in travel plans may occur as Uranus goes retrograde on August 15. It's good to stay flexible. You may need to find alternative transportation to the airport, or the arrangements you have made for your lodging may need to be changed. There may be delays due to weather.

Career changes are happening, yet it's likely your income will remain stable for the time being. A new direction is unfolding, and you have begun to see your path forward. If you're changing jobs, there should be no gap in income (which also probably means no time off, or that you are collecting money from unused vacation time from the previous job). You can maneuver your way to a better position through this transition if you voice what you want to your supporters.

September: *Mars goes retrograde on September 9. Jupiter goes direct on September 12. The Sun goes into Libra on September 22. Saturn goes direct on September 28. Your Lucky Days are 6, 12, 18, 24, 30. [How to use your Lucky Days: On these days, plan to take significant actions, make vital phone calls, send emails. These are days when your energy and luck are high.]*

If you didn't change jobs last month, you will probably stay put now for at least a few months. You can improve your situation through visualization and open communication with those who can help you. Get ready to negotiate a change—this is something you're quite good at. It's time to challenge the expectations of others, and push back where you need to. Rabbit natives don't like confrontation, which is fine because you excel at diplomacy.

If you're in a love relationship and want to move this relationship forward, you may find it's time to have those all-important conversations about living arrangements, children, and marriage. You can strengthen your love relationship now by focusing on common ground and compromise.

You may be singled out by a group or organization for a bigger role or more responsibility. Check your schedule and see if you can fit this in.

A new friend gives you an out-of-the-box suggestion. Consider taking them up on this unique offer.

The majority of your investments are good, but during a Metal Rat year, it's a good idea to give investments your attention from time to time. Ask yourself if you would purchase this investment again at its current price. If the answer is "yes," then keep the investment. But if you would not, then it's time to divest yourself of this holding or piece of property.

A sibling or neighbor pays back a favor they owe you. You may be surprised that they are following through.

October: *Pluto goes direct on October 4. Mercury goes retrograde from October 13 to November 3. Your Lucky Days are 6, 12, 18, 24, 30. [How to use your Lucky Days: On these days plan to take important actions, make vital phone calls, send emails. These are days when your energy and luck are high.]*

Children are highlighted this month. If you have adult children, one may ask to return to stay at home for a while. Younger children need your attention and advice about a matter of dealing with friends or a teacher. You can help them a great deal simply by being there for them.

If you don't have kids, you may be asked by a friend to do some pet-sitting. Your own pets may need a little more attention now too, especially if you have a couple of animals who don't get along with each other.

Relationship energy is good, and you can consider adding some romance by setting up a regular date night with your sweetheart. It's good to break out of the usual routine and try something new like dancing, a restaurant you haven't been to before, or perhaps a couple's massage. Doing fun things during Mercury retrograde can result in you repeating the opportunity for fun in the future.

You are in the spotlight now. You may be asked to give a presentation for work, school, or a group you belong to. Even if you know you will experience some stage fright, it's a good idea to jump in and do the presentation anyway. Facing your fears now will help you grow in more ways than you might imagine.

If you are active on social media, you may see your numbers increase this month. People are listening. It's good to post positive, uplifting things now. Rabbit natives are known for their compassion. And while you might have a great interest in politics, find ways to encourage peace and understanding. This will bring you benefits in the future.

November: *Mercury goes direct on November 3. Mars goes direct on November 13. Neptune goes direct on November 28. There is a Lunar Eclipse on November 30. Your Lucky Days are 5, 11, 17, 23, 29. [How to use your Lucky Days: On these days, plan to take significant actions, make vital phone calls, send emails. These are days when your energy and luck are high.]*

You may have something to celebrate in the family this month. There may be a milestone birthday, anniversary, or a wedding to attend. Your home may be suggested as a meeting place. And happy memories can be made there.

Work is stable, and things are humming along. A person you used to work with may return and may need some refresher training before they can really help you out. You may be stuck doing routine work for the time being, but a new project is coming, maybe as soon as the end of the month.

If you've needed a new phone or computer, consider getting one soon. Mercury goes direct on November 3, so there's positive energy for acquiring new technology after that.

Your creative energy is strengthened. Redecorate the home or find a creative hobby you love to do. Invest some time and energy into your creative self.

Even though you're quite busy at this time of year, if there's an investment or financial seminar made available to you, consider taking it. If it's online, then grab the recording to review later if you don't have time right away.

Towards the end of the month, a secret you've been keeping comes out—by your own choice. This is a good thing as you are taking the opportunity to show the world your unique, wacky side. You can find several new friends or supporters once this secret comes out.

December: *Solar Eclipse on December 14. Saturn goes into Aquarius on December 16. Jupiter goes into Aquarius on December 19. Sun enters the sign of Capricorn on December 21. Your Lucky Days are 5, 11, 17, 23, 29. [How to use your Lucky Days: On these days, plan to take significant actions, make vital phone calls, send emails. These are days when your energy and luck are high.]*

You need a break. You may need several days off, or you might just need someone else to handle some of the household duties for a while. Metal Rat years can be hectic times. Make your needs known to your family and friends. Even if you live alone, it's okay to say to a friend, "Can you come by and help me with...?".

You are complimented at your job for your good work ethic. This is an excellent time to ask for an increase in salary or additional help. Have a list of your accomplishments at the forefront of your mind this month, so you can rattle them off when an opportunity presents itself. You will know when the time happens. You'll also get a second chance to have this conversation following the Solar Eclipse in mid-December.

If you're in school or if you need to take an exam for your profession, things can go very well if you call in some spiritual help for your studies and on the actual day of the test. Ask the Universe to fill your mind with what you need to know. Wear yellow on the day of the test as it's a color that aids in memory. And take an elephant charm with you, as the saying is, "Elephants never forget."

Financial matters flow smoothly now. You benefit by sticking to your budget during the holidays, Be creative, and find other ways to express your affection rather than just by buying things for the others on your list.

A healing can take place between you and a co-worker. A misunderstanding can be resolved.

January 2021: *Uranus goes direct on January 14. Mercury goes retrograde from January 30 to February 20. Your Lucky Days are 4, 10, 16,*

22, 28. [How to use your Lucky Days: On these days, plan to take significant actions, make vital phone calls, send emails. These are days when your energy and luck are high.]

Finances are highlighted this month and you may receive a small windfall from a passive income source. You may sell something, or money owed to you finds its way back into your pocket. Still, if you overspent during the past few months, you may now be feeling the pinch.

Now, at the end of the Metal Rat year, you have an opportunity to bring in more money as a result of your creative thinking or actual creative work. Consider your talents and see what you can produce, something others may want or that they have told you they want. This is also a time to sell off excess stuff. Rabbit natives can be quite sentimental, but that doesn't mean you need to hold on to your great aunt's dishes if you're never going to use them.

Work is going well. Your team is melding together nicely. If you were behind on a deadline before, you're catching up now. If you own your own business, a new system or piece of tech is working out well. It would be good to consider automating more systems in your business.

You have grown a lot spiritually and emotionally this year. You have this last month of Metal Rat year to clear out a little more emotional gunk. You can do this through journaling or perhaps a burning ceremony with friends where you each burn little pieces of paper on which you have written down what you want to release.

A friendship can turn into a romance now. If you're looking for love, this can be a great opportunity. If you're already in a love relationship, you may want to think twice before jumping into this sack.

February 2021: *Lunar New Year begins on February 12. Happy Year of the Metal Ox.*

Attract New Love

You are lucky in the love department this year. You can find love whenever you decide to look for it. The issue is you may be too busy right now to look. If your job and family are taking up all your time, love may pass by without you even realizing it. Actually, put time for love into your schedule. Write in a date night, and soon someone will arrive to fill that slot.

For you, Rabbit natives, you can find love at school, at church, or at politically inspired meetings. If attendance is light locally, consider driving a bit to find a larger group of people. This year, one step leads to another, and another, and these steps lead to love. It won't hit you all at once. It will be a gradual affair.

Traditionally, one of the best flowers to use as a symbol for attracting love is a rose. Its wonderful scent attracts, while its sharp thorns warn, "Be careful not to wound me!". From the perspective of a Feng Shui cure, the rose is the perfect flower to choose when you want to attract a new love, and you still want to be cautious, and protect your heart.

Growing roses outside your front door will attract love energy. If you can't grow them in this location, consider placing a miniature rose plant in your bedroom. If you don't feel confident about taking care of a live plant, then find a beautiful picture of roses (in your favorite color) and hang or place the picture in your bedroom.

Enhance Existing Love

You may have experienced some hard times in your love relationship during the past year. The dark clouds are starting to part, and there are blue skies ahead. What may have been an impasse between you now seems to have worked itself out. You are starting to agree more often and to do things together the way you used to long ago.

But this has been a hard fight, and you may still feel a little wounded as a result of past struggles. Rabbit natives are sensitive, intuitive souls who feel the pain of their love relationships very keenly. It's good for you to give yourself space to heal—time to take care of you.

This year you will likely make an effort to move your relationship to the next level. This could mean you decide to tie the knot or otherwise make your relationship permanent. Intimacy will now grow between you, and this can become the relationship you've wanted all along.

For those born in the Year of the Rabbit attracting new love-energy will be easy when you add a big splash of red to the bedroom. Consider getting a red bedspread or some red pillows. Red is the color of excitement and passion. Choose a shade of red that appeals to you. The spread or pillows can include other vibrant colors in a pattern, stripes, or floral design.

Looking to Conceive?`

All nuts represent the potential for fertility and children, but traditionally the hazelnut, in particular, represents this energy. Folklore throughout Europe says eating the nuts will make you both wise and fertile. Hazelnuts are rich in protein, containing thiamine and vitamin B6, making them a valuable food for when you want to get pregnant. Hazelnuts can be eaten raw, roasted, or ground into a paste and mixed with chocolate for a delicious treat.

(From Donna Stellhorn's book, *A Path to Pregnancy: Ancient Secrets for the Modern Woman*)

Family and Kids

This year, if you've wanted to change residences, you may find your move delayed. This delay could be job-related, or due to the educational needs of one of your children. You can manifest your dream of moving to a better place, but you will need to be patient.

You may be playing host to other people's kids or extended family this year. If fact, you may have more visitors this year than you've ever had in this house. Most of the visits are joyful. There are only a few times when the noise and numbers make you cringe.

Education is going well for your kids. They are doing the best they can under your helpful eye. But there are many distractions in the world today, and you need to sit with younger children just to make sure they get everything done. Older children will want your support, as well. They are probably looking more for a hug and your encouragement rather than a solution.

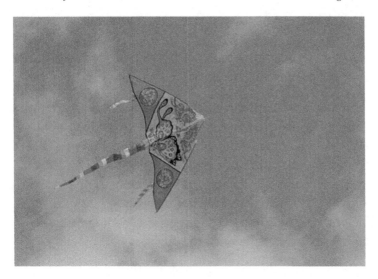

When there is a lot of energy in one life area, and you want to balance this energy between control and flying free, what better symbol is there than a kite. Kites were invented in China thousands of years ago. In ancient times kites were used for military purposes, for things such as measuring distances, communicating at a distance, and guiding troops through rough terrain. Now kites are flown for fun and to bring joy. You can display a kite in your family room or hang up a picture of kites flying in the wind. This helps bring the family together while still remaining open to the adventure of change.

Money

This is potentially a profitable money year for Rabbit natives. You are in the last year of your harvest period when money is easily acquired by the clever Rabbit. This year be open to unusual sources of money. Listen to what your friends are doing to make money and consider joining them. Money connected to internet or computer businesses is available for you this year.

Sources of money are not limited to your job this year. In fact, it's better if you branch out in the months to come and allow income to come from a variety of activities. While money is coming in, you are often quick to give it away to friends, relatives, and favorite causes. This year it's a good idea to make sure your long term accounts are fully funded before you start giving money away.

You may have been carrying a number of issues around the accumulation of money and wealth ever since childhood. This year you can clear whatever is blocking you. Think about leaving old family patterns behind you, and realize that any learned behavior can be unlearned. When you're out in the world, keep an eye on your wallet and other belongings. Don't be so caught up in the moment that you lose track of what belongs to you!

A good Feng Shui cure for attracting new prosperity energy (and attracting more money in general) is to get yourself a golden piggy bank. Choose a style that appeals to you, perhaps a classic western-style piggy bank in metallic gold, or the traditional Feng Shui piggy bank decorated with the Chinese characters for wealth and good fortune.

Place your piggy bank near your front door or in the home office, and feed it coins at least once a week (no pennies please). Place a list of your money wishes inside the bank along with the coins to bring in opportunities and positive career or wealth energy.

Job or Career

Rabbit natives need to evaluate the company they work for and the industry they are in and make a decision about these are stable for the long term future. Consider if the industry you work in will be around in five, ten, or twenty years. If not, it would be a good idea to start thinking about what you'd like to do next. This doesn't necessarily mean starting over. Many skills can be transferred to different industries. But it is important now to be aware of the trends and start to prepare yourself mentally for a change.

If a change sounds exciting, then it's time to start taking steps to make it happen. For example, you might decide to go from dwelling in a big city with a long commute to living ion a country farm or in a small town and working from home. Start to imagine and plan the life you want and see what small changes you can make in your day-to-day life now to prepare for a more comprehensive change in a few years. Often changes like these are done by shifting priorities. Once saving for land and a homestead becomes the priority, the daily lattes may not seem as important.

If you plan on staying in your current job for now, know you will likely hear about coming changes at the management level. There may be rumors of retirement or people changing jobs. Or perhaps the company you work at will be acquired by a larger firm. While your position seems stable, you may not like all the changes happening around you. These adjustments could lead to you having to spend more hours working, or add-ing travel to your schedule. To ease this energy, it's a good idea to have good relationships with the managers in the line of command above you. Not just your direct manager, but think of those further up the chain of command. Also, it's a good idea to make friends with managers of other departments. This can come in handy this year.

For Rabbit natives who own a business, this is a good year to expand your business by taking on a partner or two; or you can expand by acquiring a competitor. Remain aware and open to possibility as there are likely to be opportunities in both directions. If you're an independent contractor, you may find opportunities collaborating with others in a similar business.

For instance, if you are a yoga teacher, you may want to team up with the acupuncturist and a massage therapist and so forth. The best use for these team-ups would be joint marketing or cooperative advertising where the cost is shared. Avoid spending excessive amounts of money on slick programs promising too much. Sit down and talk with someone you like, and the two of you can find success.

The Dragon-Headed Turtle is a very traditional Feng Shui cure as this creature is not represented in any other culture. This chimera is usually depicted as having the head of a dragon with the body of a turtle, carrying with one or more baby dragon-headed turtles on it's back. This cure is used to attract wealth and success in your career.

Place your Dragon-Headed Turtle on a table in your home office, work office, or in the Wealth area of the house. Dust the figurine about once a month to re-energize this cure. You can place a few coins under the statue to focus the energy on attracting wealth.

Education

For Rabbit natives seeking to further their education, this is a good year to pursue such opportunities. Funding is available to you, though it may not match where you would prefer to study, or the subject you want to study. However, if you can make a few adjustments, you can make it work. You may appeal to the school itself for assistance and advice, as well as to friends and close relatives who will have helpful ideas for you. If you're are studying finance, banking, and business, you want to make sure your major is specific enough for a future job market. Expect to specialize.

For those of you Rabbit natives already in school, you show improved efficiency with your work and improved comprehension this year. You may have been learning how to study, or you now have fresh enthusiasm for getting your degree. The daily activity of going to school will be more enjoyable this year. You have your schedule set, and you are in the flow. There may be an opportunity to study abroad, but whether it's a good choice for you or not will become quite clear as you examine the details. Weigh your options carefully.

Legal Matters

When it comes to contracts involving money, it's always a good idea to negotiate terms. Do this gently, maintaining good relations as you proceed. Agreements for houses, employment, or vehicles will have a beneficial outcome even if you don't feel as if it's a perfect arrangement. This year any lawsuits will just be irritating. Avoid suing anyone if at all possible. Issues with custody or dissolution of a marriage may lead to happy results regarding the financial aspects of the agreement. Move slowly and deliberately, taking each step carefully, and you will experience a successful outcome.

Health and Well-Being

This is a very active year for Rabbit natives. This likely means you've found an activity you really love pursuing, and the exercise that comes with it is really improving your health. Or this may mean you are taking a very active role in your healing process. You'll find the competent health practitioners and beneficial information you seek. You may be trying new treatments or even traveling to find the help you need.

It's a good idea to take steps to reduce worry. Worry can be a problem during a Metal Rat year. You may want to practice letting go of anxiety using the tools of meditation, hypnosis, or even herbal therapy. You may consider journaling to write down your thoughts on paper (you can always burn the paper afterward if you don't want it to be read by others).

While your health is improving. You may receive less support from your significant other or closest friends. As you try new treatments or health regimens, you may find they are trying to talk you out of incorporating the changes you're embracing. This doesn't need to ruin your friendship, but it does indicate you probably need to set some boundaries so your conversations can stay on topics that support you.

If you've had issues with sleeping, you may need to make some changes to your mattress or pillow arrangement. The bedroom itself may need to be darker or cooler/warmer at night. Consider asking your doctor for a referral to a sleep clinic in the area and see if you can get professional help this year. Make getting quality sleep a priority.

Aloe plants can be found in many kitchens around the world. It is one of the best-known folk remedies for cuts and burns. This spike plant has a tradition of protection and healing energy. This year, add an aloe plant to your front garden or place a small, potted specimen in your kitchen. This will help bring healing energy to the whole household.

Dragon

February 16, 1904 -- February 3, 1905: Yang Wood Dragon
February 3, 1916 -- January 22, 1917: Yang Fire Dragon
January 23, 1928 -- February 9, 1929: Yang Earth Dragon
February 8, 1940 -- January 26, 1941: Yang Metal Dragon
January 27, 1952 -- February 13, 1953: Yang Water Dragon
February 13, 1964 -- February 1, 1965: Yang Wood Dragon
January 31, 1976 -- February 17, 1977: Yang Fire Dragon
February 17, 1988 -- February 5, 1989: Yang Earth Dragon
February 5, 2000 -- January 23, 2001: Yang Metal Dragon
January 23, 2012 -- February 9, 2013: Yang Water Dragon
February 10, 2024 – January 28, 2025: Yang Wood Dragon

Dragon Personality

When considering Chinese Zodiac anima qualities, it helps to examine the traits, behaviors, and personality of the animal—except there are no dragons to study (at least not anymore). In the Shuo Wen dictionary (200 AD), dragons are listed. We can read a description of this creature: The dragon has "the will and power of transformation and the gift of rendering itself visible or invisible at pleasure."

It is said there are three types of Dragon: one, the most powerful, inhabits the sky; the second lives in the ocean, and the third resides in dens (or caves) in the mountains. Some say a dragon can shrink to the size of the silkworm, or expand in size, lie down and fill up an entire lake! These powers describe the traits belonging to Dragon and explain why so many people envy the Dragon native.

The Dragon seems not to be of this world, and likewise, Dragon natives are seen to exist "above it all." They have big ideas and the power to make them happen. Even when young in years, Dragon will take on and carry enormous burdens and responsibilities.

Dragon natives can tap into a seemingly endless supply of energy, and they are eager to talk about their ideas. The Dragon has the potential to accomplish great things—or simply to fly around in the heavens, never allowing his or her feet to touch the ground.

Despite all of this magical power, people born in the Year the Dragon can have violent tempers (and explosive temper tantrums) when things don't go their way. Sometimes a Dragon is not diplomatic. They would much rather say what they want to say than tell others what they want to hear. When a Dragon breathes fire, everyone in the vicinity gets singed!

The Dragon native requires a very clear purpose in life. They need a cause to champion, a wrong to right. No matter what Dragon does for a living, he/she will have their pet projects and their dreams. Without these, Dragon becomes listless and depressed.

The Dragon is known to be very skillful in finance and management. Dragon very sensibly looks at long-term investing as a way to protect their assets. Good at spending money, Dragon is always on the lookout for an innovation to adopt. Dragons rise to the top of whatever field they choose. They are often chosen to be the leader, even if they're new to the organization.

Dragons hate to be trapped, with no options for change. If stuck behind a desk or saddled with a long list of rules, Dragons will revolt. For all their seeming confidence, the Dragon can feel quite insecure on the inside. There is a constant struggle between the desire for success and the fear of success. They're status-conscious and don't like to fail, especially in the eyes of others. This causes them sometimes to shoot for small goals, rather than pursue big dreams.

Dragon is by far the largest personality of the Chinese zodiac. As the only mythical animal of the twelve, a Dragon can take on many forms.

Traditionally, a Dragon could manifest as a creature the size of a gigantic cloud formation to one as small as a butterfly. Because of this remarkable ability, Dragon holds the vision for our future in this world. They see where we are heading and are aware of where we should be going.

Dragon's confidence is as big as its personality. They motivate everyone around them. They undertake the greatest adventures, eager to experience wild success—or are willing to endure crushing failure. There is no stopping a Dragon once their mind is made up. They will push right to the edge to see if they can make something happen. If things go wrong, well, that's when Dragon truly shines as a leader, the one to lead everyone out of danger.

Dragons have nothing to hide (Why should they? They have nothing to fear!). Their feelings are always out in the open for everyone to see. Dragons do not keep secrets. After they share the news, the Dragon will tell you he or she was absolutely right to reveal everything. So, if you keep a Dragon as your confidant, do be aware that whatever you have told them will come out sooner or later.

Dragons are sensitive to the climate. In pleasant weather, they are calm and levelheaded, but when a storm comes, they become easily rattled or irritated. When a storm is on its way, it's time to steer clear of Dragon! Dragon doesn't mind either way—although nearly always surrounded by friends, they are perfectly happy spending time alone.

Those born in the Year of the Dragon need a mission or a life purpose. When their life purpose is clear, Dragon is capable of soaring to heights other animals couldn't even dream of reaching. Dragon is very decisive. Once they've chosen a path is very hard to dissuade them from continuing along it.

However, sometimes Dragon is not particularly smart in the realm of business. They don't pick up on the cunning of others. Dragon natives are often unaware of the plots and schemes surrounding them. Dragon is more concerned about reaching their goal, and not at all willing to play the petty games of others.

The most challenging thing for a Dragon is the stubborn desire to do everything on their own! They never call for help, never ask for support. Dragon is powerful and can even be intimidating; natives have a fiery temper and a very fixed idea of the ways things should be. Dragon often speaks without editing, letting people know exactly what they think.

Dragon: Predictions for 2020

January 2020: *There is a Lunar Eclipse on January 10. Uranus starts moving direct again on January 11. The Lunar New Year begins on January 25. Your Lucky Days are 5, 11, 17, 23, and 29. [How to use your Lucky Days: On these days, plan to take significant actions, make vital phone calls, send emails. These are days when your energy and luck are high.]*

The year starts off with intense energy around your job. You may find one or more of your co-workers quite irritating at this time. It's also possible a change of procedures or rules has put you off. You're starting to wonder if this is the place where you should be working. Be at peace. There's no forced move yet, but it's good to be prepared. Dust off your resume and look around a bit on the job-hunting sites. Things may calm down on their own by month's end, but it's good to be ready to take action just in case they don't.

Money flow right now is neither good nor bad; it's just the way your money energy is right now. Looking back over the past year, you see money opportunities that didn't happen—or something you tried didn't pay out as much as you had hoped. You may have been out of sync, or in some way feeling not quite ready to benefit from the opportunity that presented itself. All the options are still available to you. Go back and see whether you want to try again.

You are the focus of someone else's attention. If you're already in a love relationship, take their interest as a compliment but do no more about it. If you pursue this path, you are more than likely to stir up trouble.

If you are looking for love, this month could bring success. Your charisma level is high, and people are attracted to you. Allow yourself to be admired and discovered by love.

February: *Mercury goes retrograde from February 16 to March 9. Your Lucky Days are 4, 10, 16, 22, 28. [How to use your Lucky Days: On these days, plan to take significant actions, make vital phone calls, send emails. These are days when your energy and luck are high.]*

The year starts with you, Dragon native, being quite busy. You're in high demand. You are sought out for your talents and skills. You may have job offers, or perhaps you own a business and have people lining up on the sidewalk outside your door to get your goods and services. It's a good idea to see the parts of your career that bring you both enjoyment and benefit. There's no point in expending this much energy if it's not ticking these two boxes for you.

It's a good idea to look after your health this month. Keeping on a healthy eating plan is ideal, especially after Mercury goes retrograde. That's the time when most people return to bad habits. Exercise also needs to be on your list of necessary activities. If you're dancing for exercise, it's time to get some new dancing shoes.

You shine at your job. Recent changes in management will benefit you as people begin to see what an asset you are to the company. If you find recognition going elsewhere, you may want to look around for a new team, one who does appreciate you. If you own your own business, you may receive some very beneficial publicity. This can be due to a collaboration with a related business or with an influencer who wants to help you succeed.

It's a good idea for you to shine a light on your love relationship this month. Your partner may have been feeling a little left out. You can be magnanimous in your gestures, but sometimes your sweetheart just wants to sit and watch the game with you on the sofa. A little cuddling will be nice.

March: Mercury goes direct on March 9. The Sun enters Aries on March 20. Saturn enters Aquarius on March 21. Your Lucky Days are 5, 11, 17, 23, 29. [How to use your Lucky Days: On these days, plan to take significant actions, make vital phone calls, send emails. These are days when your energy and luck are high.]

The spotlight is on the resources you can receive from others. You are surrounded by helpful people, even though you sometimes can feel quite alone. No one can sail as high up in the sky as a Dragon native, and it's wonderful, but it can be lonely up there. Now take stock of who is around offering you help when you touch back down to earth. Look for more than just material support. Spiritual help is needed as well as a soft place for you to land when you are feeling emotional.

Metal Rat Year is a great time to create passive income sources. This month you'll have the opportunity to find people with the knowledge and ability to help you get set up. The source may be a professional organization, a teacher, or a video course. Perhaps you look into real estate or some other kind of long-term investment. Remember that during Metal Rat years, take only calculated risks, ones where you are clear about your ability to handle the downside, should it come to that.

If you're in school, tests and projects can go well. Try not to leave schoolwork until the last minute. Pulling an all-nighter is possible, it's just not advisable.

If you're looking for love, you can find interesting people to meet in places where people work out, or in the business areas of town. You may also meet people in health food stores and yoga studios.

A new pet may come into your life, or you may be looking after the pet of a friend. It's also possible you are keenly aware of a neighbor's pet at this time. If a barking dog is keeping you up at night, consider having a talk with the owner before kicking up a fuss.

April: *Pluto goes retrograde on April 25. Your Lucky Days are 4, 10, 16, 22, 28. [How to use your Lucky Days: On these days, plan to take significant actions, make vital phone calls, send emails. These are days when your energy and luck are high.]*

Relationship energy is intense this month for those Dragon natives in a love relationship. You can agree on a long-standing issue. (This is easier if your partner is not another Dragon.)

If you're looking for love, you can experience an epiphany this month, one that removes blocks to you being free to find a great match. It is fortunate to be born a Dragon, but there are challenges as well. When you are uncertain about someone else, you can place a sizable block in your own path. The solution is to have faith in yourself. It's OK to enter into a relationship. If you find you're not happy, you can get out of that relationship and find another. Trust in this process.

Your schedule needs your attention. You can be very effective, but at times you can lose focus on important projects. You can improve your progress by writing down your schedule.

Paying attention to how you are feeling, your health in general, or schedule a health exam; it's a beneficial thing to do for yourself this month. It doesn't matter whether you prefer to have your check-up with a traditional or an alternative medical practitioner. Having a massage or a spa day is good for you, as well.

There is some happy news concerning your finances towards the end of the month as Pluto goes retrograde. The money you've been expecting may be coming through.

A problematic situation is clearing at the end of the month, as well. A difficult person seems to be leaving, or perhaps a contract you've wanted to get out of finally comes to an end.

May: *Saturn goes retrograde on May 10. Venus goes retrograde on May 12. Jupiter goes retrograde on May 14. Your Lucky Days are 4, 10, 16, 22, 28. [How to use your Lucky Days: On these days, plan to take significant actions, make vital phone calls, send emails. These are days when your energy and luck are high.]*

You may be singled out for recognition or a special honor during this period. This may be related to your job, or it could relate to an organization you belong to. Or, perhaps you've published a book or put a creative project out into the world, and now you're being noticed. The more work you send out this month, the more opportunities for accolades you will attract.

There may be some challenges with an upcoming test related to work or a certification for your job. It's a good idea to get some help with studying. Find a study buddy or look for a tutor.

Relationship energy can grow contentious. It may be necessary to make some adjustments to an agreement made last month. Listen to your partner's feedback; it can help bring peace back into the home.

Dragon natives who are looking for love should consider attending events and parties when invited. Also, ask friends and relatives to help you meet new people. They can be your matchmakers.

If you've wanted to change something about your appearance, now is the time to proceed. You may have been thinking about changing your hairstyle, or even scheduling something as dramatic as cosmetic surgery. Your schedule is going to get busier in the next few months, so take the opportunity if you have time this month. It can also be a good time to travel a distance to find the right practitioner or doctor.

June: *Lunar Eclipse on June 5. Mercury is retrograde from June 17 to July 12. There is a Solar Eclipse on June 20. Venus goes direct June 24. Your Lucky Days are 3, 9, 15, 21, 27. [How to use your Lucky Days: On these days, plan to take significant actions, make vital phone calls, send emails. These are days when your energy and luck are high.]*

This month, with two eclipses, may see you falling in love. You can be struck by cupid's arrow when you least expect it. This is perhaps not the relationship you had envisioned for yourself, but here it is. If you're already in a love relationship with someone, you may want to proceed with uncharacteristic caution right now.

Your dance card is full this month. Friends and extended family are sending you invitations. A group you belong to maybe having events or meetings, requiring extra time from you. And to top it off, you may be having some issues with technology (phone or laptop) around the time Mercury goes retrograde. If you need to buy new equipment during the retrograde, make sure it has a warranty, and it's possible to return it in case something goes wrong.

You may have some remarkable dreams. The symbolism will be unclear. Ask a friend or sibling what they think about it. If you don't understand the message in a dream, consider meditating or journaling this month to draw the information to the forefront of your awareness.

Things unfold at the office just as you predicted they would. There can be changes at the very top in your company. These changes won't affect your job so much, but it puts people around you on edge. If you own the company, you need to look at the corporate culture in your business in general and see what changes should be made. You may have to issue some edicts regarding new behavior for staff.

July: *Retrograde Saturn backs up into Capricorn. There is a Lunar Eclipse is on July 4. Mercury goes direct on July 12. Your Lucky Days are 3, 9, 15, 21, 27. [How to use your Lucky Days: On these days, plan to take significant actions, make vital phone calls, send emails. These are days when your energy and luck are high.]*

You need a break, especially around the time of the Lunar Eclipse. You may be dreaming of a vacation from everyone. Dragon natives often lean towards an independent, self-reliant life. All of the social activity of the last couple of months have taken their toll, and you're ready to hide out in some mountain cabin or go camping at the beach. Find some time for yourself this month, even if your obligations don't let you disappear completely. Just shutting off your phone's notifications each evening will help.

When driving this month, keep an eye on your rear view mirror if you're a speeder. You may get pulled over.

Some troubles with electronics may still be happening. This is a holdover from last month. It's a good idea to take some time and learn to use new devices. Also, if making a purchase this month, consider getting the extra warranty—especially if Mercury is still retrograde at the time.

Younger relatives bring you joy this month. You may attend an important celebration, a wedding, or a milestone birthday. Memories are made at this time.

An irritant in your relationship seems to disappear. The points of contention seem to fade away. Now you can enjoy some peace at home. You feel the warmth of love and loyalty in the family.

August: *Uranus goes retrograde on August 15. Your Lucky Days are 2, 8, 14, 20, 26. [How to use your Lucky Days: On these days, plan to take significant actions, make vital phone calls, send emails. These are days when your energy and luck are high.]*

Work heats up, and the lead on a big project may be yours, or your team expanded. If you work a contract job, you have the opportunity to have that contract extended, as well as receiving a lead on a position at another company.

For those Dragon natives who own a company, you may have more business than you can handle. It may be time to hire help or contract out some of the extra work. Look at the profitability of each product or service you offer. You may need to streamline your offerings to focus your energies on whatever is bringing you the most money. In Metal Rat years, it's necessary to pay a lot of attention to the intersection between the practical and the profitable.

Your relationships continue to go well. Your circle of friends may expand as you meet friends of friends or the parents of your children's friends. Put some time and energy into your relationships with those who consistently admire your work and talents.

A creative project may be ready to launch soon. This may need some back end promotional work, such as websites, press releases, or publicity. This may not be the fun part for you, but it's still important. Don't skimp on the promotion.

You have an opportunity to teach, perhaps a formal opportunity to speak at a conference or a University. You may be asked by a relative to teach someone in the family one of your many skills.

September: *Mars goes retrograde on September 9. Jupiter goes direct on September 12. The Sun goes into Libra on September 22. Saturn goes direct on September 28. Your Lucky Days are 1, 7, 13, 19, 25. [How to use your Lucky Days: On these days, plan to take significant actions, make vital phone calls, send emails. These are days when your energy and luck are high.]*

You have been expending a lot of energy lately, and now it seems you want to crawl back into your lair as Mars turns retrograde on September 9. You may be turning down invitations and guarding your free time. This may ruffle the feathers of a sibling or neighbor, but Dragon natives could care less. But keep your whole family in mind when you are making your decisions about what to attend. Someone else in the family may need your help with making a connection or a good impression.

A new job is possible now. If you've been looking for a change, you may have an opportunity for an interview and offer. It may be just what you've been waiting for. This positive energy is around all month, so it's a good idea to post your resume on job hunting sites, and call back the headhunters who leave messages.

Your investments benefit from your attention. You may have an opportunity for a partnership that could bring profit in the future. You may be asked by a friend or relative to lend your money or expertise to a project. It's a good idea to be clear about the terms from the beginning in case there are disagreements later. This could be a handshake deal as long as everyone fully understands the role he or she is playing in the venture.

Education is challenging as Saturn moves forward again on September 28. Perhaps a new school or a new education program. If you're not in school, you may be asked to learn a new system at your job or to help a child with their homework.

October: *Pluto goes direct on October 4. Mercury goes retrograde from October 13 to November 3. Your Lucky Days are 1, 7, 13, 19, 25, 31. [How to use your Lucky Days: On these days, plan to take significant actions, make vital phone calls, send emails. These are days when your energy and luck are high.]*

This month it feels like you've hit the reset button. Energy and vitality have returned. Dragon natives may be excited about a new project, a new subject to study or some new person in your life. Whatever it is, you want to bottle it and sell it because you're feeling so good.

You may receive an award or welcome recognition for your knowledge and wisdom. If you enter contests now, you can do well even if the awards announcements are months away. A small windfall can come to you now. This doesn't give you a license to gamble—as gambling can be ill-advised for you during a Metal Rat year—but taking a few risks here and there may be a good idea.

There are some changes at home. An unexpected repair or a renovation project begun a while ago experiences some delays as Mercury goes retrograde on October 13. It will take an extra amount of patience when dealing with others to avoid breathing fire at them. Dragon natives often don't realize they can be intimidating. You have high standards, and not everyone around you can reach the stratosphere.

Dragon natives who work for an employer may be transferred, or a work-at-home opportunity may come up for you. Give it some thought—you can structure this change to your benefit. Have a clear vision of what you want.

Relationships are going well. Your partner may have been quite busy, but now their attention turns back to you and the connection you have together. If you want to move the relationship forward, this is the time to talk about living together or tying the knot.

November: *Mercury goes direct on November 3. Mars goes direct on November 13. Neptune goes direct on November 28. There is a Lunar Eclipse on November 30. Your Lucky Days are 6, 12, 18, 24, 30. [How to use your Lucky Days: On these days, plan to take significant actions, make vital phone calls, send emails. These are days when your energy and luck are high.]*

Things at home settle down. If you've just moved, you find you love your new place. Neighbors, for the most part, are friendly and welcoming. There may be a visit from extended family. If you haven't moved recently, you may feel like you want to spruce up the place with some new décor. Make a note that Mercury is retrograde until November 3. Changes made during a retrograde period may mean you make changes every time Mercury goes retrograde in the future.

Some difficulty with a teacher or the teacher of one of your kids can be smoothed over with a little bit of attention on your part.

You feel inspired. A new direction may be opening up for you as Mars and Neptune begin to move in direct motion. You may have come across some examples of out-of-the-box thinking online, or perhaps a friend is already trying something new. This can end up being a radical lifestyle change for you and your family. Take a survey of your family members and see how many supporters you have for your idea.

To attract money this month, add in the spiritual component by doing Feng Shui: use crystals, chant, or light candles. Focus your energy on why you want the money rather than the money itself. You will achieve some results this month and more next month.

December: *Solar Eclipse on December 14. Saturn goes into Aquarius on December 16. Jupiter goes into Aquarius on December 19. Sun goes into Capricorn on December 21. Your Lucky Days are 6, 12, 18, 24, 30. [How to use your Lucky Days: On these days, plan to take significant actions, make vital phone calls, send emails. These are days when your energy and luck are high.]*

There is a lot of energy around children and fertility for Dragon natives. Of course, with the holidays here, you may be spending time with your kids, their friends, and your extended family. If you've wanted to add to the family, you'll be happy to know there is fertility energy around you—especially towards the middle of the month at the time of the Solar Eclipse. You'll find good fertility help if needed, and/or you may look into the possibility of fostering or adopting a child.

You may also be considering adding a pet. If you already have kids and/or pets in the house, make sure everyone agrees before you bring the new little soul into the house. If you find a stray pet, make sure you check the animal out with the vet before introducing them to other animals living in the house.

Work is busy but satisfying. If you manage a team, you'll notice everyone working together more effectively. Supervisors give a nod of approval for your projects and performance.

An investment pays off. You can increase your income this month as both Saturn and Jupiter enter a new sign. Overall, the past year has been profitable. You've made more, and if you were able to channel the extra into investments, you'd see some excellent results next year.

Hosting a party at home is beneficial for you. Open your house up—even if you're not completely done with renovation or decorating projects. People want to see you, not the floor, lamps, and rugs.

January 2021: *Uranus goes direct on January 14. Mercury goes retrograde from January 30 to February 20. Your Lucky Days are 5, 11, 17, 23, 29. [How to use your Lucky Days: On these days, plan to take significant actions, make vital phone calls, send emails. These are days when your energy and luck are high.]*

As the Lunar year comes to a close, you're a little more emotional, even sentimental, than usual. The positive energy combined with Dragon native's natural luck as brought you some real benefits. There have been some challenges, but you've grown during this Metal Rat year and so has your status in the world.

You may have a job opportunity land unexpectedly in your lap. It could come from a colleague who has moved on to another company and now wants to bring you on board. You need to discuss this with the whole family, especially if it means relocating the household.

Romance is in the air, and your powers of attraction are high. If you're looking for love, you can meet new, intriguing individuals in places where people have fun, such as shopping malls, amusement parks, arcades, and sporting events. Consider going to a fun conference to explore a hobby of yours in more depth. You will meet new friends and admirers.

A child brings you a reason to celebrate. You can be proud of the influence you've had in their decisions.

You are looking for change energy to celebrate the Lunar New Year and the new energy. You probably feel like changing your hair style, altering your fashion choices, buying new clothing, or perhaps adding a new tattoo. Consider doing something bold before Mercury goes retrograde. Also, look into a fun class. Take singing lessons, painting, or jewelry making. Add some bling to your life.

February 2021: *Lunar New Year begins on February 12. Happy Year of the Metal Ox.*

Attract New Love

You only need to pay attention when you do the things you do during the week for love to come into your life. Look around when you're at the post office, notice things when you're at the grocery store, check out who's there when you're at the gym. The person for you is close by and waiting for you to catch their eye.

For you, Dragon natives, making a list can help you attract love. I don't mean a list of their qualities, but a list of how you might meet them. Use your creative genius and list 20 ways you could meet someone most randomly. Great love stories do come with a narrative. Be ready to find your love story.

When attracting a new love, use the sweet sound of a bell to call the person's energy to you. Select a bell made of metal, porcelain, or clay, but it must have a sweet sound. (You don't want to attract love with a bell that's off-key.) Hang the bell from a yellow ribbon—yellow is the color of friendship and mutual understanding.

Place the bell in your bedroom where you can ring it at least once a day. (Do not hang the bell where you're going to bump your head into it.) If you want the relationship to start as a friendship and move slowly to a deeper connection, hang your bell in the living room. Then move it to your bedroom when you are ready for the relationship to become intimate.

Enhance Existing Love

This year, your relationship seems to be on life's stage. This could mean you are getting married, or your anniversary will be celebrated by many. You may be out in the world as part of a couple now, when before it was just you out on your own. It's all good for Dragon natives, but your partner may be a different sign, and not so keen you are on display. Be understanding with them as you enjoy the spotlight.

Disagreements long past in this relationship spring up one final time. You need to be open to the discussion about where the two of you want to live, what kind of work you both, do and what your bigger goals are. Decide these things together so each of you can be happy with the choices. Discussion is key.

There may be much discussion around expanding the family, either through having kids, adopting, bringing in a pet, or having an older relative move in. One of you may feel like you want freedom, while the other wants to focus on the family. While you find the middle ground at home, show a united front when you are around others. Don't let friends and family divide the two of you on this topic.

Find some pictures of the two of you in happy situations, like on vacations and at parties, and have the pictures framed. Place the pictures where your partner can see them. (For most people, this means near the TV.) But if your partner spends all their time in their office, place the pictures there. This will send a subliminal message and increase the happiness energy for the two of you.

Looking to Conceive?

One of the gemstones associated with pregnancy is the geode. A geode is a hollow mineral mass with gemstones growing inside the shell. Outdoors, a geode often looks like an egg, and when it is cracked open, the inside reveals the sparkling gemstones.

Geodes range from a couple of inches in size to several feet in diameter. When you find a geode you like, place it in your bedroom to enhance the pregnancy energy.

(From Donna Stellhorn's book, *A Path to Pregnancy: Ancient Secrets for the Modern Woman*)

Family and Kids

Home is the most fun place to be this year, which is not typical for Dragon natives. You usually like to be out and about. But this year, you are finding the joy of just staying home, perhaps due to a family addition, such as a child or pet. You may be having more parties or just dining together as a family. Home is bringing you joy this year.

There are many projects at home these days. You may be landscaping or putting in a garden, adding on a room, or now working from home. This is the time to set boundaries between work time and family time. It's good to practice work/life balance as much as you can.

Kids are your main focus this year. If you don't have kids, you may welcome visits from younger members of the family. You may add a pet or two. Couples who want to have a child find blocks to their goal lifted. There are opportunities for you to get the help you need in this area. Adult children may add to the family by getting into a relationship, getting married, or having kids themselves.

Decorating with the symbol of a bat sounds a little wacky, but the bat is actually a traditional Feng Shui symbol used to bring wealth into a home. The Chinese word for "bat" sounds like the word for "prosperity." Bats also symbolize longevity. Most Feng Shui artwork that uses bats depicts them in quite a stylized manner, so they aren't scary the way we think of bats in the West. Hang a picture with lucky bats in the family room or kitchen to bring prosperity and longevity to everyone who lives in the home.

Money

There is positive money energy for you this year. You find it easy to choose the activities that bring profits. Most of these will lean towards the creative, but you will be more successful if you also keep the paperwork organized, and take charge of tasks related to back-office stuff. If you can't stomach these tasks, find someone you trust to do them for you, but recognize you can't divorce yourself from the mundane process and succeed.

Money will be made through partnerships this year. This may show up as you receiving help from your life-partner. Butt it may also be that you are partnering up with others on smaller ventures. Try to help and promote others, and you will receive a world of support in return. Here again, a process is attached to success, one you must be involved in. Keep track of birthdays, who has a beloved pet, or which person needs a ride to the airport; be interested in others, and you will succeed.

Savings and investments can be a source of joy or irritation for you, depending on your mood at the moment. It's good this year to have the grander goal of financial independence at the forefront of your mind. You may not make it the whole way to the finish line, but you can make progress towards this worthy goal. On the other hand, if you find bill-paying tedious and you procrastinate, gains wild disappear, and opportunities go elsewhere.

Sunstone is a gemstone formed in the molten lava of a volcano. It's said to bring good fortune and legendary luck. When carried with you, fear melts away, and you feel charged with vitality. Find a piece of sunstone jewelry, or carry a small tumbled sunstone in your pocket. Let this be your lucky talisman this year.

Job or Career

This year, Dragon native, you will be focused not just on whether your career is bringing you happiness, but if it's supporting you financially as well. Many Dragons are creative souls. They have talents and skills the rest of the world can only dream of. However, it's not always talent or skill that brings financial security. Many of you may need to push this type of activity to the evening or weekend, so during the day you can focus on bringing in money.

During the Year of the Metal Rat, focusing on money brings more benefit than just cash. It can bring important contacts, increase your creative productivity (as happens when you have a limited time to create), and it can build your confidence and prepare you for the time to leap into something you really want to do.

A lot of change is going on around you. You may be with a company that was purchased, restructured, or broadened to include a new field. You may have entered this industry recently and still feel very new at the game. Or, you may find technological innovations are changing your industry forever. Dragon native, you have no trouble changing directions when you want to. But when you are not, you'd likely rather breathe fire on the earth and demonstrate your displeasure. Try not to be an angry Dragon.

If you want to start or expand into your own business, this is the right time to begin doing it. But you must take the designs and plans you now have on paper and put them into action. Procrastination is just your brain's way of telling you it doesn't like your plan. If you are putting off taking action, re-consider your strategy overall. Figure out what needs to be changed, or what resources you need to bring together to get things moving.

For those born in the year of the Dragon, you can increase positive career energy by placing an elephant figurine (or a set of them) in your living room, home office, or dining room. Choose an elephant whose trunk is up triumphantly, and point him (or them) towards the door. The elephant doesn't have to be large, but it should be prominently displayed so you can see it when you enter the room. Dust him regularly to re-energize the positive vibes.

Education

You are lucky this year when it comes to education. Going back to school to finish a degree or obtaining getting a new degree or certification can be beneficial. It seems quite likely you will find the funding you need to help you do, so make it happen. Funds are there (though not from relatives, but through your own efforts to secure grants, loans, and scholarships). You have a vision for what this future degree will bring you. Make sure your vision really requires the education you're going to work so hard to get. Nothing makes a Dragon native more cranky than wasting effort.

There may have been some issues in the past about studying, or about the school experience itself. Perhaps you attended a school that closed before providing you with the degree you worked hard to receive, or you have student loan debt, which will require your attention for a long time to come. However, this is a good year to work on any stresses you have with education from your past. You can heal and resolve problems to your satisfaction. This energy will be around you all year, and schools move slowly, so be patient but persistent when knocking at that door.

Legal Matters

A long-standing legal matter can resolve this year. Sit down at a quiet moment with the relevant documents in front of you, and visualize just how you would like it to resolve. It would be wise to be very conservative and carefully read the contracts and other agreements thoroughly, because your luck falls in other areas of the chart this year. If you're not careful, the Universe may provide you with a lesson about signing things you haven't read.

Health and Well-Being

Very positive news for you on the health front. You are releasing old negative patterns that have kept you from experiencing healing. While this process will take most of the year, you will most likely finish the year in a much better state than you were when you entered it.

You also have more access to helpful practitioners and doctors this year. Even if you've struggled with finding good help previously, now the stars are aligned in your favor. You may even find doctors who were impossible to see suddenly have an opening for you. This very positive energy will not be around next year, so it's good to take advantage of it now.

There is a lot of pet activity around you. If you don't have pets of your own, you may be disturbed by pets owned by people living around you. Try to shift irritating thoughts to more positive ideas, as it will help your well-being greatly. If you are an animal lover, you may be acquiring a pet or helping someone with their little furry (or feathered) friend.

It's a good idea to add spiritual practices into your daily life. You'll find connecting into your intuition and higher-self actually grounds you, making you more effective in your everyday life. You do look quite busy this year, so you may have to be firm when it comes to carving out time for your daily spiritual practice.

Chamomile is a beneficial herb in Feng Shui. Sprinkle dried chamomile flowers around your property to clear it of negative energy. Place a bowl of chamomile flowers in your bedroom to help you get restful sleep. Make a tea from chamomile, let it cool and pour it into a spray bottle. Spray it around the house to attract prosperity and peace. (You can store the unused portion in the refrigerator for up to a week.)

Snake

February 4, 1905 -- January 24, 1906: Yin Wood Snake
January 23, 1917 -- February 10, 1918: Yin Fire Snake
February 10, 1929 -- January 29, 1930: Yin Earth Snake
January 27, 1941 -- February 14, 1942: Yin Metal Snake
February 14, 1953 -- February 2, 1954: Yin Water Snake
February 2, 1965 -- January 20, 1966: Yin Wood Snake
February 18, 1977 -- February 6, 1978: Yin Fire Snake
February 6, 1989 -- January 26, 1990: Yin Earth Snake
January 24, 2001 -- February 11, 2002: Yin Metal Snake
February 10, 2013 -- January 30, 2014: Yin Water Snake
January 29, 2025 – February 16, 2026: Yin Wood Snake

Snake Personality

When considering the qualities of a Chinese Zodiac animal, it's a good idea to examine the traits, behaviors, and personality of the animal. At first glance, it may seem Snake is at a disadvantage, having no hands or feet. But Snakes use their sense of smell to track their prey. Their sense of smell comes from using their forked tongue to collect airborne particles. You may already be aware your sense of smell is more acute than the average person. This is one of your advantages.

The scales covering a snake's body allow them to grip things tightly and to move swiftly along the ground. These scales are shed off periodically, revealing new skin beneath as the snake literally crawls out of its old skin. This means you can reinvent yourself whenever you want. When your life needs to change, you can change it in a big way.

People born in the Snake Year rely on their intelligence and wisdom to make their way through the world. They have a very keen intuitive sense of other people. They easily attract people and keep them near for as long as they need. Snakes can also enjoy spending time alone when they wish.

Snakes cope well with making significant life changes. It seems they can renew themselves at will. They may change careers or move to a new city, leaving everything behind. They are reborn. Snakes admire power and look to gain power for themselves. When Snake realizes they're stuck in a situation, or they feel limited in their choices, they will move on.

Snake is the wisest of the zodiac signs and relies on their own judgment. They're excellent with money and have a good sense for investments. They have a computer-like brain that never stops calculating. They are incredibly tenacious when they want to achieve something. They never forget a broken promise. Some say the Snake is paranoid, but that doesn't mean people are not plotting against him/her.

While Snake natives always have money in the bank, they are cautious about speculating and should avoid gambling. If they do gamble, they need to make safe bets.

Snakes are passionate lovers (not necessarily limited to one person). Snakes are loyal, but they will wander if they suspect the other person is not entirely devoted. When wronged, they like to crush their enemies completely. Snake natives will strike without warning, although he or she can be patient until the time for revenge is right.

People born in the Year of the Snake keep their feelings a well-guarded secret. Often seen as detached and cool, but in reality, Snakes feel things very deeply. If surrounded by negative people, it breaks their concentration, and Snake becomes suspicious and wary. But Snake has the power to win people over, and many fall into line with whatever Snake wishes.

Snake: Predictions for 2020

January 2020: *There is a Lunar Eclipse on January 10. Uranus moves forward again on January 11. The Lunar New Year begins on January 25. Your Lucky Days are 6, 12, 18, 24 and 30. [How to use your Lucky Days: On these days, plan to take essential actions, make vital phone calls, send emails. These are days when your energy and luck are high.]*

Opportunities take the form of contact with strangers this month. Reach out to people you want to know. Send an email or make a phone call. Make a connection even if you feel you're not ready to move forward. You are more prepared than you think.

Positive energy shows up in the form of a nice windfall this month. Remember, you can't win if you don't buy a ticket. In this case, your ticket is a job application, freelance proposal, or an ad campaign for your small business. Look for increased opportunities after the Lunar Eclipse on January 10.

Imaginary blocks are impenetrable, but real blocks have solutions. Use your cunning mind to see where you have obstacles and where you have excuses.

There is massive support for you this month in the area of love. Usually, when this much help from the Universe is available, it means you're in a growth period (i.e., life feels highly challenging). You are protected now, and what happens is for the best. If this means you are airing your grievances in an argument, you'll discover that in the long run, great benefits derive from it.

If you're dating and you get stood up, thank the Universe—you have been protected. If you don't get a call back when you were expecting one, you've been protected once again. Consider all of what happens this month as beneficial, and let go of whatever you think "should" happen.

February: *Mercury goes retrograde from February 16 to March 9. Your Lucky Days are 5, 11, 17, 23, 29. [How to use your Lucky Days: On these days, plan to take significant actions, make vital phone calls, send emails. These are days when your energy and luck are high.]*

The year begins with a focus on love and romance. If you're looking for love, there will be several opportunities for you in the near future. It's a good time this month, especially before Mercury goes retrograde on February 16, to update your online profile on the dating websites. When out in the world, make sure you are approachable by looking up from your phone and not always having earbuds in. Snake natives are charming and attractive. Your gaze can be hypnotic. Make eye contact and see what happens.

There is a lot of emphasis on family and children this month. Your kids may need help with studies or projects they're working on. There may be an announcement of an addition to the family through pregnancy or adoption (this includes the furry "children" as well).

You make good headway on a creative project. Don't be a perfectionist here. Let others see what you're working on.

Income can increase, especially if you own a business. Your sales and territory can expand. If you work for someone else, consider setting up a meeting to discuss your future with the company and how you can get an increase in your salary.

If you're in school, you may be feeling like you don't want to be. You may be bored or just burned out with the whole process. You don't need to drop out. Instead, change up some basic things you do, such as how you study, where you study, and who you study with.

March: *Mercury goes direct on March 9. The Sun enters Aries on March 20. Saturn enters Aquarius on March 21. Your Lucky Days are 6, 12, 18, 24, 30. [How to use your Lucky Days: On these days, plan to take significant actions, make vital phone calls, send emails. These are days when your energy and luck are high.]*

Your love relationship is going well. The lines of communication are open, and you are gaining a lot of insight into how to make this partnership better. Snake natives are wise and intuitive. You can use the information you're getting to strengthen your love. If this relationship is new, you have the opportunity now to move it to the next level. Being exclusive, moving in together, or getting engaged are all options. This topic of conversation will be welcome news to your partner as well as friends and family.

Work is going well, and you like most of your co-workers. There are hints of an increased workload in the future, but right now, you are handling everything deftly.

An investment opportunity will take a little courage to become involved. You may have gotten burned in the past, or you may just feel like this is outside the realms of your knowledge. This likely involves a long term investment. If you have the funds to spare, and Mercury is moving forward, go ahead and consider it.

You may be making travel plans, possibly even taking a trip this month. It will be good to see some new sights. It would be even better to visit some friends and reconnect.

You receive an inspiring message from a book, video, or TV show. You feel charged up and excited about this concept—a new direction for your life.

April: *[note: Pluto goes retrograde on April 25. Your Lucky Days are 5, 11, 17, 23, 29. [How to use your Lucky Days: On these days, plan to take significant actions, make vital phone calls, send emails. These are days when your energy and luck are high.]*

Finances improve, and you may receive a small windfall. Don't consider this a regular source of income going forward, but this is a good month to give some thought to other sources you could access. Connect with others who have knowledge about passive income methods and get some education about what you would need to get involved.

You are looking good and your powers of attraction are high. Someone in your circle approaches you and confesses feelings for you. If you're already in a love relationship, it would be good to use caution here.

Snake natives can attract love or increase love in a relationship this month by using spiritual tools such as visualization, goal boards, or affirmations. While you, Snake native, may love science, you have an innate understanding of magic. Time to bring magic into your daily life. You can do this by taking the time to focus your intention and practice visualizing.

You may be offered a resource (one you really want) by a person you admire. You're perhaps a little concerned about what the strings are, though this person may just be trying to pay it forward for their own reasons.

A new workout routine captures your attention. Now you're keen to buy new equipment, workout clothing, or sign up for a gym membership. Your health is important. If you're excited about this system, then go for it.

May: *Saturn goes retrograde on May 10. Venus goes retrograde on May 12. Jupiter goes retrograde on May 14. Your Lucky Days are 5, 11, 17, 23, 29. [How to use your Lucky Days: On these days, plan to take significant actions, make vital phone calls, send emails. These are days when your energy and luck are high.]*

Education is highlighted now. You may be taking final exams or studying for a certification test for your job. This can possibly be something connected to your children and what they are doing in school. While studying is very important now, it's not going to help you (or the kids) to nag. Stay positive and remind yourself you love to solve problems. If you're having trouble sitting down to get the study time in, especially with three planets going retrograde this month, look at it as a problem to solve. Check out the research on best practices for studying and retaining information. Share what you find with family members if they need your support.

If you're involved in a legal matter, you probably need to focus on some paperwork to make something official. You may be signing a contract for a purchase, or a new job. Last-minute changes to the agreement are possible. You can negotiate for what you want if you have a clear vision of your goal in mind.

You may feel your investments aren't going well. Snake natives can be risk-averse, and during Metal Rat years there's a lot of pressure to take chances with investments. But remember, you're in it for the long haul. Unless you cash out now, you still have opportunities to turn this around.

You're quite busy this month, and you're having trouble staying on schedule. Timing improves as the month goes on. Make sure to schedule in some time to spend in nature. It refuels you at a core level. That and sleep are the elixir of life for you, Snake native.

June: *Lunar Eclipse on June 5. Mercury is retrograde from June 17 to July 12. There is a Solar Eclipse on June 20. Venus goes direct June 24. Your Lucky Days are 4, 10, 16, 22, 28. [How to use your Lucky Days: On these days, plan to take significant actions, make vital phone calls, send emails. These are days when your energy and luck are high.]*

There is a focus on friendships this month, and you have a chance to enlarge your circle of friends. You might be asked to join an organization, or new hobby of yours puts you in touch with a bunch of new people. Look at groups involved in some form of movement, dance, walking, or hiking. Also, intellectual discussion groups are good for you. Consider attending lectures by noted authors and great thinkers.

You love life heats up, and what may have been a casual connection suddenly takes a more intimate turn after the Lunar Eclipse on June 5. They may have confessed some secrets to you, and things are getting physical. Intensity is building, and this could get interesting.

Your career is getting better, and you receive recognition from a supervisor or someone fairly high up in the company. If you own your own business, you may receive some positive publicity or a write up from an influencer. Increase your good fortune by letting everyone throughout your social media channels know, or informing your customers about your success in a newsletter or other form of communication.

A decision about your home or living arrangements is made, signaling a move in the next few months. Or perhaps someone is moving in or moving out. You might want to save money by getting a roommate or moving back in with parents (which could help them out as well).

July: *Retrograde Saturn backs up into Capricorn. There is a Lunar Eclipse is on July 4. Mercury goes direct on July 12. Your Lucky Days are 4, 10, 16, 22, 28. [How to use your Lucky Days: On these days, plan to take significant actions, make vital phone calls, send emails. These are days when your energy and luck are high.]*

Children or younger relatives are on your mind this month as one makes an announcement that shakes the family up. There may be a divide happening around the time of the Lunar Eclipse, and others in the family are pressuring you to pick a side. Or possibly an adult child may be moving on their own, and others in the family doubt they are ready. Don't sit on the sidelines on this one. Your opinion is valuable.

If you want to add to the family, this is a good time to pursue options for fertility or adoption.

A friend of yours makes a surprising request. Snake natives don't usually like surprises, so it's fine to say "No," or to respond with, "Give me a few days to think about it."

Someone in your professional life compliments your knowledge and your charisma. This is genuine admiration. Instead of discounting the comment or pushing it aside, see if you can bring this person into your inner circle. They can be of help to you.

You need to act regarding paying off debt, bill consolidation, or to fight an erroneous medical claim or invoice. You can win this. Do your research and compare options. Maintain open communications with others about this, and you will buy yourself more time to reach the solution you want.

A possible love match is becoming known to you. You may be hesitating because of something in the past. But this is something new and definitely worth exploring.

August: *Uranus goes retrograde on August 15. Your Lucky Days are 3, 9, 15, 21, 27. [How to use your Lucky Days: On these days, plan to take significant actions, make vital phone calls, send emails. These are days when your energy and luck are high.]*

Things settle down considerably, and you feel a sense of peace at home as well as among your friends. Now is the time to host a party! You may think about inviting some extended family members, including the in-laws, but keep the energy light. Invite a good mix of happy people to share in your good feelings.

Work is going well, and your co-workers admire you. The workload may not be quite as high now, but it's more likely you've used your innovative abilities to find ways to streamline operations or automate procedures. Snake natives don't usually like getting stuck with day-to-day chores, and when you see a way to get a chore off your list, you don't hesitate to implement a new way of doing things.

You may have pets in the home or lots of animals on your property. It will be necessary to find ways to help both humans and animals to live in harmony. This is doable. It may take a little patience and a little understanding, but peace will be restored in just a few weeks.

A friendship may turn romantic, and if you're looking for love, it may feel like you've been slipped a love potion. Be aware this feeling may be mutual. It could be the moment you've been waiting for.

If you're already in a love relationship, things are going well. There could be a heated discussion about politics or some other ideological concept. Snake natives tend to think in big terms, seeing the whole forest, while others may only see the pine needles on one tree. It's okay to have a lively disagreement at times, but keep it pleasant and stick to the bigger picture.

September: *Mars goes retrograde on September 9. Jupiter goes direct on September 12. The Sun goes into Libra on September 22. Saturn goes direct on September 28. Your Lucky Days are 2, 8, 14, 20, 26. [How to use your Lucky Days: On these days, plan to take significant actions, make vital phone calls, send emails. These are days when your energy and luck are high.]*

The focus is on you this month, especially your health and physical appearance. You may want to update your wardrobe or try out a new exercise routine as you focus on getting in shape. Time to tweak your diet, as well. Adding in more veggies is always a good idea and will make a difference in your energy levels and vitality throughout the day.

Snake natives can expect a possible job offer, whether you are looking or not. A person you used to work with may have moved on to another company and would like you to join them. Or, you may receive a call from an old boss asking you to come back to do a job you've done before. The Metal Rat year is a time to consider making some adjustments. And success comes more readily when you open up to the possibilities of change.

A project may be coming to completion as Jupiter and Saturn both start moving forward in direct motion this month. You have been working on this project for quite a while and are happy to have it done. Don't let your desire for perfection hold you back from pronouncing it complete. You could spend months trying to get everything just right when you've already done more and done it better than most people could have done.

A lover from your past may return, this time just looking for friendship. They have most likely moved on to another relationship, but for sentimental reasons they couldn't get you out of their mind. Keep this connection platonic as rekindling a fire now could burn the house down.

October: *Pluto goes direct on October 4. Mercury goes retrograde from October 13 to November 3. Your Lucky Days are 2, 8, 14, 20, 26. [How to use your Lucky Days: On these days, plan to take significant actions, make vital phone calls, send emails. These are days when your energy and luck are high.]*

You want a break. It feels like you've been going non-stop for weeks, and now you want to lock the door, close the blinds, and binge watch your favorite TV series. That's perfectly fine if you can get away with it, but your phone is buzzing, and others are looking for you. You may have to get out of town if you want to get some rest.

Your health is improving during this Metal Rat year, especially now. A shift in diet or exercise you made a few months ago is paying off. But towards the middle of the month, Mercury goes retrograde and threatens to put you off your good routine. It's going to take some willpower to avoid falling back into old habits. It's a good idea to set up your environment to support you by removing temptation from the kitchen. Plus, pack your gym bag the night before, and keep it by the door. That way, it's easy to grab on your way out.

Transportation in general, or specifically your vehicle, may require your attention this month. It's not lucky to buy a car during Mercury retrograde. However, getting regular maintenance taken care of is fine, as well as re-upping transit passes or toll road transponders. If you need to, renew your license. Try to do it online; or take an interesting book with you to the DMV, because during Mercury retrograde, the waiting time and the line itself is often very, very long.

Your children or kids in the neighborhood are making their presence known. You could be driving them to games and sporting events, or perhaps you are hosting a block party? Or, the neighborhood kids are just making a noticeable amount of noise. Try to tune it out so as not to lose your temper.

November: *Mercury goes direct on November 3. Mars goes direct on November 13. Neptune goes direct on November 28. There is a Lunar*

Eclipse on November 30. Your Lucky Days are 7, 13, 19, 25. [How to use your Lucky Days: On these days, plan to take significant actions, make vital phone calls, send emails. These are days when your energy and luck are high.]

Your partner may be quite happy at this time, and this is helping your relationship overall. This is a reason to celebrate.

It's a good time to travel now that Mercury is direct, and you may want to take a trip to visit relatives or friends in other cities. You can also plan a trip to an exotic location for the holidays. You may want to lock in the tickets early to get the best deal.

Finances improve, and you show increased income now. You may receive a bonus or other remuneration from your job. Profits from a side business may come through. And there is positive energy around investments and passive income sources for Snake natives.

Your career is under the light of the eclipse at the end of the month. It's a good time to do some research on the "health" of your company and the industry you're in. There may be changes over the coming six months, and you, Snake native, do not like surprises. You have many opportunities opening up for you. It's a good idea to reach out through career websites like LinkedIn and connect with past colleagues, managers, and people you would like to meet. Any connections you make now will pay off in the future.

There's a lot of passionate energy happening for you. You could be having a lot of fun behind closed doors. Put down the romance novel and find someone to have fun with.

December: *Solar Eclipse on December 14. Saturn goes into Aquarius on December 16. Jupiter goes into Aquarius on December 19. Sun goes into Capricorn on December 21. Your Lucky Days are 7, 13, 19, 25. [How to use your Lucky Days: On these days, plan to take significant actions, make vital phone calls, send emails. These are days when your energy and luck are high.]*

A person you admire tells you how much they admire you. It is likely not an expression of a romantic interest, just someone who thinks you're great. Snake natives can sometimes be at a loss for words in the face of a compliment, and in this case, you can simply say, "Thank you!"

You may be in the process of a job change this month or preparing to make a switch in the next few weeks. You have made many adjustments during this Metal Rat year, and this one will bring you the most benefit and success. Even if you're just changing departments, getting a new team, or switching offices, any change now will be good for your success going forward.

If you own a business, it's time to take a critical look at your overall marketing. It is probably not possible for you to delegate this task. You may have to spend a few hours understanding who your customer is and where they hang out online. The hours you spend now on this project can pay real dividends. Even though your schedule is busy, make every effort to fit this into it.

Your children are active and around you more than usual. This may be due to the holidays, or one may be moving back in.

Getting a new car or new mode of transportation is beneficial after December 21.

January 2021: *Uranus goes direct on January 14. Mercury goes retrograde from January 30 to February 20. Your Lucky Days are 7, 13, 19, 25. [How to use your Lucky Days: On these days, plan to take significant actions, make vital phone calls, send emails. These are days when your energy and luck are high.]*

As the Metal Rat year comes to a close, you are already starting to feel the new positive Metal Ox energy on approach. Things in your life are going more smoothly, and the pieces are starting to fall into place. You are getting more help around the house. People around you are offering to share resources with you. Things are getting easier overall, and they will continue to improve.

See what you can do about getting more restful sleep—maybe doing some renovations in the bedroom to make it more of a sanctuary. You may need a new mattress or pillows. Consider a white noise machine or some black-out curtains. The more restful sleep you enjoy at night, the more productive and happy you will be during the day.

Your relationship is in a good place; you enjoy more harmony at home. You feel you and your partner are on the same page when it comes to the kids and extended family. You may be adding some new décor to the house, or finishing up a renovation project. Keep the budget in mind. What you want may be found at a cheaper price if you do just a little research, and are willing to accept a slightly longer delivery time.

You're busy at work, but you have more work/life balance now and that feels good. The people you work with, for the most part, are pulling their weight. They often come to you to ask for your opinions and insights into what's going on. You impress others with your decisive nature and quick wit. You being there makes the office a better place for many.

February 2021: *Lunar New Year begins on February 12. Happy Year of the Metal Ox.*

Attract New Love

If you've been looking for love for a while, your search is just about done. Now someone is looking for you! They are serious, business-like, and have a long list of things to do. They don't often take time for love, but for you, they'll stop in their tracks. When they do, it will be your turn to smile back. This is the only thing needed to get things going.

Good places to find love this year are where people have fun. Check out amusement parks, shopping malls, and movie theaters. You may even find love at a casino or a pool table. There are also love opportunities for you where parents take children—such as your child's school, parks, and arcades. Your child might even lead you to love this year.

Burn a red candle in your bedroom about once a month (possibly at the time of the New Moon) to stimulate the energy for bringing a love relationship into being. You can use a tea light or votive candle for this purpose, or you can choose a large pillar candle to burn over a series of days.

Enhance Existing Love

Those Snake natives already in a relationship will find the romance growing. You are more in sync this year than you have been in some time. But while you may feel more connected, you may be missing important messages your partner is sending you about what they care about now; what they need and what they want.

There is a focus on hearth and home this year, and it's quite possible the two of you may be moving, buying, or building a home. That's a wonderful thing, but communication is necessary and will help you find and unify the vision each of you has of what home is. Many considerations about this big decision can change in October or November. But if you've talked about it extensively, issues will now arise, and you'll be able to sail right through the process.

There will be several options for expanding your family this year. Perhaps you'll add a child? Or, maybe it's time for a new pet? The dynamics of the relationship change for the better. There is also a sizable creative project you and your partner may tackle together—successfully, I might add.

Quan Yin (also spelled Kwan Yin) is the embodiment of a goddess representing loving kindness. She is often depicted holding a small vase of healing waters. Place this statue in your bedroom to bring good energy for a happy, loving relationship.

Looking to Conceive?

There are many foods associated with fertility. One is the watermelon—specifically the seeds. You've probably heard the old saying: "Swallowing watermelon seeds can get you pregnant!". Rather than swallowing them, I suggest you take seven seeds, clean them and dry them.

Place the dried watermelon seeds in a small pouch, along with a metal charm shaped like a child (you can find these at party stores, in the baby shower section). Place the pouch under your mattress, so when you lie down, your belly is right over the pouch. This will bring good conception energy.

(From Donna Stellhorn's book, *A Path to Pregnancy: Ancient Secrets for the Modern Woman*)

Family and Kids

Children and their success are a focus this year. If you don't have kids, you may give your attention to nieces and nephews. You will find it brings you great happiness to watch them push through challenges and come up with creative solutions for any issues they have.

Fun comes to your home. You may have more than one party at your house this year. While it may be a lot of extra work, and the clean up is definitely a drag, the treasured memories make it absolutely worth it. You may make your home the site for classes, the local book group, or for the office poker night. You may even hold political meetings or Bible study at your house this year.

While you are most likely staying put and not moving this year, there are rumblings beneath the surface, which could indicate a move is coming in the next few years. The reason may be a result of changes in the neighborhood, or changes in your job. You'll have plenty of time to sit down with your family and come together to unify the vision of what you all want to attract.

The large white flower of the magnolia tree is a symbol of a happy family. This blossom elevates the family to a place of nobility and respect. You can display real magnolia flowers in the dining room. If you choose silk flowers, keep them well dusted; or consider a painting of these beautiful flowers and hang it in the dining room or family room.

Money

This year will be much more lucrative for Snake natives. Your strong business acumen reveals numerous opportunities to you—most of which others seem to be completely unaware of. However, having contact with other people leads directly to money for you. You may identify these contacts or information links online, but you would do well to have in-person meetings with some of them (for some Snake natives, this will mean traveling some distance, but the connection can be worth it).

You will be tempted to sink much of your hard-earned savings into real estate or land. Carrying out your due diligence and taking the time for careful research will ensure you don't make this purchase based on your emotions. Metal Rat years bring a desire to move quickly, but you don't have to rush as much you think. More than one good buy will be presented to you this year. On the other hand, if you're considering selling an investment property, this is the time to move on it.

This year, allow yourself time for creative thinking. Money opportunities will be revealed. Working hard will not bring you as much as a well-crafted email letter, tantalizing sales pitch, or clever cover letter. It can also be a good idea to consider adding some esoteric or spiritual activities known to attract money energy, such as meditation, lighting candles, or chanting. There's money to be made if you put your mind to it. You are programmed for success now. You see opportunities where others walk right by.

A good Feng Shui cure to attract wealth and money is to have the representation of flowing water in the house. A fountain is a good example, and you can find small, table top fountains just about everywhere. Place a table-top fountain in your entryway or home office to attract prosperity energy to the house. Run the fountain at least a few times a week for the best results.

Job or Career

This can be an exceptional career year for Snake natives. You have more business sense than most, and you can feel the winds shifting. Business opportunities present themselves to you. You may not have the time and resources to grab each one in the moment, so jot down your ideas and go back over your list later.

Inspiration may come in an article or blog post you read. You might hear a friend or colleague mention something that gets you thinking. Or, you may attend a presentation or conference that offers you lots of ideas. Keep in mind any new venture you start should proceed without using your own funds. Find others to help you.

Your strong business sense will also provide clues, letting you know whether the company you work for and the industry you work in are still strong. You see many changes on the horizon as new technologies become mainstream, and the world shifts politically. When you sense these changes on approach, it's time for you to quietly start preparing your exit. Start making contacts in your industry so you will be ready to slide seamlessly into a new and better position.

An even greater change is possible, perhaps starting your own business or moving from an office to working out of your home. You may need to put in more hours for a time while family members and friends try to pull you into their activities. Instead of being irritated that they are not boosting your efforts to reach new goals, try being more productive and efficient in your work (a particular skill of Snake natives.) You will then have time for leisure.

Snake natives who are planning to retire this year would do best to ease into it by going part-time for a while, or trading a work schedule for a strict exercise schedule to stay healthy.

If you'd like to change your position, get a new job, move up in the company you currently work for, or expand the market share for your own business, consider displaying a globe. The globe can be a small one, the size of a paper-weight, or it can be a larger free-standing model. Make sure the one you choose is in keeping with your overall décor, so if a large globe looks out of place in your home, choose a smaller version.

The globe can be any color, but should display the continents clearly. Place the globe in sight of your front door. Once you have your new job, you can move the globe to your family room or home office to help maintain the positive energy.

Education

If you're thinking about going back to school, short, quick programs are ideal this year. Real estate license programs, getting proficient at video production, or developing some other marketable skill can help you get ahead in your career. Consider study-at-home programs and online classes. Snake natives have good business sense and understand the value of incremental learning. Keep yourself on track with your studies by setting aside a short study period each day.

If you're already in school, you can make some wonderful contacts this year. It's possible that some of your peers or teachers now can become important mentors in the future. During the school year, you will need to stay aware of any student debt you are currently incurring, or have already incurred. You may feel it necessary to participate in some options that have the potential to be very beneficial in the long run. But be aware you may need to make some adjustments this year in the type of loan or payment schedule you choose. A big creative project can pay off. Enter academic and creative contests.

Legal Matters

This year you may be surprised by someone bringing a suit against you. If this happens, it will occur early in the year. Once past March, you're in the clear. But if someone does try to sue you, don't ignore the paperwork; go through it step by step, and you will have a good chance of the suit being dropped or being won by you. A large financial purchase brings contracts to consider. You may be getting a house, car, RV, or boat. You may feel rushed at the time of signing, so try to slow the energy down and give yourself enough time to understand what you're signing.

Health and Well-Being

Your sign is naturally one of the healthiest of the 12 zodiac signs. This year it's a good idea to increase your physical health by focusing on your mental well-being. This year you'll need a change of scene in some regard. It would be a good idea for you to take a trip—either to a very beautiful place, or one you know makes you happy.

This is a year for changes and adjustments. You may have had your current health routine for many years, but this year you show change energy, so it's good to consider new things you can do to improve the way you take care of yourself. This may be related to eating habits, or it could be exercise based. Allow your intuitive sense to guide you to places where you uncover helpful information or interesting people.

You are likely to have some interaction with the medical community. This may be for regular medical procedures, or to complete a healing begun in a previous year.

Don't underestimate the importance of friendships and of interacting with animals for your overall health. The more joyful moments you can rack up this year, the more energy and positive health you'll experience.

Obsidian is natural glass formed by the heat of a volcano. Its mirror-like surface is a reminder to look at yourself and your own behaviors before looking at others. Obsidian is a grounding stone. It helps you stick to practical routines and good habits. You can place specimens of obsidian in your home gym, or carry a small tumbled piece in your gym bag. Clear the stone every few months to re-energize it. See the chapter on clearing crystals at the end of this book.

Horse

January 25, 1906 -- February 12, 1907: Yang Fire Horse
February 11, 1918 -- January 31, 1919: Yang Earth Horse
January 30, 1930 -- February 16, 1931: Yang Metal Horse
February 15, 1942 -- February 4, 1943: Yang Water Horse
February 3, 1954 -- January 23, 1955: Yang Wood Horse
January 21, 1966 -- February 8, 1967: Yang Fire Horse
February 7, 1978 -- January 27, 1979: Yang Earth Horse
January 27, 1990 -- February 14, 1991: Yang Metal Horse
February 12, 2002 -- January 31, 2003: Yang Water Horse
January 31, 2014 -- February 18, 2015: Yang Wood Horse
February 17, 2026 -- February 05, 2027 Yang Fire Horse

Horse Personality

When considering the qualities of a Chinese Zodiac animal, it's a good idea to examine the traits, behaviors, and personality of the animal. There are many myths and legends about horses in our culture. Humans began to domesticate horses around 3000 BC, so many cultures have horse stories and traditions which help us identify specific traits and behaviors of these beautiful animals.

Horses are sensitive creatures; they can sense danger and know how to flee. They can sleep standing up, giving them the ability to run at a moment's notice. Even baby horses—foals—can run soon after birth. Horses have enormous endurance and are highly intelligent.

Those born in the Year of the Horse are attuned to the moods and motivations of others. They are quick to take offense and can explode with anger. But once Horse feels safe again, they quickly forget their rage. Horses want to move things forward, sometimes rushing others. They become impatient when results manifest too slowly.

They prefer things done their way. While they believe in the pursuit of happiness for everyone, their way is the best way. They will become aggressive if you try to block them, or pull them off their chosen direction.

Horse natives are great at business—especially from the perspective of sales and promotion. They are sociable beings, eager to connect people for the benefit of all. However, they're not good at sticking to a schedule, nor do they like adhering to procedures. The more stimulating the job, the better! Once involved in their tasks, Horse much prefers to keep working on a project until it's done, and then take time off to play.

Horse natives are better at short-term projects; they may not have the staying power to tackle lengthy processes. Break goals down into quick steps. Horses are great at solving problems, and they love to get things done—no endless projects, please! Horses are curious and enthusiastically interested, or they're not interested at all. Once they lose interest, they're out the door. (This goes for love as well as business.)

Horses need both mental and physical exercise. They are graceful and elegant in their movements (and in their decision-making). They can be defiant nonconformists. When you try to put them in a box, they become hot-tempered and headstrong.

Their biggest problem is their lack of focus and their readiness to jump to another project when something seems to move too slow. They will abandon the original goal and then wonder why they are not making much progress.

Horse natives excel at making money. They are strong leaders who allow people the freedom to work on their own thing. They can be extremely generous with their time and energy, but if Horse doesn't like what you're saying (or doing), he won't think twice about trampling you.

Horse: Predictions for 2020

January 2020: *There is a Lunar Eclipse on January 10. Uranus moves forward again on January 11. The Lunar New Year begins on January 25. Your Lucky Days are 1, 7, 13, 19, 25, and 31. [How to use your Lucky Days: On these days, plan to take necessary action, make vital phone calls, send emails. These are days when your energy and luck are high.]*

There's a great deal of activity going on at home. You may be considering moving or doing a major renovation. Someone may be moving into the house, or an adult child may be leaving home. There's a turning point in your family (and perhaps one which gives you a reason to celebrate). The changes happening in the house will prove to be very beneficial for you, and perhaps the entire family.

You are focused on money and find opportunities to expand your income this month. You will encounter some obstacles to this expansion and may need to put some additional effort into this endeavor if you want it to succeed. There may be no signs of growth or success until early next month. The period around the Lunar Eclipse finds you irritated and doubtful, but it is reasonable to take risks this month. Even if your efforts don't pay off immediately, you will still learn valuable lessons which will help bring profits in the future.

You have general happiness in love relationships now. While it's good to spend time with other members of your extended family, you may find your weekends monopolized by family events or obligations. Don't neglect your beloved, or there could be hard feelings between the two of you towards the end of the month. Plan a trip (even if it's to see family); a change of scene will bring a fresh spark to your love life.

February: *Mercury goes retrograde from February 16 to March 9. Your Lucky Days this month are 6, 12, 18, and 24. [How to use your Lucky Days: On these days, plan to take significant actions, make vital phone calls, send emails. These are days when your energy and luck are high.]*

Concerns about changes at your job are starting to happen now. They are turning out to be better for you, Horse native, than you had imagined. There are some possible changes in both personnel and procedures, and while these changes don't make much sense at first glance, they will make your life easier in the long run.

There is a lot of energy and activity at home. You may be giving a party or hosting friends overnight. If you were planning some redecorating or renovation, you may experience some delays when Mercury goes retrograde during the latter half of the month. Now is an excellent time to declutter, but be careful not to toss out something valuable stored in an odd place or a non-typical container (like money in an old coffee can or jewelry in an old handbag).

Finances improve this month, even though you receive an unexpected invoice. Perhaps this is an annual bill, but it could also be a mistake—so be prepared to contest any bills that don't seem to be right, and may not actually be yours.

You experience healing energy concerning a long term relationship. As a Horse native, you can have a quick temper, but you're also very quick to forgive. You may have voiced your opinions too abruptly the last time you spoke, and have stepped on someone else's feelings. You can smooth everything over now by listening to their concerns, and soon you can be galloping together towards the sunrise.

March: *Mercury goes direct on March 9. The Sun enters Aries on March 20. Saturn enters Aquarius on March 21. Your Lucky Days are 1, 7, 13, 19, 25, and 31. [How to use your Lucky Days: On these days, plan to take significant actions, make vital phone calls, send emails. These are days when your energy and luck are high.]*

Relationships of all kinds are the focus this month. There's no need to chase after what you want. Your powers of attraction are strong. You are the belle of the ball! Set your intention and visualize the kinds of relationships you want so you can spend your time strengthening quality connections.

Family life is humming along. There's a lot to do with members of the household, all pursuing various interests. You may be invited to attend several different types of events or functions.

There can be a little stress on the horizon as something which was of value to one person, is considered merely trash by another. Use caution if decluttering, and give everyone a say in what's discarded.

Finances continue to build, and you may want to pursue an investment in residential property or land. You may be tempted to follow the herd towards an investment fad, as many people give you their (unasked) investment advice. But Horse natives are smart. Do your own research before committing a chunk of your savings.

Work is busy, but you have a good team working alongside you. If you own your own business, you can find helpful people to support you by either hiring or outsourcing some of the daily tasks. Take the time to explain what you want to have done, so everyone is clear. Create a support system for yourself by being unambiguous about what you want.

You may receive a surprise gift from a friend. Just say thank you rather than trying to return the favor.

April: *Pluto goes retrograde on April 25. Your Lucky Days are 6, 12, 18, 24, and 30. [How to use your Lucky Days: On these days, plan to take significant actions, make vital phone calls, send emails. These are days when your energy and luck are high.]*

Social opportunities continue to come in, but you feel tired or bored with the same old routine events. You're looking for a break, a change of pace, or perhaps you just want to draw the curtains and pretend you're not home. Horse natives sometimes believe they want some isolation, but in truth, you are quite social, and when the crowds disappear, the silence can get on your nerves. It's better to change things up a little by reaching out to some friends you haven't connected in a while.

Financial opportunities show up for you, but you might be feeling a little skittish now. This seems to be outside of your comfort zone. Consider getting some more information or take a class and teach yourself about the investment or money-making opportunity instead of just chucking the idea into the bin. Look for information online as well as in your community. Play the devil's advocate and look at it clearly from both sides of the issue. You are known to be practical and realistic about new ideas. Use that common sense here.

A relationship can become serious. If you've been dating, you can now raise this connection to a new level. You may discuss making the relationship exclusive, moving in together, or perhaps even getting engaged.

If you're already in a love partnership and have been hoping to grow the family, there is good energy for this if you're willing to "work" at it. That may mean finding medical assistance with fertility, or sitting down with your beloved and talking about the changes your lives will experience when you add a child into your home.

May: *Saturn goes retrograde on May 10. Venus goes retrograde on May 12. Jupiter goes retrograde on May 14. Your Lucky Days are 6, 12, 18, 24, and 30. [How to use your Lucky Days: On these days, plan to take significant actions, make vital phone calls, send emails. These are days when your energy and luck are high.]*

There is energy around travel this month, and you may be on the road for some portion of this period. It's also possible someone is coming to visit you from some distance. Either way, this can be an enjoyable time. If you're in a new relationship, this may be the first trip you make with your sweetheart. It may be more fun if you can go at the beginning of the month than at the end when Venus is retrograde.

If you're looking for love, this an outstanding month to update your online profile, or at least to activate the dating apps on your phone. Attend some mixers, especially ones at fun venues like concerts, art shows, and comic book conventions.

Friendships abound, and this is a month where your circle of friendships is likely to expand. If you're invited to coffee, consider saying "Yes." Horse natives prosper when they can count themselves as one of a large group of friends. Consider picking up a new hobby, and you'll meet a whole community of people.

It's time to be aware of any changes in your investments, debt, or retirement options. All the information you need is available, but it will take some time to sort through it all. You will be happy in the long run if you take the time to do your homework now. You can set things up to benefit yourself and your family later.

An adult child may be knocking on your door for advice or assistance. Maybe not a surprise, as you were expecting something like this to happen. You might want to establish some boundaries this time.

June: *Lunar Eclipse on June 5. Mercury is retrograde from June 17 to July 12. There is a Solar Eclipse on June 20. Venus goes direct June 24. Your Lucky Days are 5, 11, 17, 23, and 29. [How to use your Lucky Days: On these days, plan to take significant actions, make vital phone calls, send emails. These are days when your energy and luck are high.]*

This month, around the Lunar Eclipse on June 5, it seems more than one person is telling you what you should and should not do. You're often the leader, and all this "advice" feels like having dust kicked up in your face. The Lunar Eclipse has brought this energy to remind you of your real goals and not to get caught up trying to please everyone else. If someone tries to block you, now you can just leap over them and fly above the fray.

An educational project may be coming to an end. If you're graduating, then congratulations! However, if this is just a break between semesters, you may want to examine your school plan to make sure you're still heading towards the destination you want. You don't want to lose steam. A test or set of tests can go well because of the hard work you've put in.

You may spend more time with younger relatives now, involving changes in your schedule to accommodate everyone.

The Solar Eclipse marks a time when something new is brewing at your job. You're in good shape when faced with change, but right now, most of what is going on is just talk; Mercury retrograde is holding back the change energy. Even as you implement new processes, they seem to dissolve back into the old ways pretty quickly. You may see a change in management you are less than happy about. However, this will turn out better for you in the long run. Try to be patient even if you think the new boss doesn't quite have it all together.

July: *Retrograde Saturn backs up into Capricorn. There is a Lunar Eclipse is on July 4. Mercury goes direct on July 12. Your Lucky Days are 5, 11, 17, 23, and 29. [How to use your Lucky Days: On these days, plan to take significant actions, make vital phone calls, send emails. These are days when your energy and luck are high.]*

You have strong feelings about finances this month related to a side business or a hobby you're trying to build into a stable source of income. This month it's a good idea to make a budget (even if you don't stick to it to the letter). By having a written budget, you can have a profitable money month and be more in harmony with the prosperous energy of the Metal Rat year.

Travel comes up again as a possibility. Maybe an invitation to a friend's city, or perhaps there's a conference or event you want to attend. Adventure awaits. Consider getting out of your comfort zone rather than lamenting you're stuck at home.

Someone close to you knocks on your door, asking for help. You handle this with your usual aplomb. Your life may change as a result of this contact. In a few months, you'll become aware of a significant improvement in both of your circumstances. Horse native, you are a guiding light to those around you.

For those Horse natives in a love relationship, there can be an even greater increase in romance after Mercury goes direct around the middle of the month. Look for something you can do together that brings you closer, like dancing, dining, or a romantic movie night. Consider doing something new and exciting behind closed doors.

If you're looking for love, consider attending sporting events, concerts, and festivals.

August: *Uranus goes retrograde on August 15. Your Lucky Days are 4, 10, 16, 22, and 28. [How to use your Lucky Days: On these days, plan to take significant actions, make vital phone calls, send emails. These are days when your energy and luck are high.]*

Your life path is lit up this month, and it's easier to make progress towards your bigger goals now. Contact influential people who can give you a hand up. You can plant many seeds and watch them grow into beanstalks reaching the sky. That said, this energy is so positive and easy, you might just let it slide. Make an effort to not pass up this good energy by putting off until tomorrow what you could be working on today.

You may be feeling more settled at home as a renovation project comes to completion, or out of town visitors leave to return to their homes.

There are possible changes to your income. You may be in line for a promotion or bonus. Or this increase may be related to commissions earned a while back being paid to you this month. Horse natives are naturally good with finances, and it's wise to pay down debt at this time and put extra funds into investments that will only grow.

For those Horse natives in a love relationship, you grow closer now by doing more things together, even mundane activities like folding laundry or washing the dishes. Open up discussions about finances and the future. You can now find yourselves on the same page in key areas of this partnership.

There is increased activity with friends. You may be invited to join a new group or to take a leadership role in an organization you already belong to.

September: *Mars goes retrograde on September 9. Jupiter goes direct on September 12. The Sun goes into Libra on September 22. Saturn goes direct on September 28. Your Lucky Days are 3, 9, 15, 21, and 27. [How to use your Lucky Days: On these days, plan to take significant actions, make vital phone calls, send emails. These are days when your energy and luck are high.]*

There are career opportunities this month, and if you're looking for a new position, you may find more than one door opening for you. It's a good idea to update your resume and post it to job hunting sites. Contact headhunters who have reached out to you in the past few months and reestablish that connection.

There is positive spiritual energy now, as well. You can find benefits by doing meditation, lighting candles, chanting, or visualization. This practice may aid you in many areas of your life, and it's specifically powerful if it's done daily after Jupiter goes direct around mid-September. The energy will build. Results will start to manifest in a few weeks.

Love is around you. You may be approached by someone who has been interested in you for a while. Or you may find you have a sudden interest in a person you hadn't considered before. This could hit you like a lightning strike, leaving you feeling a bit overwhelmed (as well as excited). Avoid getting involved in some ill-fated relationship from your past if possible, especially while Mars is retrograde. Instead, use this positive energy to find someone new to explore love with.

You can collect money owed to you this month—you may even end the month with a small windfall. Horse natives can be quite generous. When you have extra money in your account, you start to think about helping others rather than paying down debt or investing in your future. You are generous and can make brash decisions. Make sure you've set aside some for your future before handing out gifts to everyone else.

October: *Pluto goes direct on October 4. Mercury goes retrograde from October 13 to November 3. Your Lucky Days are 3, 9, 15, 21, and 27. [How to use your Lucky Days: On these days, plan to take significant actions, make vital phone calls, send emails. These are days when your energy and luck are high.]*

This month provides a chance to improve friendships with several people. You can make new friends, especially if you take the opportunity to meet friends of your friends. Getting involved in a new hobby or interest will put you around new people as well. Horse natives are naturally popular, and you are entertaining to be around. It's easy to make new friends now.

Take care of yourself this month. Eat healthily and find time to exercise. Also consider a new hairstyle, outfit, or perhaps a new tattoo. Find something that changes your look or freshens up your style. This will help you feel more confident and puts a spring back in your steps.

A deep emotional connection is possible with someone you care about. You can learn some things about this person you really weren't aware of or didn't understand before. Now you see things from their point of view. Knowing this about the person helps you trust them more and gives you a feeling of a greater connection.

If you own a business, the Mercury retrograde period is a good time to increase your knowledge about marketing and social media. You have an opportunity to expand your business. While you could delegate the tasks, you do better if you have at least a working knowledge of the channels you want to broadcast your message through.

If you work for someone else, you may find current projects or instructions to be on the vague side. Get clarification before you go too far down the rabbit hole.

November: *Mercury goes direct on November 3. Mars goes direct on November 13. Neptune goes direct on November 28. There is a Lunar Eclipse on November 30. Your Lucky Days are 2, 8, 14, 20, and 26. [How to use your Lucky Days: On these days, plan to take significant actions, make vital phone calls, send emails. These are days when your energy and luck are high.]*

Your powers of attraction are strong. If you're looking for love, this could be one of the best months for you. It's good to post your profile online or attend some social mixers through Meetup.com. If you're already in a love relationship, you can connect to your sweetheart on a deeper level. Communication can be lively and fun. Consider doing some new things together to spice up the relationship.

You may be making more money or receiving money from several sources. However, you still have some concerns regarding an insurance issue or something to do with a passive income source. You can resolve things by getting more information from knowledgeable friends. You may also get help through a social or government organization. This matter will ultimately resolve in your favor, but it will take your attention for a little while.

Home life is good. You may have out of town visitors as well as local people coming by. Horse natives thrive in social situations, and so it's already known among your friends that you can throw a great party. Your pantry is probably already stocked.

Your spiritual energy is in harmony with the greater energy field. As Neptune goes direct, you can access manifesting energy. Update your vision board or add an entry to your affirmation journal. You can now bring in positive energy into your life and attract opportunities with ease.

December: *Solar Eclipse on December 14. Saturn goes into Aquarius on December 16. Jupiter goes into Aquarius on December 19. Sun goes into Capricorn on December 21. Your Lucky Days are 2, 8, 14, 20, and 26. [How to use your Lucky Days: On these days, plan to take significant* *actions, make vital phone calls, send emails. These are days when your energy and luck are high.]*

You may be thinking about buying a new vehicle or changing up your method of transportation. Think about how you get around most of the time and find new ways of getting yourself from one place to another.

Communication is in focus right now. You may receive recognition for some writing or public speaking. If you've always wanted to sing in the choir or perform somewhere, this is the time to take steps to make it happen. All that said, some care is needed when you send emails or texts, especially around the Solar Eclipse on December 14. Make sure you're sending to the right person, or you may have some explaining to do later.

Finances improve, and you may receive a bonus or an increase from your job. The extra money jingling in your pocket combined with warm feelings of the Holiday season may tempt you to the mall and result in a shopping spree. Keep your goals in mind before you open your wallet.

Your sweetheart wants to spend more time with you. It's been difficult for the last couple of weeks because you've both been busy. Now is a good time to snuggle up on the sofa for some quality time together.

If you're looking for love, attend charity events, church functions, or professional organization holiday parties. Break free of your usual crowd and meet some new people. Venture out alone if no one will go with you. The more you do socially, the greater chance the Universe has to put you together with someone wonderful.

January 2021: *Uranus goes direct on January 14. Mercury goes retrograde from January 30 to February 20. Your Lucky Days are 1, 7, 13, 19, 25, and 31. [How to use your Lucky Days: On these days, plan to take significant actions, make vital phone calls, send emails. These are days when your energy and luck are high.]*

The Metal Rat year comes to a close, and you may already feel the new energy of the Metal Ox year approaching. This year is when you have had to stomp your feet a little harder to get the attention you deserve. Now, in the shifting energy, you find you've learned much about how to promote yourself and your work. This will be beneficial in the new year.

A person from your past returns. If this was a lover, they may want to get things going again. If they were a close friend, they may be moving back to your area. Either way, this could be interesting.

Your child or a younger relative may come to you for help with school or finding a job. But they may be more interested in having you listen to their side of the story than hearing your advice.

If you're in a committed relationship, it's a good idea to get together and have a conversation about finances. When the two of you are on the same page, you can create some real prosperity. You can make progress this month by talking about your goals to repay debt or accumulating retirement savings.

Renovations or repairs on the home front may have to be postponed. Mercury is retrograde at the end of the month, and you may have trouble finding reliable service people to help at this time. Or you may just want to wait until this energy clears, and you are sure which changes you want to make to the house. You may also be interested in selling or possibly downsizing. It's a good discussion point, but wait to take action until after Mercury goes direct in February.

February 2021: Lunar New Year begins on February 12. Happy Year of the Metal Ox.

Attract New Love

This year you may be looking for sex and find love. Or you may be looking for love and just find sex. It will be helpful for you to be clear about your intentions this year. Love can hit you like a ton of bricks! You may find your new person even before you're fully out of your old relationship. It could get complicated, not that Horse natives mind. You like a bit of excitement and romance in your life, and this year there are many indicators you will get your wish.

There is a chance a past love returns during February, June, or October. You may consider giving it one more shot, especially if you have enjoyed   a good intimate relationship with this person in the past. They seem to have changed, but the old dynamic can return if you're not careful. Don't gallop into anything without talking it over with your closest friends.

The symbol of a monkey riding a horse combines the energy of monkey's cleverness with Horse native's power, strength, and popularity. This is a good Feng Shui cure to improve your romantic endeavors this year. Find a small figurine of a monkey riding a horse or choose a couple of stuffed animals, one monkey, and one horse and placed these in your family room or bedroom. This will clear the way for new love to find you, and then you only have to make time in your busy schedule for dating.

Enhance Existing Love

It's likely your relationship has gone through a healing process over the past few months. While there's still work to be done, you're both on the right track now. Communication improves, and you feel more connected to each other. A weekend getaway helps bring the two of you together.

There seem to be issues with extended family not supporting your relationship. It will be important for the two of you stand together as you win people over to your way of thinking. That said, it looks like you receive more support from the younger generations than others in the family.

Travel is perfect for the two of you this year. Consider taking more than one trip during the Metal Rat year. Away from the job, the home, and the day-to-day grind, you can clearly see what's working in your life and build on that. Long-distance travel or extended trips are best, but even a day away will help.

Double Happiness is represented by a pair of Chinese characters. The single character translates as "joy." When two of these characters are written together, it is associated with love unions and weddings. It's called "Double Happiness." This motif dates back to the Song dynasty (960-1279 AD). You can find this pair of symbols in artwork, on vases, rugs, or brass sculptures like the one shown here. Hang a Double Happiness symbol in your bedroom to enhance your current love relationship.

Looking to Conceive?

What could be a sweeter fertility symbol than honey? The ancient Egyptians associated honey with love, happy marriage, and fertility. Honey was considered a gift from the divine.

o enhance fertility this year, place a jar of honey in your bedroom near the entrance (on a dresser or shelf), and pair it with a silver spoon. Give your partner a taste of honey to set the mood and attract conception energy.

(From Donna Stellhorn's book, *A Path to Pregnancy: Ancient Secrets for the Modern Woman*)

Family and Kids

Things are solid at home. You've worked hard to make them so. Renovations, if not already done, will be completed soon. The house looks the way you want it to look. Of course, you could sell now for a tidy profit. But you could also settle in to stay for the next five or six years.

The family looks larger than it did last year. There may have been an addition in the previous 12 months. A child, grandchild, or new pet may have come into your life or your extended family. As the family grows, so does happiness. You couldn't be prouder of this family of yours.

One or more of your kids will receive some recognition this year at their job or school. You've kept a watchful eye on their progress and guided them along the way. The results are in.

You did a good job. You will have reason to celebrate their success and the family overall.

The date palm tree is a symbol of abundance and protection. These trees go back to ancient times. The dates are eaten, the seeds are used to produce things like soap and cosmetics, and the leaves are woven into mats and screens. It's said the date palm symbol represents wisdom and a connection to a higher source.

If you have a yard and are in the right climate zone, you could plant a date palm on your property. But if this isn't possible, consider decorating your living room or family room with pictures of palm trees or fabric decorated with images of palm fronds.

Money

This year you may be finishing projects that directly lead to a paycheck. Or, you may be completing a level of school which will bring you more money in the workplace. However, now is the time to avoid putting the cart before the horse. Put in the time to finish what's right in front of you, and then it will be the right time to receive the reward you've been waiting for. Don't skimp on this step.

When it comes to money in this Metal Rat year, you profit when you share unified goals with family members. Some in your family may want to change the way money is handled on a day to day basis. You, Horse native, are the soul of optimism and generosity, but this may not be something that makes your family comfortable now. Be pragmatic with your money. Follow wise leads, and you will have success this year.

You may be tempted to put a lot of money into fixing up a home. And this is fine if the money is just sitting there in your savings account, but try not to add to debt this year.

You benefit when you meditate on creative solutions to money issues (even long-standing ones from childhood). Ask yourself good questions like, "What is a unique way for me to cut expenses?" or "What is a new way I can make more money?"

When you want to figure out a way to bring new money into your life, imagine you are unlocking a magic door. Behind this door are all the opportunities for money you could imagine. What better symbol could there be than a key to unlock the magic door? Indeed, the perfect Feng Shui cure to attract more money into your life this year will be a symbolic key!

Find an old-fashioned key. It can be large or small; it can be a replica key—even a key on a necklace or a key chain. You might find your key made into a piece of jewelry, or you might find an old key at a swap meet or in an antique shop—any store where you buy things for your home may have decorative keys you can use as your Feng Shui cure to attract wealth and money.

Once you have found your key, either hang it by your front door or on the wall in your home office area; or place the key on the desk or table where you work (or pay your bills). Having the key there will constantly remind you to keep looking for the magic door to wealth and abundance. (You'll know as soon as you find the door, you already have the key to unlock it).

Job or Career

It is said the opposing year in the Chinese zodiac (like the one you will experience this year as a Horse native in the Year of the Metal Rat) is a challenging year. The reason it's said to be difficult is that everyone is turned away from you and paying attention to the opposing sign, in this case, Rat. But this is also the first year of your harvest period.

There are so many options for you to think about, to choose from. Opportunities are fresh, ripe, and easy picking. This is what your career energy is like this year. You may have to try a little harder to get people's attention, but when you do, there will be great options for you when it comes to jobs offering higher pay.

If you've wanted to do something more creative or add some excitement to your current job, this is the year. While suggestions you make to your boss may be regarded with some initial skepticism, they will heartily accept them when you show positive results.

You can also focus on a creative business on the side. Sell your photos on a stock photography site, put your handmade pottery up on Etsy, refinish furniture, and sell it on Facebook marketplace. Consider a side business with one of your older children. They can help you with the technology, or you can help them with marketing. No one is better at making contacts than a Horse native.

If you work for a company, you may have been looking for a promotion for some time. Unfortunately, this won't bring you the stability or security you may be hoping it does. Rather, you can secure the job you want by getting to know people in higher positions in your organization. Network and socialize.

If you own a business, think about expanding by teaming up with companies that allow you to automate or streamline your back office. The more time you have in front of people and less behind the scenes managing your office, the better. Also, keep your eyes open for a surprising source of support. It may come courtesy of a family member, a former boss, or a competitor.

Clocks help us keep track of time. They can remind you to stay on the path towards your goals. You may already have a clock in your home office or work office. But this year consider getting a special clock, one you enjoy looking at. Remove other clocks and hang this clock where you can see it from your desk or workspace. For added positive energy, attach a list of your goals to the back of the clock. When you look at the clock, you will be affirming what you want to the Universe.

Education

There will be many opportunities for you to receive help or assistance, Horse native. This may come in the form of peer tutors, mentors, or helpful teachers. This is coming at absolutely the right time for you, as you seem more distracted this year than in previous ones. Perhaps you are also working a job or have a lively social life that's keeping you hopping. However, your studies can suffer if you don't find a way to have undistracted study time.

You may be offered options for studying abroad. If studying in another country has long been a goal of yours, this is a year to pursue opportunities.

If you're thinking about going back to school because you want to improve your resume or increase the number of career options available to you, you can do it. Be mindful of your time, and don't overload yourself with too many tough classes at once. If you can maintain a balanced schedule, you will do well, but if you put too much on your plate, you may find yourself rebelling and get little done.

Use visualization techniques and daily meditation to improve your concentration, memory, and comprehension. You can do very well on tests and projects by calling in spiritual help before the event through meditation or affirmations.

Legal Matters

There is not a lot of energy around legal matters this year. This may be a sign you don't have many contracts to sign, and there aren't any lawsuits taking up your attention. But, if you are already involved in a lawsuit, you may be so weary of the process you no longer are putting any energy into winning. Perhaps this involves a custody suit or patent/copyright issue. If you're putting out creative content this year, find out about any protections offered. You may want to trademark or patent something, and this year it's best to do it officially.

Health and Well-Being

There is a positive flow of energy around health for you this year. You may feel the urge to change your eating habits, adding more vegetables, and cutting back on the junk food. You have opportunities to learn to cook and/or to share meals with others. It would be a good idea to set up some regular dinners with family a few times a week.

Helpful exercises for you this year would be swimming, biking, dance, and martial arts. You can make some new friends by joining a hiking club or taking dance lessons. You may have a home gym, but being out among people is preferable for you, Horse native.

There is some stress as you focus on some larger goals in your life. But, like a horse running free on the prairie, the challenges are exciting and get your heart pumping. That said, taking time out for quiet meditation or taking an easy evening stroll is good too. Give yourself the time to rest between sprints.

Many cultures know about the mystic knot. The knot is known throughout Asia, the British Isles, and is even mentioned in Greek mythology. The mystic knot is a decorative knot tied in such a way it seems to go in an endless loop. It represents eternity or longevity.

Mystic knots come in various colors and a variety of materials, such as rope, wire, or yarn, but the best color for our purposes is bright red. Hang your mystic knot in the kitchen, bedroom, or family room to bring positive health energy to everyone in the home.

Sheep/Goat

February 13, 2007 -- February 1, 2008: Yin Fire Sheep/Goat
February 1, 1919 -- February 19, 1920: Yin Earth Sheep/Goat
February 17, 1931 -- February 5, 1932: Yin Metal Sheep/Goat
February 5, 1943 -- January 24, 1944: Yin Water Sheep/Goat
January 24, 1955 -- February 11, 1956:Yin Wood Sheep/Goat
February 9, 1967 -- January 29, 1968: Yin Fire Sheep/Goat
January 28, 1979 -- February 15, 1980: Yin Earth Sheep/Goat
February 15, 1991 -- February 3, 1992: Yin Metal Sheep/Goat
February 1, 2003 -- January 21, 2004: Yin Water Sheep/Goat
February 19, 2015 -- February 7, 2016: Yin Wood Sheep/Goat
February 6, 2027 – January 25, 2028 Yin Fire Sheep/Goat

Sheep/Goat Personality

When considering the qualities of a Chinese Zodiac animal, examine the traits, behaviors, and personality of the animal. For this sign, we need to consider two animals—Sheep and Goat. They both have distinctive qualities. We'll start with Sheep.

There are many traditions and stories about Sheep. (A ram is a male sheep, and a ewe is a female sheep, and lambs are both the male and female young.) Sheep are gregarious creatures who enjoy living in a flock. They can become stressed when separated from others in their flock. They have a natural inclination to follow a leader. Sheep are not territorial, but they do like to stay in familiar spaces. They flee from danger, but when cornered they will charge and "ram" you.

Even though the traits of Ram represent the masculine expression of the sheep family energy, people born under the sign of Sheep tend to appreciate the more "feminine" expression of their essence. By this, I mean qualities such as shyness, sensitivity, tolerance, and compassion. Sheep natives strongly represent these attributes.

While Sheep can come across as thin-skinned, they will willingly forgive when they sense the honesty in an apology. Sheep do not like to be hemmed in, preferring not to be under someone else's rule or schedule. Neither do they care to rule—often opting for the supporting role.

Sheep is a generous sign; known for their kind heart. Despite their generosity—or perhaps because of it—they always have a good home, plenty of food, and money in the bank. Sheep spends their life helping others, and are generously reciprocated.

When Sheep make a list of their material goals and share it with others, people step up to help Sheep make these goals a reality. Sheep often receive legacies from people not related to them.

The only time a Sheep is straightforward in word and deed is when they are angry. Most of the time, they will take a circuitous route to tell you what they want or think. They may tell you their story in the most expressive and creative of terms, yet never come right out to say what they need or expect of you.

Sheep are devoted to their families and their friends. They remember birthdays, celebrate occasions, and are quick to send help when they sense trouble for the people they care about. Often not reciprocated, their birthdays or their special events are often forgotten by those around them, and this hurts the kindly Sheep very profoundly.

Sheep natives tend to worry and perceive future events as being dark and potentially disastrous. They can spend many hours— even days—stuck in a dark depression. They benefit greatly by talking over their difficulties with others, but many Sheep try to hold everything inside, and this can cause physical issues such as fatigue and low energy.

Sheep can receive money, but they often spread it around quickly, leaving themselves with just the minimum to meet their needs. They often attract money in the first place because of someone else—someone they love needs it. It's imperative that Sheep plan for their future financial security, although they rarely do so.

Sheep are astute in business and are masters of the soft sell. They're able to get beyond objections and help others come to a decision.

People born under the sign of the Sheep spend time waiting for the right moment to take action on their goals. They can wait for quite a while to get what they want. Committed to doing things the "right way," things often do not get done at all.

Sheep tend to be hypercritical of their own actions (and sometimes the actions of others,) and this leaves them feeling vulnerable, as well as causing them a great deal of suffering. They need to take chances more often. They are more sure-footed than they realize.

In some parts of the world, the creature symbolizing this section of the Chinese Zodiac is the Goat—not Sheep or Ram. While many of the qualities ascribed to Goat are similar to those of Sheep or Ram, the energy of Goat has some different attributes overall. A person born in the year of the Sheep/Goat can access the attributes of the Goat as well as the Sheep.

While Goat is a different animal than a Sheep, goats are a sub-family of sheep. A simple way to tell the difference is by noting a goat's tail points to heaven, and a sheep's tail points to earth. When you are acting more goat-like, you can focus on climbing to new heights; you seek to get to the top and see the view below. When you are more Sheep-like, you tend to want to stay home and stay in your comfort zone, your routine.

Goat forages for its meal, sheep graze on grass. People born in Sheep/Goat years may find they spend time investigating lots of new things, new foods, new places, and new people. Then they might spend months at a time doing the opposite—sticking to a routine and the places and people they know well.

One of the valuable qualities of Goat we see in people born in Sheep/Goat years is curiosity. This quality allows you to explore and examine opportunities all around and to find out whether or not they may be viable for you to pursue. Curiosity keeps you interested in the motivations of the people around you. Your life is enriched as you find yourself entranced by new topics and ideas. This keeps life very interesting.

Goat/Sheep: Predictions for 2020

January 2020: *There is a Lunar Eclipse on January 10. Uranus moves forward again on January 11. The Lunar New Year begins on January 25. Your Lucky Days this month are 2, 8, 14, 20, and 26. [How to use your Lucky Days: On these days, plan to take necessary actions, make vital phone calls, send emails. These are days when your energy and luck are high.]*

The actions you're taking this month (ones you've been planning to take for a while) come at the right time. The results will be quite beneficial, so full steam ahead, Captain. Watch out for naysayers. You often go out of your way to avoid any conflict, especially with loved ones. But this month, you have an opportunity to make real progress on your path.

There's the most energy in your area of money this month, more than any month in the previous 12. You can ask for the raise, promotion, or transfer now, and gain positive results. Now is not a time for your usual Sheep native peaceful nature. Action is key to getting what you want. Sometimes you hold yourself back, not willing to risk criticism or the displeasure of others, but this month the summit is in sight. Climb, baby, climb.

You are at a loss as to why your partner is upset with you—because it has nothing to do with you. There is a misunderstanding, or someone is projecting their issues onto you. For kind-hearted Sheep natives, this is rather distressing until you realize it's not about you. Still, your feelings could be hurt—but before you fall into melancholy, recognize your partner is not perfect. You can struggle through this together.

If you're looking for love, you may feel the search has not resulted in you finding anyone even close to the type of person you want to spend time with. But the truth is, you've been hiding at home, just taking the same route to and from home, from home to the gym, and back home again. Break free of the pattern, and love will be able to find you.

February: *Mercury goes retrograde from February 16 to March 9. Your Lucky Days this month are 1, 7, 13, 19, and 25. [How to use your Lucky Days: On these days, plan to take significant actions, make vital phone calls, send emails. These are days when your energy and luck are high.]*

If you're looking for love, you may have an opportunity with someone from your past as Mercury goes retrograde towards the middle of the month. Proceed with caution to see if this person has made the changes they said they have. Sheep native has a sensitive, generous heart, which is wonderful, but it is also a heart worth guarding against empty promises.

If you're in a long-term relationship, you find you're growing closer as you both put your efforts behind a single goal. As you work together side by side, making the effort and perhaps sacrifices, you see how you can trust and rely on each other.

There is a lot of activity around finances this month. You find opportunities to receive payment from more than one income source, but it will take the application of a little energy to get the check in your hands. This could mean you are selling some items, working a side job, or just reminding someone they owe you money. The funds come through, and payments are received during the retrograde Mercury period at the end of the month. And this source may pay you again in a few months.

You may be in the market for a new vehicle. But purchasing a vehicle during Mercury retrograde periods can be problematic. You may want to postpone your transaction until next month.

A neighbor or sibling makes their feelings known to you. They may be bringing a problem to you with the hopes you can find a solution to their issue. Since you're probably not directly involved, you can step aside if you choose.

March: *Mercury goes direct on March 9. The Sun enters Aries on March 20. Saturn enters Aquarius on March 21. Your Lucky Days are 2, 8, 14, 20, and 26. [How to use your Lucky Days: On these days, plan to take significant actions, make vital phone calls, send emails. These are days when your energy and luck are high.]*

There is a lot of activity around communication this month. You may be asked to present a report, lead a meeting, or do some public speaking. If you don't feel up to this, try to delegate the task to someone else. Otherwise, remember that stepping outside your comfort zone is the best way to grow.

There's a lot of romance around you. If you're in a love relationship, there will be fun after dark with your sweetie. If you're looking for love, consider going out to night clubs, theater, or dine at high-end hotel restaurants at night.

Things are going well at your job as you find you are working side-by-side with people you like. There is a lot to do, but there can be real cooperation now with fellow employees, and that makes working there much easier.

If you're not as happy with your career, find ways to acquire new skills through online learning or local classes. If a long educational program sounds tedious, consider a short, self-study program for something that doesn't require certification.

Your health is improving. You may be following a new diet or exercise program which benefits body, mind, and spirit. Mercury goes direct on March 9. and you may feel tempted to stop your new program, but keeping it up will improve things a great deal for you in the long run.

April: *Pluto goes retrograde on April 25. Your Lucky Days are 1, 7, 13, 19, and 25. [How to use your Lucky Days: On these days, plan to take significant actions, make vital phone calls, send emails. These are days when your energy and luck are high.]*

Things are busy at home. If you're moving, you can gather friends and extended family together to help you pack and move to your new place. If you're doing renovations or construction on your property, you can expect to find helpful workers now (though they may not come cheap). Sheep natives have good taste when it comes to home and décor; you have exceptional luck at finding skilled craftsmen to help you realize your vision.

If you're in a love relationship, your partner may surprise you by agreeing to a trip or adventure you've been asking for. This again is confirmation that you married well.

You may be taking a test or some certification for your job. Or perhaps you're traveling to a conference this month. Some unusual events disrupt your routine, and this has thrown off your rest cycle. When this task is done and off your list of things to do, you need to schedule yourself a break.

Your finances remain strong; however, there may be a large expense as you purchase a high-ticket item, or you put a deposit down on something important. This money is an investment as much as it is an indulgence, and it's a wise idea to balance the price with how much enjoyment it will add to your life.

A close friend or older relative may be visiting you or invites you to visit. It may be difficult to fit this into your already busy schedule, but, Sheep native, it will be worth your time.

May: *Saturn goes retrograde on May 10. Venus goes retrograde on May 12. Jupiter goes retrograde on May 14. Your Lucky Days are 1, 7, 13, 19, 25, and 31. [How to use your Lucky Days: On these days, plan to take significant actions, make vital phone calls, send emails. These are days when your energy and luck are high.]*

There are opportunities for love and romance this month. If you're looking for love, it's the right time to be out in the world. Try attending events and going to new places. Look up from your phone and smile at the world. Your charisma is high now.

If you're already in a love relationship, it's time to shake things up, especially as Venus goes retrograde around mid-May. Suggest a date night and push yourselves out of the rut you might be in. Consider toasting with champagne in a hot air balloon, watching the sunset over a secluded lake, or teaming up together to solve a case at murder mystery dinner theater.

Your finances get a boost through an agreement or contract. This may be for employment, or from a passive income source like rental property. You have opportunities now to create streams of income in this Metal Rat year. The information you need can be found online rather than through a conventional class.

There is a spiritual guide helping you through a matter requiring you to speak up. Don't hesitate to agree to lead the meeting, teach a class, or give a presentation. You know your material, and the experience will help you grow.

Keep an eye on your vehicle and where you park as Saturn and Jupiter are retrograde this month. Parking in questionable spots could get you a ticket or a scratch on your car or truck.

Your health benefits now from some exercise. See if you can get a walk, run or hike into your schedule regularly.

June: *Lunar Eclipse on June 5. Mercury is retrograde from June 17 to July 12. There is a Solar Eclipse on June 20. Venus goes direct June 24. Your Lucky Days are 6, 12, 18, 24, and 30. [How to use your Lucky Days: On these days, plan to take significant actions, make vital phone calls, send emails. These are days when your energy and luck are high.]*

A change in finances is probable this month. You can boost your income by taking some calculated risks. It's time to implement plans rather than just doing more planning. Launch the website, call the meeting, or phone up the prospect. Benefits come to you when you get out of thinking mode and into the doing mode.

A legal matter can be resolved quickly and easily, but it should not be ignored, especially if it comes around the time of the Solar Eclipse. If you feel unsure about how to proceed, find professional legal help with the issue.

A difficult situation at work now has the potential to clear up without any effort on your behalf. If this is about a co-worker, the problem seems to resolve itself.

You may feel like growing in your life, and this may mean taking a class or two or making a move. You're seeking change, but you're not sure, so research seems like the best solution. However, much of the change you're looking for (and especially getting unstuck) is accomplished by doing new things. Go to some meetup groups, get involved in a new hobby, find a charity to support. Anything involving other people will bring satisfaction to your life right now. The best time to start is after Venus goes direct on June 24.

Children or younger relatives figure prominently this month. There may be milestone celebrations to attend. This is a welcome break in your routine, even if you have to travel to get to the event.

July: *Retrograde Saturn backs up into Capricorn. There is a Lunar Eclipse is on July 4. Mercury goes direct on July 12. Your Lucky Days are 6, 12, 18, 24, and 30. [How to use your Lucky Days: On these days, plan to take significant actions, make vital phone calls, send emails. These are days when your energy and luck are high.]*

This month, Sheep natives may experience a profound spiritual experience. You may feel quite intuitive and connected to a higher power. Your spiritual guides and angels are present. You may feel their counsel and protection at this time. This may be a result of you attending religious services, or you may be practicing spirituality in your home through prayer, meditation, chanting, smudging, or lighting candles. Overall you feel more peaceful and self-assured. It's as if you're the recipient of a big hug from the Universe.

While spiritually, you feel things are working out, the practical aspects of life go on. You need to focus some attention on some paperwork, especially since Mercury is still retrograde until July 12. A contract or other agreement may be involved. It could relate to family members, and everyone may need to find consensus before everything can be signed and sealed. You may want to engage professional help to get this all done. You have luck on your side, and so with some effort, there can be a satisfactory conclusion to this process.

Romance is available to you if you want it. If you're in a love relationship, there's more than just some cuddling going on. If you're looking for friendship, there is a chance of romance, too. It's up to you, Sheep native, to decide whether it's right or if everything is moving too fast.

Finances improve during this period. You may be able to pay off an old debt, inspiring you to focus on paying down other debts too. Maybe sell off some excess items to make a little extra cash.

August: *Uranus goes retrograde on August 15. Your Lucky Days are. 5, 11, 17, 23, and 29. [How to use your Lucky Days: On these days, plan to take significant actions, make vital phone calls, send emails. These are days when your energy and luck are high.]*

This is a hectic period. There is a lot of communication going on. You may be talking to family members and extended family. Maybe you're planning a family reunion or a milestone event for a family member. A short trip can be involved, or people may be coming to visit you.

In addition, you may be speaking to a group or doing some public speaking at a work event. You may not like being in the limelight, but it's good every once in a while to stretch and expand your comfort zone.

Things with your career are going well. You are admired by those you work with, and the supervisor gives you a sign that he or she is pleased with your performance. There may be talk of a future promotion, but you. Sheep native, you may prefer to try for some perks like a more flexible schedule.

Your health improves since you've been more active the past few weeks. Perhaps you're working out at the gym, or you've been hiking with friends. Dancing is a possibility as is swimming; in fact, any physical movement is good at this time.

Your partner surprises you with a gift you were not expecting. This gesture shows the love in your life right now. Sheep natives are known for their luck in relationships, and you have chosen well.

If you're looking for love, consider going to new places and trying new activities. You have a lot of luck meeting new people when you do something out of the ordinary while Uranus is retrograde.

September: *Mars goes retrograde on September 9. Jupiter goes direct on September 12. The Sun goes into Libra on September 22. Saturn goes direct on September 28. Your Lucky Days are 4, 10, 16, 22, and 28. [How to use your Lucky Days: On these days, plan to take significant actions, make vital phone calls, send emails. These are days when your energy and luck are high.]*

Work is busy now, and you may have some opportunities for extra shifts or overtime. Your team may be short-handed now, putting a lot of extra work on your shoulders. You're a team player, but no one should take advantage of your peaceful, accommodating nature. Let management know what you can and cannot do, and ask for more help where needed.

Your life may be even busier at home as Mars is retrograde early in the month. You may be moving or making substantial changes to the home, like renovating a kitchen or gutting the main bathroom. This is disrupting your normal routines and making everything you normally do take longer. It's going to be great when it's all done, but in the meantime, you'll need to muster the patience to get through all the inconveniences and little irritations.

Your love life is healthy. There is positive partnership energy around you. If you're dating, you may be taking the relationship to another level by becoming exclusive, moving in together, or getting married. There's a reason to celebrate, but this is also a little stressful. Don't lose your nerve. You are heading in the right direction.

There are opportunities to spend time with friends you haven't seen in a while. Yes, you're super busy now, but find the energy deep inside you and go be social. You will be making some good memories.

October: *Pluto goes direct on October 4. Mercury goes retrograde from October 13 to November 3. Your Lucky Days are 4, 10, 16, 22, and 28. [How to use your Lucky Days: On these days, plan to take significant actions, make vital phone calls, send emails. These are days when your energy and luck are high.]*

October is an excellent month to work with your investment and retirement plans. You can find good help and information from financial professionals. If you've wanted to try your hand at investing, you can take some small risks now as that's in harmony with the energy of the Year of the Metal Rat. It's also the time to look into employer-based plans and see what benefits you can tap. You may have an opportunity for a 401K match or a stock purchase plan. Other banking opportunities may be available such a debt consolidation loans or business financing. Review your financial goals and set aside some time to look into making things happen.

Children, younger relatives, or dear pets figure prominently this month. Expect an addition coming into the family, possibly even into your very household. Adult children may be visiting and asking for your guidance. Younger children may be bringing friends home who ask to stay overnight. New pets household may need some training or special care.

An issue with your vehicle may come up again as Mercury goes retrograde around the middle of the month. If you need to take the car or truck to the mechanic, ask for a warranty for the work done. Repairs done during Mercury retrograde periods often need to be redone at a future date.

If you're looking for love, this is one of the best months of the year to be seen. Post your profile on dating apps and be noticeable on social media. Go out to social events in your area. Look for singles groups and meetups around your hobbies.

November: *Mercury goes direct on November 3. Mars goes direct on November 13. Neptune goes direct on November 28. There is a Lunar Eclipse on November 30. Your Lucky Days are 3, 9, 15, 21, and 27. [How to use your Lucky Days: On these days, plan to take significant actions, make vital phone calls, send emails. These are days when your energy and luck are high.]*

Pay Attention to your passive income sources, investments, and banking this month. If you worked on this area last month, you may have some new opportunities to capitalize on. You could find new sources of income available to you, possibly through a family connection. If you did not work on this last month, there may be some issues around banking security and passwords. It's a good idea to change banking passwords periodically and especially during a Metal Rat year. You may find investments you were considering last month have now increased in value. Move on what you feel comfortable with. Don't bet the farm, but also don't avoid it all. Find the balance between risk and security.

If you're in a love relationship, there are some good times ahead this month. There is a lot of laughter and fun in the house. You may also be entertaining friends, coming together for a holiday meal or a dinner party.

You are sleeping better. This quality rest is really helping your mood and decision-making. It's good to make sleep a priority now.

Your job is humming along. Your projects are going well, and you can get help when you need it. At this rate, you may be in line for a bonus or raise towards the end of the year or in January. However, If you're at the top of your pay scale, consider planting seeds now to make a change next year. No reason to be stagnant.

December: *Solar Eclipse on December 14. Saturn goes into Aquarius on December 16. Jupiter goes into Aquarius on December 19. Sun goes into Capricorn on December 21. Your Lucky Days are 3, 9, 15, 21, and 27. [How to use your Lucky Days: On these days, plan to take significant actions, make vital phone calls, send emails. These are days when your energy and luck are high.]*

You are looking good and your powers of attraction are high now. If you're looking for love, it's a good idea to attend social events, charity functions, and office parties. Wear a bright color, smile at the world, and see who is attracted to your light and energy.

You are also attracting new friends. Several people may have been acquaintances up until now, but you find joy in creating a deeper connection with them. You are expanding your circle of friends and are part of a bigger tribe.

Finances improve, and you have the opportunity for a windfall. That said, there may be a disruption in finances around the time of the Solar Eclipse halfway through the month, but it's probably one you've been expecting. A contract may be finishing up, or a side income may be coming to an end. Other sources of income are on the horizon, and you will probably be making more a year from now than you are at this time.

It's useful now to pick up some tech skills. It's a good idea to learn more about posting on social media, and about the apps on your phone or other devices. It may not be your favorite thing to do with your evenings, but having an understanding of how these devices work and how best to use them in your daily life is a proper use of your time right now.

January 2021: *Uranus goes direct on January 14. Mercury goes retrograde from January 30 to February 20. Your Lucky Days are 2, 8, 14, 20, and 26. [How to use your Lucky Days: On these days, plan to take significant actions, make vital phone calls, send emails. These are days when your energy and luck are high.]*

Income opportunities are around you, and you can collect money from several sources this month. You may also be selling some property or other large ticket items, which is bringing you some cash.

A neighbor or sibling is in communication with you—a welcomed connection. You can receive good advice or assistance now from this person.

There is a lot of activity around relationships for Sheep natives already in a love connection. You may be moving in together or otherwise making the partnership official. This calls for a party.

There are some changes in management or a shift in supervisors at work. This is not the first managerial change you've been through, and it's not the last. Things will settle down again in a few weeks. Just take a wait-and-see attitude. No reason to plan any big changes for yourself now.

The energy of the new year, Metal Ox, is almost here. Ox is the opposing sign to your own. The world will begin to turn away from all things Sheep so they can put their attention on Ox. Sheep natives prefer to have company rather than feel alone. As the energy shifts, it's essential that you reach out to friends and family. Going forward into the next year, you'll have to be the one who initiates contact, suggests the get-together, picks the restaurant, etc. It's more work for you, but it will gather to you the people you enjoy.

February 2021: *Lunar New Year begins on February 12. Happy Year of the Metal Ox.*

Attract New Love

Beautiful love is possible this year. There is magical energy around you, Sheep native. You can feel the threads that connect all living beings. Tug on one thread, and you can pull the one for you closer and closer. It's good to visualize, but make sure you're visualizing the meeting and first date, not your wedding day. Give the universe clues on how to get you together with a great love.

You can connect with a new love when you're doing creative work outside the home. Take art classes, volunteer at the local community garden, audition for a play. You can also meet this person by volunteering for a charity organization or community program. May and June are particularly strong months for this.

If you are looking for a serious relationship with a person to settle down with, then consider using the Wedding Ring cure. Find a replica wedding ring (you can often find these at party stores in the bridal section), and place the ring under the mattress on the unoccupied side of the bed. Just lift the mattress and slide the ring underneath.

If you're not ready to settle down, but you still want a romantic new love in your life, place a copy of your house key under the mattress instead of the ring. Put it under the side of the mattress where your new lover will rest their head. If you decide later you want to make the relationship more permanent and official, change out the house key for the replica wedding ring.

Enhance Existing Love

Expect the unexpected in your relationship this year. What you may have thought was over begins again, and sails along like it never has before. Likewise, if you're completely sure nothing can rock your relationship, be aware you are too complacent and may be missing important clues.

The best part is the excitement and feelings this can inject back into your love life. The more interesting things you do together as a couple, the better. Push outside your comfort zones. Consider travel, moving, changing jobs, starting a company, or adding to the family. Think change and that energy will bring you closer together.

It's also a year to put the fun back in your relationship. Dress up and pretend like you're dating each other again. You can also bring energy to this relationship by getting involved in a money-making activity together.

Amethyst is the purple quartz stone of peace. It's said to raise hopes, calm the mind, and bring soothing energy to your life. Amethyst can help you be more intuitive and connect spiritually. This is a good gemstone for Sheep natives, who are looking to improve their love relationship.

Place a specimen of amethyst in your bedroom. Place it on the dresser or on a table where you can see it from the bed. You can also wear amethyst jewelry this year to help you connect with your partner in a deeper, more meaningful way.

Looking to Conceive?

Olives and olive oil have long been a symbol of fertility. Eating olives was said to increase sexual potency in men. Consider adding extra olives to your lover's salad or chop up some olives and sprinkle them over a savory dish.

In the past, women would wear wreaths of olive leaves on their wedding day to increase fertility. If you have olive trees nearby, you can cut some small branches and put these in your bedroom. Use extra light olive oil (which has no scent) for a massage before and during love-making.

(From Donna Stellhorn's book, *A Path to Pregnancy: Ancient Secrets for the Modern Woman*)

Family and Kids

Happiness reins at home for Sheep natives this year. While there will be the occasional ups and downs, for the most part, there is fun and harmony in family matters. Please note: there will be change, but these changes are welcomed and supported by most of the family (the very young ones may not agree, but they will adapt).

Changes in and around the family can mean someone is moving in or moving out. If you have adult children, one or more may be leaving the nest. There also may be relatives or friends staying with you at home for longer than their usual visits. Again, this looks harmonious and pleasant, even if you get very little notice before their arrival.

There may also be changes around the family as one of your older children gets into a relationship. It's also possible you meet a new friend or friends who, over time, seem to become part of the family. The hardest part about your home and family this year is getting out of the house. You're more of a home-body than usual this year.

The lotus flower is a sacred symbol of wisdom, purity, and spirituality. This year use this symbol to bring protection and harmony into your home. You can use pictures of lotus flowers or find a figurine of a beautiful lotus blossom to place on a table in the family room or living room. It's also said that a lotus flower can unlock a locked door. This symbol is to help you unlock better relationships with everyone at home.

Money

You are often lucky with money, but this year you find some situations (perhaps not of your own making) quite irritating. This can be relative to the small bills—they just keep increasing year after year. The income doesn't seem to be keeping up with inflation. Your family may be on a different financial page than you. Fortunately, most of these things are slight irritations rather than major obstacles.

Your income can increase this year though it seems connected to tasks you don't like as much. Perhaps you need to ask for more money, and you are hesitating. You may need to delegate tasks or be creative about their completion. As more money does flow in, you need to investigate investment options that will help your money grow. If you've been too conservative in the past to invest—this year, the Metal Rat year, take a class or study on your own until you feel ready.

This year you may have some large expenses such as the purchase of a new car for yourself or a family member. There may be repairs at home to do, or an adult child may need some help with their expenses. Money can come in to cover these, Sheep native. It's helpful to ask yourself if there's a non-financial solution before you open your wallet. There are trade and barter options available for you if you look.

Around the world, seaports are still the most popular places to live and work. Even though we no longer rely on ships for personal transportation, much of the goods we use come into the country via boat. For this reason, one Feng Shui cure is the 'Wealth Ship,' representing prosperity sailing into your life. This is one of the most potent symbols for attracting what you want.

When using the symbol, you can choose a model of a wealth ship or find a picture or painting you like of a ship. If you're feeling ambitious and craft-minded, you can build a model ship from a kit. If you have the inclination, you can paint a picture of your own wealth ship. Any of these would make a fine Feng Shui cure.

Place your cure near your front door or in your home office. Position the ship or picture, so it appears to be sailing into the room, not out the door. If the ship is sailing out the door, it will take a lot longer for it to return and for wealth to find its way to you.

Job or Career

Of all the signs of the Chinese zodiac, Sheep natives may value security the most. For a while, you've felt the rumblings of change. Perhaps you've been nervously holding on to work that's really not that great a job. Remember, you're a sure-footed climber. As change happens, you will find your footing easily and make your way to higher ground. Keep your resume handy. Find and connect with people in your industry who may be working for companies you're interested in. Explore connections through professional organizations. This is the path to security.

That said, this is going to be an amazing year for you career-wise. Opportunities can drop into your lap in a way you've never seen before. Some of these may be a whisper heard at the office, or the result of a phone call from a friend. Know your goals and priorities. When offers come, you can evaluate which ones are worth taking. If you've wanted a higher position, that path may indeed open up. But there are also possible connections to having your own business or working for a promising startup.

If you already own a business, there may be some changes in partnerships. You may part ways with someone who's been with your company for a long time. You may bring in someone to bring new life to a department. You may close offices and work at home to save expenses or move out of the garage to open a shop or warehouse. You are prepared for this type of change. The changes coming are the ones you've wished for. Now they are here, so don't put your head in the sand.

In choosing a Feng Shui cure, remember the universal rule: "Like attracts like." This concept allows you to use representations of things to attract the real thing. For example, as you are looking for your new job, visualize yourself showered with money when they make you the offer.

To complete the picture, find a wind chime made of Chinese coins. Choose a chime with many coins—this is to represent a shower of money.

Hang the wind chime outside your front door, or if you're in an apartment, hang it from your balcony/patio. As you hear the coins tinkle and chime in the breeze, imagine the sound of raindrops showering money on your roof and your windows. While it's best to hang the chime outside your front door, if this isn't a viable option where you live, hang your wind chime on your back porch or balcony.

Education

If you've had any thought at all about going back to school, or even just taking a single class, the answer is "Yes!" Your intuition is correct—it's time to add to your skillset. You can choose fun, creative courses, or you can go back to get a higher degree. There is so much helpful energy for you in this area it would be a shame not to take advantage of it. The Universe will open doors for you to get you into the right school and the right instructors. All this positive energy doesn't mean you should throw caution to the wind when it comes to funding your education. Be your usual prudent self and find ways to get the education you want without going into too much debt.

If you're already in school, well done. You are on the right track. This year will require effort and to bring your game up because the course you've chosen does show it challenges you. Sheep natives don't mind a climb, so get help when possible concerning better study habits and time-saving tips. When choosing classes, check with past students about which teacher would be the best. Make connections with academic counselors for additional advice. If you're going to a campus, you do show some issues around commuting or parking. These can be solved with some diligent effort at the beginning of the semester.

Legal Matters

You show legal activity centered around real estate, moving, and family estates. There may be contracts to sign and agreements to review with family members. You may have to get some family members on your side to move forward on an important matter. Lawsuits are unlikely this year, but if there's a legal matter that's hungover from a previous year, you may have to pay some money to get it finished and solved.

Health and Well-Being

You have access to healing energy this year. You may be recovering from some issues picked up last year. During this Metal Rat year, you may find new treatments or great new practitioners to help you on the road to wellness. The best months for actively working on your health are from September to November this year.

Difficulties this year stem from negative self-talk rather than other sources. It's not helpful to be hard on yourself, Sheep native. Be as kind and considerate of yourself as you are to so many other people in the world. You may explore some helpful techniques to rid yourself of the bad habit of negative thinking. Try meditation, tapping, and hypnotherapy as alternative methods of disrupting old mental patterns. Also consider getting more exercise, especially doing enjoyable activities out in nature.

To clear old energy out of your home and bring in positive healing energy, consider using Smudge Spray this year. You can make your own Smudge Spray, also called Sage Spray, by making tea using white sage leaves; when it's cooled to room temperature, put the sage tea into a spray bottle. This spray will stay fresh in your fridge for about three days. Smudge Spray you make yourself will smell very woodsy like sage. You can also find commercially sold Smudge Sprays created by some very good herbalists. These types of Smudge Sprays use an alcohol base and a light floral scent. They last a long time and don't need to be refrigerated.

Use the spray at least once a month. Spray around doorways, especially the front and back door. Also, use it in the bedroom. Be careful spraying around delicate fabrics. Using Smudge Spray will help you clear the energy and bring in positive health vibes.

Monkey

February 2, 1908 -- January 21, 1909: Yang Earth Monkey
February 20, 1920 -- February 7, 1921: Yang Metal Monkey
February 6, 1932 -- January 25, 1933: Yang Water Monkey
January 25, 1944 -- February 12, 1945: Yang Wood Monkey
February 12, 1956 -- January 30, 1957: Yang Fire Monkey
January 30, 1968 -- February 16, 1969: Yang Earth Monkey
February 16, 1980 -- February 4, 1981: Yang Metal Monkey
February 4, 1992 -- January 22, 1993: Yang Water Monkey
January 22, 2004 -- February 8, 2005: Yang Wood Monkey
February 8, 2016 -- January 27, 2017: Yang Fire Monkey
January 26, 2028 – February 12, 2029 Yang Earth Monkey

Monkey Personality

When considering the qualities of a Chinese Zodiac animal, examine the traits, behaviors, and personality of the animal. Of all the Chinese Zodiac animals, the most agile and adaptable is the Monkey. Monkeys can live on the ground or in the trees. They have dexterous hands and feet. Monkeys are also known for their ability to mimic behavior.

The Chinese Zodiac sign of Monkey is the sign of intelligence. This Zodiac animal rules the inventor—one who is intelligent enough and innovative enough to solve complex problems with ease. Monkeys have an excellent memory and proficiency in communication. They can give you an inspirational speech that motivates you, or they can give you a dressing down, which leaves you feeling about two inches tall. Monkey is a problem solver. He or she will not provide you with sympathy but will offer you a solution instead.

Monkeys do well in business because they are connectors. They find people who can help them achieve their goals. They know how to play the system, trading favors as part of a strategy for success.

Monkey always has a plan, often several. Monkey wants to do more than merely survive, he or she wants to prosper! The Monkey native will avoid confrontation if it is possible you can be of assistance in the future. Once wronged, they will exact revenge, but only when the time is right.

A Monkey is susceptible to incentives and bribes. To get them on your side, you need to offer something they want. You can criticize the Monkey, and they will not pay any attention. They are incredibly confident in their talents and abilities.

Monkey can justify their actions to achieve or obtain what they want. For this reason, people find it hard to trust Monkey, and this can affect Monkey's career and personal life. They are rarely discouraged by failure nor envious of the success of others.

Monkey's love a bargain. They're good with money and would rather save it than spend it. They prefer to find their own solution to spending cash. This choice shows up in their home where innovative decorating ideas and creative uses for cast-offs abound. They do love a party at home (BYOB); if you're invited, you can expect an evening (or night) of stimulating conversation and lively music.

Monkeys are into self-preservation. This can give them a nervousness or hyperactivity, causing them to leap out of any situation they don't feel right about. They can get themselves in trouble by trying to avoid what they perceive as trouble.

But no matter what mistakes they may make, they are quick to rebound. Overall, the Monkey native gets what they want without too much effort or struggle. If there's no apparent benefit, they just lose interest.

Monkeys are at one moment a passionate lover, the next moment they've forgotten you entirely. When in a long-term, committed relationship, they can be a devoted partner; however, they like a lot of fun and attention, and they can get caught up in the moment. This can lead to jealous feelings; Monkey doesn't notice, and in a moment he's back at your side as if nothing ever happened.

Monkey's love projects. They can renovate their home continuously. They love to create new things or make improvements to old things. Sometimes they just like to move the furniture around to get a different look. Otherwise, the combination of half-finished projects and Monkey's love of new stuff can make for a very messy house.

Monkey: Predictions for 2020

January 2020: *There is a Lunar Eclipse on January 10. Uranus moves forward again on January 11. The Lunar New Year begins on January 25. Your Lucky Days this month are 3, 9, 15, 21, and 27. [How to use your Lucky Days: On these days, plan to take essential actions, make vital phone calls, send emails. These are days when your energy and luck are high.]*

The New Year begins with you feeling great about yourself and your future. The Year of the Metal Rat energy is very harmonious with Monkey energy.

It's a great idea to do some decluttering of your space. Focus on getting rid of paper clutter first. Shred private information and toss the rest. See where you can go paperless. Then move on to household goods and consider selling things you're not using. The open space you create at home will bring positive opportunities during the year.

You may find that money seems to disappear: a check is late, or a credit card is lost. Don't panic, but take appropriate action to right whatever is going wrong. By the end of the month, you see how resourceful you can be, and this adds to your confidence.

You share positive communication with your partner this month. This is a good thing because it's not always easy to connect with other members of the family. There is a lot of movement of people and things around your dwelling. Choices are being made, and you may not have a say in what is decided. Generally, Monkey natives don't need to feel in control. A little spontaneity can feel good.

You can create excitement at home by throwing a big party. Invite lots of friends and family. This activity could bring positive energy to the whole family.

If you're looking for a relationship, don't turn down any party invites this month. Seek out groups to join (or at least attend a meeting and check them out). Wear red to enjoy positive attention.

February: *Mercury goes retrograde from February 16 to March 9. Your Lucky Days this month are 2, 8, 14, 20, and 26. [How to use your Lucky Days: On these days, plan to take significant actions, make vital phone calls, send emails. These are days when your energy and luck are high.]*

You can have an amazing year this year as the energy of the Metal Rat is quite harmonious with your quick-witted, optimistic, inventive mind. This month there will be opportunities to plant seeds for making money, to advance in your career, and to meet truly interesting people. Monkey native, you are never one to hide or shy away from the limelight, but more than ever this year, you want to step up to the stage and grab the mic.

This month your energy is high, and you show opportunities for additional income or sources of financial gain. You may need to make a phone call here and there or send out an email to make a connection, but these are easy for Monkey natives to accomplish. As money flows in, it's a good idea to keep track of the funds, channeling extra income to useful places.

There are some beneficial changes at work. There may be new people on the team or a new system in place. This will shift your routine, but overall this will be good for you. You weather change better than most people. You may feel uncertain about some aspects of these alterations, but the energy will soon settle down.

If you're looking for love, consider changing gyms or workout routines so you can meet new people. Look for exercise classes or a facility that has a lot of members. Or take regular walks through your local mall. Skip the shopping and instead engage in conversation with strangers.

March: *Mercury goes direct on March 9. The Sun enters Aries on March 20. Saturn enters Aquarius on March 21. Your Lucky Days are 3, 9, 15, 21, and 27. [How to use your Lucky Days: On these days, plan to take significant actions, make vital phone calls, send emails. These are days when your energy and luck are high.]*

Romance is near. If you're looking for love, it's time to activate the apps and memberships in online dating sites. Update your profile and get some good pictures up on the site. The Universe is offering a helping hand in your search. Make a list of what you're looking for in a true love but also list how you can meet that person. Ask yourself what situation or circumstances can happen that would make you feel comfortable enough to ask a stranger to coffee.

There is energy around kids and/or pets. The house is filled with noise and activity—there may be a party or a celebration. A new addition may be coming into your life and home. If this happens before Mercury goes direct on March 9, you may have more than one party this month.

Your communication skills are tapped by someone of importance. This may cause your social media following to increase, or you may be noticed for a lecture or class you gave. This can all be parlayed into something more significant for your future. Step forward and be noticed.

Your job is going well, and changes from last month are now proving to be helpful to you. Monkey native, you may have an opportunity to ask for more flexibility in your schedule as

Saturn moves into a new sign towards the end of the month. If you work for yourself, adjust your schedule so you can have a little more time for self-care. You will find this makes you more productive and ultimately increases your bottom line.

An email comes into your inbox with an attractive offer. This is something you may want to consider.

April: *Pluto goes retrograde on April 25. Your Lucky Days are 2, 8, 14, 20, and 26. [How to use your Lucky Days: On these days, plan to take significant actions, make vital phone calls, send emails. These are days when your energy and luck are high.]*

You may have a disagreement with a loved one or partner, business partner, or close friend. If you live with this person, the trouble could be over the division of duties or how the household is run. If the issues lie with a friend, there may be a difference in ideology, or perhaps they disagree with how you're living your life now. In both these situations, it's very possible to find common ground and repair the rift. It's worth investing a bit of time and effort into preserving the peace.

If this disagreement is about work and involving a business partner, it's a bit more serious. You may feel your partner is holding back progress or unwilling to take chances to grow the company. During Metal Rat years, calculated risks can bring great opportunities, but risk isn't everyone's cup of tea. You may have to sit down with your partner and go over the fine print of deals or review spreadsheets of the numbers.

While this is going on, however, income is still coming in. There are good prospects for financial success in the upcoming months (with the occasional downturn every once in a while just to keep you on your toes). Expand advertising or marketing into new territories or shift up the marketing message to make it fresher and more targeted to your ideal customers.

There is some work to do at home and you, Monkey native, may be doing some small renovations or repairs. There is also a lot of activity in the dwelling. Friends or relatives may be visiting and staying in your home.

May: *Saturn goes retrograde on May 10. Venus goes retrograde on May 12. Jupiter goes retrograde on May 14. Your Lucky Days are 2, 8, 14, 20, and 26. [How to use your Lucky Days: On these days, plan to take significant actions, make vital phone calls, send emails. These are days when your energy and luck are high.]*

Your health is improving. If you've needed medical advice or want an annual physical, now is the time to get that all scheduled. Mercury is retrograde next month, so it's better to do it now than wait. This month you can find expert help in diet, exercise, and physical care. It's okay to change doctors at this time if you wish. You also may consider seeing alternative medicine practitioners, such as acupuncture or massage therapists, especially if this is something new for you.

There is energy around your vehicle or your usual means of transportation. You may be in the market for a new car or truck. It might be fun to explore alternative ways of getting around. Perhaps walking, biking, or rideshare can work for you as an option.

Your relationship is going well. The air has cleared from the previous month's difficulties, and everything is moving forward smoothly. Monkey natives are naturally efficient, especially when it comes to daily tasks. Everything regarding home maintenance gets easier when you have less stuff. Consider more decluttering and clear out some space.

After a talk with your boss, you have a clear view of your career. Your supervisor may have outlined a path for you to move up in the company, or he or she makes it very explicit to you that you're at the top of your pay scale, and now there's nowhere to go. Trust what they are saying and take action now since you now have the information you need in order to plan for your future. This is a Metal Rat year, very harmonious energy for your career. It's good to take risks and boldly ask for what you want.

June: *Lunar Eclipse on June 5. Mercury is retrograde from June 17 to July 12. There is a Solar Eclipse on June 20. Venus goes direct June 24. Your Lucky Days are 1, 7, 13, 19, and 25. [How to use your Lucky Days: On these days, plan to take significant actions, make vital phone calls, send emails. These are days when your energy and luck are high.]*

After the frank discussion with your manager last month, it's not surprising you're full of ideas for various strategies for your career situation. The Lunar Eclipse early in the month brings some more information and lights the way. By the time the Solar Eclipse comes around, you have your plans in place. Monkey natives are survivors, you can move quickly and decisively. This year is a lucky one for you, so the opportunities being presented can really happen. It's more about which direction you want to go and not waiting for someone to move out of your way before you start the process.

Socially, you may feel blocked in ways that surprise you. People who have been supportive in the past may seem to be standing in your way. But nothing stops the determined Monkey native. You don't even have to pause to convince your friends and family. Just leap into action and follow your heart. You will be able to look back and see your loyal supporters scrambling to catch up with you.

While you are feeling some impediments in your life right now, home is still a safe place to rest and relax. You may find your beloved is also feeling the outside world is less than helpful now. If so, band together and form a united front by staying at home and caring for each other.

When it comes to looking for love, it's good to incorporate movement. Go dancing, biking, or rent a boat and sail into the sunset. The sense of movement will help things flow to connect you to new people.

July: *Retrograde Saturn backs up into Capricorn. There is a Lunar Eclipse is on July 4. Mercury goes direct on July 12. Your Lucky Days are 1, 7, 13, 19, 25, and 31. [How to use your Lucky Days: On these days,* *plan to take significant actions, make vital phone calls, send emails. These are days when your energy and luck are high.]*

While this is a healthy money month, the Lunar Eclipse early in the month has you doubting the needed resources are going to come through. You may be looking for a bank loan, payment from an investment, or proceeds from the sale of a big-ticket item. Monkey natives are efficient, and so delays can make you quite impatient, especially if the delays are for no clear reason. But this is one of those cases when taking a moment to pause may pay off in a big way. Allow things to unfold in their own time, and you'll see why the Universe created the delays.

There is some intriguing romantic energy about someone you find quite attractive. If this connection was started while Mercury was retrograde, it may not last, but it will be fun for a while. Mercury goes direct on July 12, and you'll see then whether things will pop or fizzle.

Monkey natives tend to rack up lots of skills and experience. A humanitarian organization or charity may tap you for some help. Check your schedule and see if you can fit in this good cause.

Work continues to hum along. You may be close to the time of an annual review, or a new project may be launched soon. Have your career goals in mind when you meet with your manager. Consider updating your vision board at home. Look at your career path and see if you're heading the direction you want. A manager is willing to help if you can present a compelling idea.

August: *Uranus goes retrograde on August 15. Your Lucky Days are 6, 12, 18, 24, 30. [How to use your Lucky Days: On these days, plan to take significant actions, make vital phone calls, send emails. These are days when your energy and luck are high.]*

The energy settles down. You may even find you're a little bored this month. This is the perfect time to take a quick trip. Consider a weekend getaway to someplace where there is excitement (like Vegas) or adventure (like climbing a mountain).

This is also a good time to add some art or creativity to your life. Consider taking an art class or get out a creative project you've been working on and devote some time to getting it finished. The more new experiences you give yourself this month, the more opportunities you will attract over the next few months.

Finances continue to be steady, but perhaps you feel less satisfied with your savings rate. Time to look at where your money is going. Monkey natives are excellent money managers. It's good to periodically give yourself an audit to see if money can be directed to debt repayment or places that will bring you future passive income.

There are some shifts at home, and you may be feeling a change would be good. There may be adult children leaving home, or an older relative may be moving in. Some changes in the neighborhood have an effect on where you park or how you use your own outdoor spaces. Remember, you are co-creating with the Universe. State what you want through affirmations, prayer, or by lighting candles. Then let the Universe alter the circumstances to make things better in your life.

September: *Mars goes retrograde on September 9. Jupiter goes direct on September 12. The Sun goes into Libra on September 22. Saturn goes direct on September 28. Your Lucky Days are 5, 11, 17, 23, 29. [How to use your Lucky Days: On these days, plan to take significant actions, make vital phone calls, send emails. These are days when your energy and luck are high.]*

Monkey natives can move very quickly. You are good at thinking on your feet and rapidly assessing a situation. Answers to problems come to you in a flash. On September 9, Mars turns retrograde, and the world holds up a hand, indicating it's time for you to stop. Many other people in your life want more time before they make a decision or begin an action. You may feel the same way about some things, but in many cases, you're not willing to slow down. This will be very much the case when it comes to dealing with children. You may see them taking much more time to do things than you think is necessary.

Mars moving backward isn't helping your mood. You're ready to snap, and your quick mind has a lot of opinions about other people right now. It would be a good idea not to voice those thoughts out loud! Be careful of late-night texts or emails sent when you're feeling impatient. Toward the end of the month, Mars is still moving backward but will at least be moving at its regular speed, and you'll feel a little less irritated.

On the plus side, this is a strong money month for you. You may have an additional source of income. A small windfall is possible. It's okay to take calculated risks in business. And it's especially good to reach out and make meaningful connections with people you admire professionally.

Now is a favorable time for a change in a health routine or eating habit. It's okay to do something really different and break a family tradition when it comes to your health, especially if your birth family has a common health issue.

October: *Pluto goes direct on October 4. Mercury goes retrograde from October 13 to November 3. Your Lucky Days are 5, 11, 17, 23, 29. [How to use your Lucky Days: On these days, plan to take significant actions, make vital phone calls, send emails. These are days when your energy and luck are high.]*

There is a lot of activity around children, fertility, and creativity this month. If you're hoping to get pregnant or add to the family through adoption (even a pet), explore your options this month. Note, Mercury does go retrograde on October 13, so agreements entered into during the retrograde period can fall apart or end up being something you're ultimately not so happy with.

If you've been working on this project for some time, realize the retrograde may delay some of the progress, but it probably won't derail the entire project. Try to be patient. On the other hand, if you're making a sudden decision to adopt a litter of kittens or to let your adult son and his girlfriend move into the master bedroom of the house—and Mercury is retrograde— you may want to think more than twice.

Creative energy is increased this month, and that means you can tap into this energy to solve problems. These may be challenges with your job or a side business. To really use this energy, state the problem clearly before you retire for the evening. Monkey natives are likely to wake up with a solution by morning.

New friendships are possible this month. It's a good idea to accept invitations to parties or meetings. Plan to attend conference or workshop in a subject you're interested in (perhaps not work-related, maybe involving a hobby). You are quite magnetic now, and your powers of attraction are strong. Make yourself seen, and you can attract more than just a friend. You may even meet a future long-term relationship.

November: *Mercury goes direct on November 3. Mars goes direct on November 13. Neptune goes direct on November 28. There is a Lunar Eclipse on November 30. Your Lucky Days are 4, 10, 16, 22, 28. [How to use your Lucky Days: On these days, plan to take significant actions, make vital phone calls, send emails. These are days when your energy and luck are high.]*

Finances are particularly improved this month. You can get a better position or secure a raise. You may learn about a bonus or other company perk. Your daily workload may be changing as well as some point of automation is added. This frees you up for more interesting work, especially around communication with others or being a liaison between various parties.

The Lunar Eclipse at the end of the month can bring a change in a close relationship. You have an opportunity to sit down and talk to this person and clear the air. Monkey natives are very good at communication, and you will make the most headway if you're clear about what you want from the start. The energy will feel blocked at first and then give way, like a dam collapsing, the water spreads out over the landscape. As you both open up, there is a feeling of relief, like the pressure is being released. Take a deep breath. Ultimately, this is a good thing.

Your children or younger relatives are very active now, and you are involved. This may be due to sports or other extra-curricular activities. This may mean an overnight trip or some short distance travel for you. You are making memories, and even if these events are difficult to fit into your schedule, it's worth making the effort to attend.

December: *Solar Eclipse on December 14. Saturn goes into Aquarius on December 16. Jupiter goes into Aquarius on December 19. Sun goes into Capricorn on December 21. Your Lucky Days are 4, 10, 16, 22, 28. [How to use your Lucky Days: On these days, plan to take significant actions, make vital phone calls, send emails. These are days when your energy and luck are high.]*

The Solar Eclipse this month brings change to your life in a very personal manner. You feel like you want to go in a different direction. You may be longing for freedom from a boring job, a bad manager, or a dead-end position. You may have been sending up a prayer to the Universe to light up a new path for you.

Now the path appears, and you are more than ready to take it. This could come in the form of a new relationship for those looking for love. But it's most likely a different way of looking at the events in your life that suddenly lifts a burden from your shoulders. You can understand now that there's so much within your power to change. Monkey natives, your new path is waiting.

You might have been silent last month, but in December, your tongue lets loose. Monkey natives are near geniuses when it comes to oration. No one can stand up to your quick mind and sharp words. But watch where you aim your blows. Don't say things just to release steam. If you're going to say something, say it with the idea of making a lasting change.

There is an opportunity for romance and intimacy behind closed doors. If you're single, go out and see who crosses your path. If you're already in a love relationship, consider checking into a fancy hotel with your partner and having a good time.

January 2021: *Uranus goes direct on January 14. Mercury goes retrograde from January 30 to February 20. Your Lucky Days are 3, 9, 15, 21,*

27. [How to use your Lucky Days: On these days, plan to take significant actions, make vital phone calls, send emails. These are days when your energy and luck are high.]

January brings the end of the Metal Rat year, and you can look back on the amount of progress you've made. You'll soon feel the energy of the Metal Ox year. This is more challenging energy for Monkey natives, though you do love a challenge. You can feel the energy slowing down and becoming more practiced and methodical. Monkey energy rarely moves so slowly, and you can swing through the crowd as everyone else is starting to plod along.

Finances are good this month. You can also see how there have been pretty consistent gains throughout the year. Look at budgets and see if there are any easy adjustments you can make.

There is positive energy around education. If you're in school, you may find renewed interested in getting through your classes, projects, and tests. Consider looking into how to improve study habits or find a new study partner. If you're considering going back to school, there may be some resources to help you pay for the education. Or, if a degree isn't crucial, check into free online schools.

Dating energy abounds this month. If you're looking for love, it's looking for you now. Don't hide at home or bury yourself in your job. Time for meeting new people, especially in places like gyms, yoga studios, spiritual retreats, and business conferences. When you're out in the world, show people your positive, witty energy. Don't hide with your head buried in your phone. Lift your eyes and smile at the world. The world will be dazzled.

February 2021: *Lunar New Year begins on February 12. Happy Year of the Metal Ox.*

Attract New Love

It's a bold thought, but you can be in love by the end of 2020. This is probable, as you've been working to clear past issues, and you are more ready to move forward into a healthy, loving relationship. Your magnetism is strong, but you would do well not to focus on a person who needs to be won over. Be available for someone who wants to chase you.

Monkey natives can find new potential relationships just by stepping out the door. Work may be keeping you very busy, or you may have a new money-making side project that has captured your attention. But remember to put some time in your busy schedule for love. Love can be found at gyms, home improvement stores, and hiking groups. When you are in these places, look up from your phone and greet the world. Quickly, you'll find potential friends and even a lover staring back at you.

In Feng Shui, we often use wind chimes to call new energy. The material the wind chimes are made of will tell us what kind of energy it will specifically attract. When looking for new love, choose a silver-tone wind chime. The color silver attracts relationship energy.

Hang your wind chime outside of your front door, or outside your bedroom window. (If this is not possible, then hang the wind chime in your bedroom window inside the house.) Listen for the chimes or chime them manually to call love to your door.

Enhance Existing Love

The two of you are in the eye of a storm, one not of your own making. It could be that family members are warring with each other, or there is disruption due to a job change. Either way, you are clinging to each other, bringing your partner comfort, and helping the two of you grab hold of opportunities.

This is a very good year for you to sit down together and really talk about what you want to do as a couple over the next one year, three years or five years. Goals set this year can attract many opportunities to help you manifest. In this case, you're stronger together. What you agree on will manifest more quickly than things you want just yourself.

There may be a brief separation due to a family matter or work project. But as you stay in constant communication with each other, you will have no issues with the relationship. Make sure that large purchases are discussed before being made, especially if they're made while you are apart.

If you're in an existing relationship and you want to increase the fidelity energy and overall happiness, you can place a pair of Mandarin Ducks on your bedside table or dresser. These ducks are known to mate for life, and they are a symbol of marital bliss.

Mandarin ducks are primarily used as they are considered the best of the species in intelligence and beauty. Their energy symbolizes felicity. They are usually displayed with the lotus blossom, the flower that emerges from the mud pure and clean.

Looking to Conceive?

Find a necklace made of cowrie shells. Cowrie shells have long been associated with pregnancy, due to their uterus-like shape. Small, usually white cowrie shells are made into necklaces and bracelets.

You can also find larger cowrie shells; these may be striped or spotted brown and white. Place one or more of these larger shells on your bedside table. Cowrie shells are not only reputed as fertility cures but also have been used as currency in some cultures, so the shell will attract good money energy, too.

(From Donna Stellhorn's book, *A Path to Pregnancy: Ancient Secrets for the Modern Woman*)

Family and Kids

This is a good year for Monkey natives when it comes to home, family, and kids. You usually love to be out in the world, but this year you find a lot of comfort and joy in staying at home. There may even be a work-at-home opportunity to give you even more time within your four walls.

You enjoy more goodwill and harmony with relatives, including extended family this year. You may be put in charge of some family project, like a reunion or important birthday, but you will be able to pull together a support team, and this will include financial support as well as a team to help you complete tasks.

There are lots of activities around children or younger family members this year. You may travel to see relatives regularly. Be cautious about overspending to decorate or renovate the home. It would not be advisable to tie up a lot of money in the home investment this year.

Sometimes in Feng Shui, we combine multiple symbols to create a powerful cure. The symbol of a bowl is to "welcome something new into our space." If the bowl is made out of brass, we have the energy of success and prosperity.

So, for this cure, place a small brass bowl on your entryway table. You can leave the bowl empty or put coins and crystals in it. You can also place a list of your wishes regarding home and family in the bowl.

Money

There's positive energy for Monkey natives with regard to finances this year. You receive money from several good sources. A project or venture you've been working on for some time starts to show real returns. Additionally, old sources of income still flow in (even though you may have thought one or more of those were lost). This could be a job, pension, or some government check.

As more money flows in, there is the temptation to spend more. This will be a challenge to avoid during the year as you think of many practical, useful things to acquire. You also may be tempted to travel more than usual, and this could get expensive if not carefully planned. Spontaneous, throw-caution-to-the-wind Monkey natives like yourself aren't known for waiting. To show a "plus" in your financial books at the end of the year, start the year money-smart.

With some of your money producing projects, the work has just begun. This could be related to your business, or it could be a profitable hobby. You've ironed out the details and acquired the skills; now you know how to build the money machine. You are still in the harvest period of your 12-year cycle, and so this is a great year to gather the team and get to work.

There are a lot of symbols, both universal and cultural, we can use to attract luck and good fortune into our lives, and one of these is the horseshoe. Hang a horseshoe over your front door—inside or out—with the ends of the horseshoe pointing upwards. This creates a U-shaped form, (figuratively a firm, empty, yet defined space in which to catch all the luck).

Job or Career

Monkey natives are usually high-spirited doers, ready to swing into action, but this year when it comes to your career, it's a time to pull out pen and paper and design what you want. It's time to make a plan. It could be you need to do your business plan to get funding or your education plan (listing why this will lead to a better job) or your marketing plan so you can determine if all the time and energy you're putting into Instagram is really worth it. Planning will be key, and a monthly review will help you stay on track.

There's just enough not right with your career this year to bring you a bit of irritation. You may want to work at home, but the boss won't allow it, or you do work at home, but it's too noisy. You might want to spend more time on special projects, but you're bogged down with routine paperwork. You may have co-workers who bore you to tears. All these irritations are to inspire you to look at what you can change. This is the year to post your resume and update your Linkedin profile. Opportunities are coming. Make it easy for you to be found.

Your positive financial outlook may not come from your job, but other things you do on the side. Get together with smart and creative friends for brainstorming sessions. Look at innovations that interest you and consider how you might capitalize on new trends. The essence of Monkey energy to stretch yourself, to find new ways of doing things, and to do them with ease (as Monkeys always do). Look at what could be an adventure. Make a plan and then make the leap. Monkey natives who opt for retirement may end up making more money with side businesses than they did when they worked a regular job.

Gold Flakes remind us of the accumulation of wealth and abundance through seemingly small actions. You can attract positive career energy by placing a vial of real gold flakes on a table near your front door. (Gold flakes are available in gem and mineral shops and online.)

Write out your career goals and place them under the vial of gold flakes. Every few days as you pass the table, pick up the vial and shake it; watch the gold flakes sparkle in the light and think about your goals for a moment. This will increase the positive career energy.

Education

If you're in school, you may be looking for the exit door. Perhaps you're at the tail end of the program, or maybe you're smack dab in the middle, but you're getting pretty tired of the whole program. It's time to sit down and consciously focus on remembering why you are doing this in the first place. Get back on track with your study habits or get some help. You may consider online tutors or check out study productivity videos on YouTube. If you find that your heart is just not into school, consider taking a semester off or doing a gap year. You will be on track again in the future. It may not be necessary to stick with something now that's causing you so much irritation.

If you're thinking about starting school and you haven't been in a formal education program for a while, this is a very good year to start. You are looking for a change, and school can shift your environment and the people you are around. Online classes in technology subjects are okay, but other subjects may not offer enough change energy to help you make the effort to sustain the academic program. You can find funding options, even in some unexpected places. Consider the usual online search for grants and loans, but also reach out to older friends and relatives for ideas on how to find financial assistance for your education.

Legal Matters

Possible contracts for long-term and short term employment are highlighted. You may contract with more than one company. Consider starting your own firm so you can contract with competing companies. If you are involved in a lawsuit, or you bring suit against someone, you are likely to be victorious. However, you may find the amount of time and energy you expend to win isn't covered by the amount of money you are awarded.

Health and Well-Being

Monkey natives are generally healthy and tend to have boundless energy. This year your energy is electrifying. You may be bouncing out of your chair at times. Find a way to express the energy through creative activities or exercise; otherwise, you may find yourself irritated by the smallest things.

This is a favorable year to change basic habits you've had for years. You may decide to start getting up at sunrise, or perhaps you'll take up daily meditation. You may start journaling every day or calling friends and family regularly. What you set into place this year will bring you benefits for years to come.

There are indications of a potential setback in your health habits in October or November of this year. Stay mindful during this time. Don't berate yourself if you fall off whatever good habit wagon you had been riding. Just get back up into the wagon, whether that's back into daily exercise or healthy eating. Whatever you can do to keep your healthy habits in November is worth doing.

A pagoda is a many-tiered sacred building popular in the far East. They are often religious or spiritual structures, some dating back to BCE times. Often the very top pinnacle comes to a point and was made of metal to channel lightning strikes. In Feng Shui, the pagoda symbolizes peace and harmony. You might display a small replica pagoda or have a picture of a pagoda. Place this in your living room or family room to attract positive, healthy energy. You can also find stone pagodas to place in the garden for the same purpose.

Rooster

January 22, 1909 -- February 9, 1910: Yin Earth Rooster
February 8, 1921 -- January 27, 1922: Yin Metal Rooster
January 26, 1933 -- February 13, 1934: Yin Water Rooster
February 13, 1945 -- February 1, 1946: Yin Wood Rooster
January 31, 1957 -- February 17, 1958: Yin Fire Rooster
February 17, 1969 -- February 5, 1970: Yin Earth Rooster
February 5, 1981 -- January 24, 1982: Yin Metal Rooster
January 23, 1993 -- February 9, 1994: Yin Water Rooster
February 9, 2005 -- January 28, 2006: Yin Wood Rooster
January 28, 2017 -- February 15, 2018: Yin Fire Rooster
February 13, 2029 – February 02, 2030 Yin Earth Rooster

Rooster Personality

When considering the qualities of a Chinese Zodiac animal, it's a good idea to examine the traits, behaviors, and personality of the mythic creature we are discussing. While most animals in the Chinese Zodiac do not differentiate between male and female, the Chinese sign of the Rooster is the male. (No one ever says they're born under the sign of the hen or the chicken.)

When we look at the personality of this creature, we think of Rooster as the boss of the hen-house. Roosters are polygamists; they can have many 'hens' under their care. He also will guard and protect all he sees as his from any interlopers. He will oversee from a high perch, keeping a sharp lookout, sounding his distinctive alarm if predators approach.

Because of the substantial duties a Rooster always seems to have (particularly that of keeping an eye out for others,) the Rooster personality is to be a perfectionist, someone with a sharp eye for detail and the ability to keep an accounting of everything (and everyone). In matters of money, Rooster excels. Roosters are adept at handling finances, protecting assets, and making sound investments.

As perfectionists, Roosters are intolerant of even the smallest error. They will aggressively go after what belongs to them, from a small overcharge at the bank to a raise or bonus they believe is owed them at work. (It's best not to owe a Rooster money unless you can pay them back.)

Roosters like to look good and equate looking good with respect from others. Roosters open their pocketbooks to add things to their lives to make others take notice. Money is well spent when it's for a flashy car, or a nice suit, or a piece of sparkling jewelry.

Roosters prefer routine over surprises. Surprises are seen as a warning of danger and are perceived on a range from merely irritating to stressful. Those born under the sign of the Rooster like to be prepared. They will keep extra things in their home or their handbag just in case—everything from change for the parking meter, to remedies for headaches, to extra pens.

Rooster natives like to be seen as the person who has it all together. Because of this, they can be convinced to take part in projects which prove to be impossible tasks.

Rooster natives are very inquisitive. They end up taking on more and more and still find the energy to do it all. They give parties, volunteer for groups, and decide to make their own bread, possibly all in one day. Overall, they keep a calm demeanor—unless things go very wrong. You will witness their extreme distress and hurt, seemingly erupting from out of nowhere.

If we can find fault with Rooster, it would be their sense of entitlement. It's true, Roosters do a lot, but then they also want a lot of praise and compliments for their actions. Roosters can be prone to jealousy when others seem to be in the limelight, causing the Rooster to take actions which don't benefit him like being insensitive or even vengeful.

When a Rooster falls in love, it's serious business. He follows his practical manner in his approach. This can lead to great disappointments in Rooster's love life as it's hard to categorize and schedule emotions.

Many Roosters find that being in a relationship is preferable to being alone. It's not that they need the romance, it's more their life, and the house just seems to run better when there's two. Rooster loves an orderly and tidy house. To romance a Rooster, share kitchen duties, and he'll pronounce it, "true love."

Rooster: Predictions for 2020

January 2020: *There is a Lunar Eclipse on January 10. Uranus moves forward again on January 11. The Lunar New Year begins on January 25. Your Lucky Days this month are 4, 10, 16, 22, and 28. [How to use your Lucky Days: On these days, plan to take essential actions, make necessary phone calls, send emails. These are days when your energy and luck are high.]*

This is a busy month for Rooster natives. The requirements of work and home life collide, forming a long list of chores, tasks, and projects. You are a little disturbed to find someone in your life has let some vital matter go on past its deadline. This could be related to a contract, license, or taxes. You need to rush in and save the day. (Fortunately, that's no problem for super-efficient Rooster!)

The year starts well financially, and you are encouraged by the flow you see happening. You've invested wisely, and when markets have fallen, you've picked up investments at a bargain.

There may be rumblings in the financial news; it's imperative you don't buy into fear. Many a savvy Rooster has made a fortune in an uncertain market. Trying to control everything will get you nowhere. Instead, hedge your bets and study the downside before moving forward. Don't dwell on worst-case scenarios. Just get a plan and stick to it.

Relationship energy is powerful right now. Going into the new year, you feel alert, decisive, and super-efficient. Okay, these aren't the most romantic qualities, but they do help you keep the household running like a clock. This, in turn, takes the pressure off your beloved and you get heaps of praise.

If you're looking for love, consider visiting comedy clubs, music festivals, and art shows. Go where creative, unique people hang out.

February: *Mercury goes retrograde from February 16 to March 9. Your Lucky Days are 3, 9, 15, 21, 27. [How to use your Lucky Days: On these days, plan to take significant actions, make vital phone calls, send emails. These are days when your energy and luck are high.]*

This Metal Rat year is a robust time for Rooster natives, but a clear direction is needed. You are practical, down-to-earth yet able to see and seize upon trends. It's a good idea to spend a little time this month considering possibilities. Tune out and turn off distractions; visualize your options. As pictures come to mind, ask yourself what these options would look like if it were easy. Ask what it would be like if it were fun.

Children or younger relatives are changing. One or more may come to you for advice or help. You may consider assisting them with school or starting a business. You may choose not to advise them, as some in the family may disagree with the choices the children are making. If you can keep the peace while imparting wisdom, then go for it.

The Metal Rat year begins on a sound financial note. You're more visible now and can ask for a salary increase at work. If you own a business, there is an opportunity to expand your sales by increasing the number of products you sell or expanding into a new territory.

Relationship energy is perhaps the strongest now. If you're looking for love, it's good to get out of the house, weather permitting, of course. You are attracting positive energy. As you are out in the world, you can meet many lovely and fascinating people. Do the things you like to do rather than trying to go where you think the people are. But still, be social. If your favorite evening is sitting at home in front of the TV, try changing it up and visit a local pub where you can watch TV with others.

March: *Mercury goes direct on March 9. The Sun enters Aries on March 20. Saturn enters Aquarius on March 21. Your Lucky Days are 4, 10, 16, 22, 28. [How to use your Lucky Days: On these days, plan to take significant actions, make vital phone calls, send emails. These are days when your energy and luck are high.]*

Communication is highlighted, and you may be asked to give a speech, teach a class, or lead a meeting at work. Rooster natives get admiration when they step up to the podium. Though it may not be your favorite thing to do, this month, if asked, say "Yes." Unexpected benefits will come from you taking on this responsibility.

Creativity and fertility energy increase. If you're looking to add to the family, this is a good time to pursue help in this area. It is true also if you are choosing to adopt (even a pet). Mercury goes direct around March 9, so consider waiting to sign contracts or agreements until then.

A love relationship gains a more solid footing. For those Rooster natives who are dating, you may have the opportunity to take your relationship to the next level. Maybe you are introducing your sweetheart to your family and friends. It could mean moving in together (though this energy comes up stronger later in the year.) It could mean getting engaged. But this is a time to be patient about the progress of this union. Let it unfold naturally. Don't push.

If you work from home, there may be a space crunch, or it may be time to redo your work area. Perhaps your business has expanded, or you've had to bring home equipment from the office. If there's clutter, it needs to be cleared away to welcome in new growth and customers. Get organized, and things will flow.

April: *Pluto goes retrograde on April 25. Your Lucky Days are 3, 9, 15, 21, 27. [How to use your Lucky Days: On these days, plan to take significant actions, make vital phone calls, send emails. These are days when your energy and luck are high.]*

Sizable changes happen this month as both Saturn and Mars are in new signs. You may suddenly feel you want to change your financial picture for the better. Changes can include austerity measures so you can pay down debt more rapidly, or so you can gather funds for an investment. This is beneficial, and while others may think you're going overboard, you know how to pinch a penny—and you actually enjoy it. It's okay to swing in this direction as far as you like as an experiment. You can make a course adjustment later in the year.

You are more empowered at work. Management has noticed your ability to handle responsibility, and so you may be offered more. There may not be an actual change of title, and if it does not, it would be good to get at least a promise it will happen in the future. Rooster natives are hardworking and efficient, thus deserve to be compensated. If it seems unlikely to happen in the next six months or so, you may want to think about moving on.

If you're in a partnership, your beloved may need a little more TLC this month. They may be having some trouble with an extended family member, and they are coming to you for support (more for support than guidance). This is not a time for debate or saying "I told you so." Just be a shoulder to lean on, and your relationship will grow stronger because of this.

Purchasing large ticket items is not advised at this time unless you've done a great deal of due diligence.

May: *Saturn goes retrograde on May 10. Venus goes retrograde on May 12. Jupiter goes retrograde on May 14. Your Lucky Days are 3, 9, 15, 21, 27. [How to use your Lucky Days: On these days, plan to take significant actions, make vital phone calls, send emails. These are days when your energy and luck are high.]*

Everything was moving forward in your life so nicely, then suddenly comes to a halt; Several planets started moving in retrograde motion, moving backward in the chart. Now is the time for patience on your part. The best thing to do is work on other projects while you wait for others to get paperwork in order, contracts signed, or job openings posted.

Your health benefits as a result of a change either in diet or exercise routines. Consider following in a friend's footsteps—after all, they are getting good results. Start moving more, perhaps you want to dance, swim, cycle, or practice martial arts.

This month it's a good idea to review investments and insurance. Check fees and automatic withdrawals to make sure everything is in order. It would be okay to make a change in investment manager or insurance agent if you feel you're not being represented fairly or getting the support you deserve. Consider making a change even if you've been with the same broker for years or have the same insurance agent your father had.

Romance is highlighted. Plan a romantic evening with your sweetheart. Go out on the town. Try a new restaurant. Consider having some alone time away from the kids or other members of the family. If you have several generations under your roof, perhaps book a hotel in town for a few nights. If you're looking for love, consider visiting a few of the city's hotspots for drinks and dancing.

June: *Lunar Eclipse on June 5. Mercury is retrograde from June 17 to July 12. There is a Solar Eclipse on June 20. Venus goes direct June 24. Your Lucky Days are 2, 8, 14, 20, 26. [How to use your Lucky Days: On these days, plan to take significant actions, make vital phone calls, send emails. These are days when your energy and luck are high.]*

You may find you need a bit more rest during this month. It's good to carve out some time for yourself now. Take a vacation, even if it's a short one, and practice some mindful self-care. The Lunar Eclipse early in the month highlights your need for some "me time."

Finances are healthy, but you're not feeling as confident as usual. Perhaps there's bad news in the world, or you've had some unusual expenses. But overall, your prospects are good, even for collecting some income from a side business or new source. Don't let other people's panic mess with your head. Take stock of where you are financially of course, but mostly believe in yourself, Rooster native.

There may be a change in a significant relationship towards the middle of the month when the Solar Eclipse occurs. Rooster natives are alert and intuitive, so you may have seen this coming. Whatever door is closing, know another door is opening. This doesn't mean your current love relationship is dissolving; in fact, it may be your relationship needs to grow to get stronger. A stronger relationship often means having a deeper understanding of your partner.

Mercury goes retrograde around the middle of the month, Rooster natives looking for love may be surprised to find a love return from the past. Or, maybe a new you meet has an uncanny resemblance in some way to a past love. Move forward with caution. You don't want to fall into the same hole twice.

July: *Retrograde Saturn backs up into Capricorn. There is a Lunar Eclipse is on July 4. Mercury goes direct on July 12. Your Lucky Days are 2, 8, 14, 20, 26. [How to use your Lucky Days: On these days, plan to take significant actions, make vital phone calls, send emails. These are days when your energy and luck are high.]*

You feel empowered this month. Your charisma is strong, and people are ready to listen to you. July is a good month for standing on stage and showing off your talents. You may also consider launching a creative project out into the world. Others applaud, and your ego gets a boost.

The Lunar Eclipse brings a relationship opportunity for those Rooster natives who are in the market. It's good to be seen now. Post your profile on the usual dating sites. Consider attending social events in your community. But mostly, release fear about entering into a partnership with someone. It may go much better than you think.

Mercury moves forward again around the middle of the month. Travel plans that were delayed are suddenly on again. A contract or agreement you have been waiting to shows up on your desk, now with a ticking deadline. Everyone is suddenly in a rush. Fortunately, you are decisive, and you can use their time table to your advantage by stating what you want, and for the most part, standing your ground.

Some financial pressure is off you as payments come in or income is higher than usual. But this is not a time to forget about the budget. Set extra money aside to pay down debt or to add to savings. You may be able to sell a high ticket item now.

There is a lot of activity at home. You may be finishing up a renovation project, or doing some serious decluttering. A family get-together is possible.

August: *Uranus goes retrograde on August 15. Your Lucky Days are 1, 7, 13, 19, 25, 31. [How to use your Lucky Days: On these days, plan to take significant actions, make vital phone calls, send emails. These are days when your energy and luck are high.]*

You may be feeling self-conscious this month as others go out of their way to compliment you. Friends, family, and even superiors at work seem to be everywhere, singing your praises. This is all deserved, and you should feel proud. Yes, some may use this opportunity to ask you to pick up an extra shift or cover for them at the local Homeowners Association meeting. But the compliments you received are still deserved.

Showing your confidence now actually can open some doors for you. If you've been looking for a new job, it's good to give yourself an upbeat talk in the morning. Whether you feel completely qualified for the job or not, there's no reason to doubt your ability to give it all you've got. Getting a job offer is quite possible this month. Once you have the offer in hand, then you can start negotiating for a higher salary, more time off, or other perks.

If vehicle repairs or even the hunt for a new car was delayed over the last few weeks, it can now resume. You can find yourself a good deal as well as finding a buyer for your old vehicle. Also, look into alternative forms of transportation such as trains, rideshare, or biking.

The spotlight is on investment or passive income sources. If this isn't your strong suit, spend a few hours this month studying the basics of investing. You have the drive to succeed, and success comes quicker if your money is working for you. This month you can find a knowledgeable friend to help you.

September: *Mars goes retrograde on September 9. Jupiter goes direct on September 12. The Sun goes into Libra on September 22. Saturn goes direct on September 28. Your Lucky Days are 6, 12, 18, 24, 30. [How to use your Lucky Days: On these days, plan to take significant actions, make vital phone calls, send emails. These are days when your energy and luck are high.]*

You are lucky in love this month. If you're already in a love relationship, you have some happy evenings ahead. You may be feeling more romantic, and so is your partner. Consider having a date night or spending some time cuddling together on the sofa.

For those Rooster natives who are looking for love, there is positive energy around you for meeting new people. Consider taking a class or attending some spiritual function. You may also meet someone while doing something charitable involving a large group of people. What's most important is getting out of the house. There seems to be a lot of extra reasons to stay home, but this could cause you to miss out on meeting someone extraordinary.

Finances are doing well, though there may be a little crunch at the end of the month due to an extra or unusual expense. You're good at handling money, so you may have been saving up for this outgo. But just the same, you may be feeling the pinch. If the purchase is important to you, then it's good to move forward. But if you've just blown a bunch of money on a stylish new leather jacket or a pair of boots, hang on to the receipt and see if you want to return this purchase early next month.

If you work outside the home, you may be very busy with new clients while at the same time moving furniture around your office or workspace. You may need to shift how you do things so you can be more efficient in the long run.

October: *Pluto goes direct on October 4. Mercury goes retrograde from October 13 to November 3. Your Lucky Days are 6, 12, 18, 24, 30. [How to use your Lucky Days: On these days, plan to take significant actions, make vital phone calls, send emails. These are days when your energy and luck are high.]*

Share the focus between work and home this month. Starting with home, some changes are happening. You may be moving, or someone may be moving in or moving out. You may be getting a new pet, or perhaps you celebrate the arrival of a child in the family. These changes have made you want to stay closer to home and to spend time with loved ones.

At the same time, there are circumstances at work where you are needed. You may be temporarily be put in charge of a project or department while your manager is away. You may be preparing for an inspection or an important meeting with someone quite high up on the organizational chart. All this goes very smoothly though the preparation causes you to move a little faster than even your usual quick speed.

Mercury goes retrograde around the middle of the month, bringing back an issue with a friend you thought was resolved. It seems they were more hurt than you previously were aware of. You can be quite patient, while others say they're half of the story, and this is a time to give them some attention. You can smooth over bad feelings just by letting the other person know you've heard them.

Cupid has an arrow pointed at your heart, and you may find you're smitten with someone who previously was just a friend or acquaintance. Things could get sticky if you're already in a love relationship. If you have wanted to share a loving relationship, this may be the time to move forward decisively and ask the person on a date.

November: *Mercury goes direct on November 3. Mars goes direct on November 13. Neptune goes direct on November 28. There is a Lunar Eclipse on November 30. Your Lucky Days are 5, 11, 17, 23, 29. [How to use your Lucky Days: On these days, plan to take significant actions, make vital phone calls, send emails. These are days when your energy and luck are high.]*

Mercury starts moving forward again early in the month, and a paperwork or contractual issue seems to dissolve. No reason to fret or have sleepless nights for fear it will come back. You can handle whatever comes pertaining to this matter.

Your children or younger relatives want extra attention now. They may want advice, but tit's more likely they want your help from a monetary standpoint. Older kids may be looking for a loan to help them start a business or to get through a rough patch of bills. Younger children may be asking for new tech devices to use with schoolwork or to keep up with their social circle. There can be good reasons to help them, but only after setting some boundaries on these requests.

Mars goes direct in the middle of the month, and you get a burst of energy. This comes at a good time, as there may be people coming for the holidays. There's a long list of things to do before that. Or you may be in a seasonal business and feeling a push to maximize sales.

You are doing well at work and may receive an award or formal recognition of a job well done. You may reach a critical sales goal or company milestone. Take a few moments to bask in the accolades since you rarely give yourself the time to enjoy your successes.

December: *Solar Eclipse on December 14. Saturn goes into Aquarius on December 16. Jupiter goes into Aquarius on December 19. Sun goes into Capricorn on December 21. Your Lucky Days are 5, 11, 17, 23, 29. [How to use your Lucky Days: On these days, plan to take significant actions, make vital phone calls, send emails. These are days when your energy and luck are high.]*

Behind the scenes, a lot is going on in your life. You may be working on a large project, one that isn't ready to be revealed. There is no way to rush this process. It's a little like being pregnant—the baby comes when it's ready (well, traditionally that's how it works).

Love and romance can hit you like a thunderbolt this month. If you're looking for love, consider getting dressed up, and being social. Find new Meetup groups, social clubs, or go where there is a lot of people. The Solar Eclipse around the middle of the month can open the door to a whole new experience with someone unlike anyone you've known before.

Work is hectic now. Perhaps you're rushing to get everything done before a well-deserved vacation—or everyone else is on vacation, and you're the one holding down the fort. During this period getting quality sleep will help. Consider upgrading your mattress or mattress pad. Get an ergonomically correct pillow if needed.

The best thing you can do for yourself this month is to make some adjustments to your rules. Rooster natives can live by a code, and that's admirable, but some of your rules may be out of date. Don't allow rules in your life to block you from doing what you really want to do. Either start breaking some rules or rewrite the rule book.

January 2021: *Uranus goes direct on January 14. Mercury goes retrograde from January 30 to February 20. Your Lucky Days are 4, 10, 16, 22, 28. [How to use your Lucky Days: On these days, plan to take* *significant actions, make vital phone calls, send emails. These are days when your energy and luck are high.]*

The Lunar year comes to an end, and the new year begins. You may start to feel the energy of the Metal Ox year throughout this month. This will be very harmonious energy for Rooster natives. But it's not quite time to move forward yet. There are still loose ends to tidy up. Try to get as much of your old life cleaned out as possible.

To clear clutter, get rid of debts or past obligations, answer emails, and clear out your inbox. Mercury goes retrograde at the end of the month will bring any missed items back to you. February will be much less stressful if you are mindful of what needs to be completed in January.

Finances improve, and you find opportunities for additional sources of income. You may see only small amounts come in now at the beginning, but it's a sign of better times ahead. You can be optimistic even while those around you are wallowing in doom and gloom.

Something is changing at home. Someone may be moving out, or you may be able to clear out some extra space. This shift in energy is quite positive. It opens up good prospects in the home. There is more peace (not that this person was so disruptive—but now there is one less voice in the house).

Romantic energy continues. There can be fun behind closed doors. If you're already in a love relationship, a lot some time to spend with your honey. Sit by the fire together and talk. Play a game and share a laugh. Spoon together in front of the TV and cherish each other.

February 2021: *Lunar New Year begins on February 12. Happy Year of the Metal Ox.*

Attract New Love

This year it looks like love is waiting for you to take notice. Love comes from an unexpected source. You may find it in a neighbor or reconnect with someone you grew up with. You may find this person attending the same educational project as yourself, or they may simply be sharing an Uber with you.

Rooster natives usually have their lives pretty well planned out, but love seems to break all the rules this year. You may be blown away. This is not the type of person you are usually attracted to, but here they are, and you can feel the pounding of your heart. Let go and allow some excitement in your life.

For those of you born in the Year of the Rooster, promote love energy in your home by adding orchids. Orchids have gained great popularity in recent years. You can find orchids in garden shops as well as the local grocery store. Orchids have long symbolized love, luxury, and beauty.

Choose an orchid with beautiful blooms and place the plant in your bedroom or family room. When the orchid loses its blossoms and goes into it's resting phase, continue to water and care for the plant.

When temperatures drop, a well-cared-for orchid will develop a bloom spike. It will continue to grow in cold weather, then produce blooms as temperatures turn warmer. Most orchids bloom once per year. If you can't wait for the new blooms to appear just buy another orchid to display.

Enhance Existing Love

A surprise opportunity causes you both to really assess where this relationship is heading. You will most likely stay together, but your thinking seems miles apart. Differences in how you see problems and how you handle challenges will come up this year. Rooster natives are known for their ability to solve problems, but this year focus on listening rather than just giving advice.

As you listen to your sweetheart, a healing is taking place in this relationship, bringing the two of you closer together. You may find it's easier than ever to act together and speak with one voice. But there may be a short period this year when one of you is surer of the relationship than the other. During this time, it's good to be understanding and patient with your partner. Give them time to catch up.

There may be some disagreement about the friendships your partner keeps. Even if they've been friends for ages, you see these connections as less than helpful for your family. Try not to openly criticize—rather pull your partner aside and discuss this in private.

The common herb, ginger, has been used for centuries to magically add a little heat to your desires. If you live in the right climate, you can grow ginger in your garden. Or, place powdered ginger in a clear, glass jar and set it in view on your kitchen counter to rekindle the passion of your relationship. Every so often, take a pinch and add it to a meal to pit this fire magic inside both of you.

Looking to Conceive?

If you're looking to get pregnant this year, place gemstone eggs in the bedroom. You will be able to find gemstone eggs at rock and mineral shops, or check online where you'll be able to find a variety of stone carved in the shape of eggs. The egg shape represents a baby. Reasonably priced eggs carved from Agate, Jasper, and sometimes Rose Quartz are easy to find.

(From Donna Stellhorn's *book, A Path to Pregnancy: Ancient Secrets for the Modern Woman*)

Family and Kids

Home is your refuge this year. The outside world represents a lot of responsibilities and activities, even more than usual for you (who usually has the longest to-do list of all the 12 animals of the zodiac). Home is a place to rest and heal from the demands of your job and/or school. For this reason, pay particular attention to your bedroom. Make sure it's just as you want it to be.

While home is the place you want to be, you may find you are not near some members of your family you really care about. This separation could be due to a job or school opportunity you couldn't pass up. Keep in mind there will be opportunities for visits, and you can maintain the connection through lots of calls.

If you're looking to expand your family through pregnancy, adoption, or adding a pet, it's a good idea to think through the situation carefully and discuss it with all involved. There are some good alternative methods for achieving what you want. Think creatively if you are blocked in the pursuit of making things happen this area for a while.

Jasper is an opaque gemstone in the quartz/chalcedony family. It comes in many colors and has is associated with a great deal of lore. It's believed to protect the family—especially the children in the home. It also helps bring positive thoughts and mutual understanding within a group. The red jasper is the most protective, the green jasper is for healing, and the brown jasper has a grounding effect.

It's not an expensive stone, so get several specimens and place them in a bowl in your living room or family room. Have at least one stone per person in the household (but each person could have more than one). Clear the stones a couple of times a year to re-energize them.

Money

There are significant positive changes for you this year in the area of money. This begins with your commitment to a creative venture. You may have been considering such a commitment for years, perhaps your entire life; now, finally, you've decided to pursue it. And while it's good to keep your "day job" as you do so, you will find moving forward on this new path is both emotionally satisfying and profitable.

If you're not sure what this creative venture is, just look at the thing you've been saying, "Someday I'll do...". That's the thing. You may have been putting things off because you need funding or resources you don't currently have. Your contacts will help get you going. Start researching options on the internet.

You also have good energy around investments and passive sources of income. If this is an area you haven't explored yet, it's time to get an education. It's true, you are very busy this year, but having your money work for you would save you time and energy in the long run. A period of good luck and synchronicity follow you this year. This will help you make the right connections to bring in profits. Be cautious, however, of real estate investments this year. Don't jump into buying property without doing a lot of due diligence.

This year, bring positive career energy by burning a metallic gold candle approximately once a month. From a Feng Shui perspective, metallic gold represents large sums of money, and a candle, or anything on fire, focuses your attention. You can find small metallic gold candles in the wedding department of your local party store or online.

You can 'carve' or write your wish for wealth energy into the wax of the candle. Take a pencil or a sturdy toothpick and write your wish in block letters along the side, or from bottom to top of the candle. As you write, picture your desires coming true. Burn the candle in your home office or the entryway of your home. If you feel uncomfortable burning candles in the house, you can use a battery or plugin type. Remember, these aren't nearly as powerful, so if you are using an electric "candle," keep it switched on for the entire month.

Job or Career

If you've been looking for a behind the scenes job for a large company, where you'll be able to work away without much interference this year, you, the wish is about to come true. There may be a good reason you want just such a job. You may have a side business that takes most of your creative energy, or you may have a growing family taking much of your time. Sometimes taking a position where you're a cog in the wheel makes sense.

If you are looking for a more satisfying main job, it's time to spend a little time looking at your vision board! If you don't have a vision board, it's a good idea to create one. Put together a collage of pictures, each one representing your ideal job in some way. If you have a career vision board and it's more than a year old and hasn't yet manifested what you want for your career, you may be procrastinating. Rooster natives have luck when it comes to manifesting a good career. Roosters are great managers of people and time. They learn quickly and make useful contacts with important people. You have the drive to get where you want to go. Now it's time to think about what is in your way.

Add some magic to the mix this year. Make a new vision board, or write out what you want. Then outline the beginning steps for each item on your list. Make the beginning steps so easy, so quick, you have no excuse not to do them. Then light a candle, talk to the moon, or pray a prayer, and picture yourself making the first steps. The most amazing things will happen when you start doing this. You will see people come from out of nowhere to offer you what you want. You will see the pieces come together just when you need them. The lessons you learn about goal setting this year will help you for years to come.

Even though you have lots of positive energy for your career this year, you want the energy to flow smoothly and continuously. Hang a windsock or flag outside, either by your front door or on your patio/balcony. Choose a colorful one, something bright that makes you happy when you see it. You might also switch out the banner at each holiday, or at the change of every season to bring more energy. Or, you can choose one in the form of a fish (fish represent abundance in Feng Shui). This will attract a constant flow of energy and bring you even more opportunities.

Education

You may be dreaming about going to school or continuing your education this year. The strongest fields of study for you this year are creative courses—things like acting, art, computer animation, and graphics. There is also a lot of energy around medical studies. However, these are more about the care of people, the environment, humanitarian aims rather than spending time in a lab. You may find funding options limited, but you can manifest the money you need by creating a clear vision. Do Feng Shui or meditation to bring in helpful people who can point you in the direction of resources.

If you're already in school and studying medicine or some creative program, you're good. Keep up the excellent work! If you're studying something more related to collecting and handling data and hard numbers, you may need to balance the energy with a creative class or activity to keep going. It will not be a waste of your time or energy. You may find you receive more benefit from the concepts or the people you meet while studying something that's not part of your actual major. A financial planner can benefit greatly from a class on story-telling. A drawing class can help an engineering student. A law student can find value in an improve class.

Legal Matters

Financial gain forms a central focus of most legal matters for you this year. You may draw up a contract to sell a large item, possibly even to sell a business. Negotiations for most of the contracts you draw up this year will move frustratingly slowly, and you will feel very tempted to rush. You may feel pressure from the other parties to get things moving just when you want time to review details. There may be talk of lawsuits this year, but these are more threats on paper than actual suits. However, if you're in a suit begun during a previous year, you may need to review a lot of paperwork in order to move forward.

Health and Well-Being

You'll focus a lot of energy on your health. It's time to make changes and move toward a healthier lifestyle. This can mean changing how you eat. You may want to take up cooking, or use a meal prep service so you can dine at home more regularly.

The months of June, November, and December have positive change energy around your physical self. You may begin a new exercise program or find a sport you enjoy doing. This is an opportunity to be social as well as getting in shape. You're more likely to show up at the gym if you know some friends are going to be there.

It's also essential to get enough quality rest this year. Take steps to make sure your nighttime routine helps you relax and fall asleep quickly. Experiment with darkening the room or cooling it down and see if you wake up more refreshed.

Consider adding a salt lamp to the home to bring in good health energy. Salt lamps are made from solid pieces of Himalayan rock salt. A hole is carved into the bottom of the block of salt, and a small light bulb is placed inside. When lit, the lamp glows with a soft peach-colored light. Also, the heated salt emits negative ions into the air, like a miniature version of the air at the ocean.

The combination of the heavy object (the rock salt) and the negative ions it produces will bring stability and peace to an environment. Place the salt lamp in the living room or bedroom and keep the light on for long periods during the evening hours. You can also display several salt lamps since they come in many interesting shapes and sizes.

Dog

February 10, 1910 -- January 29, 1911: Yang Metal Dog
January 28, 1922 -- February 15, 1923: Yang Water Dog
February 14, 1934 -- February 3, 1935: Yang Wood Dog
February 2, 1946 -- January 21, 1947: Yang Fire Dog
February 18 1958 -- February 7, 1959: Yang Earth Dog
February 6, 1970 -- January 26, 1971: Yang Metal Dog
January 25, 1982 -- February 12, 1983: Yang Water Dog
February 10, 1994 -- January 30, 1995: Yang Wood Dog
January 29, 2006 -- February 17, 2007: Yang Fire Dog
February 16, 2018 -- February 4, 2019: Yang Earth Dog

Dog Personality

When looking at the qualities of a Chinese Zodiac creature, it's a good idea to consider the traits, behaviors, and personality of the animal itself. When considering the qualities of the Dog, many of us have some idea about dog personalities and behavior.

Dogs came to live with humans around 100,000 years ago. Humans found dogs to be very valuable—helping to hunt and herd, pull loads, and even protect their people from wild animals.

Sometimes we confuse the personality of dogs in general, with the individual characteristics of specific dog breeds (most of which are only a few hundred years old). We want to consider the energy of a dog in general as we think about the personality traits of natives born under the Chinese Zodiac sign of the Dog.

The animal dog is known for companionship; similarly, individuals born during the Year of the Dog are usually very well-liked and friendly. They have a deep sense of loyalty and fair play. They are happier around people than on their own. They go with the flow, being less demanding, always meeting others halfway, so everyone gets something of what they want.

Early humans brought dogs into their lives to increase their chances of survival. The dogs would help them find food, keep them warm at night, and protect them from dangers. Those born under the Chinese Zodiac sign of Dog are protective of their friends. They watch over them and are willing to fight for them. Dogs are eager to take up a cause, whether on behalf of an individual, a group, or an organization.

Because they take loyalty so seriously, Dog natives choose their friendships very carefully. Accepting a new person into their circle takes time. At the same time, many people want to be their friends. Dogs are often in positions of influence and connected with people of power. Dogs are rarely selfish, and when they crave power or money, there is usually a person or cause who will benefit from everything Dog creates.

Dog natives are known to work hard and to play hard. They have to be cautious to avoid overindulgence in food or overspending. They generally like competitive sports, and they often love a good hard workout. They don't mind a night out dancing, followed by an early morning yoga session. They like a stylish home, but their home may not be neat—it doesn't matter to them since they're not at home that often.

Dogs make good lawyers, always looking for justice and fairness. These characteristics also make them excellent employees. They're particularly good at managing several projects simultaneously. They won't gossip at the water cooler, nor will they speak ill of others. Dog prefers to be a team player, and if you're part of the team, you can count on them.

Dogs alternate between aggressive spending and aggressive saving. When it comes to investments, they are better at investing in property, or precious metals or stones, and other tangible things rather than intangible derivatives.

Most in life, Dog wants loyal, honest, intelligent friends, who will share a dinner or attend the theater, or join them on an impromptu trip to the Bahamas for the weekend. They love to be treated fairly, and honestly, they don't like to be questioned too deeply about their reasoning and thinking processes. They'd love to have enough money—in fact, so much money they never have to think about what things cost!

Even when Dog seems happy, they are pessimists by nature, capable of worrying a great deal, including the small things. They can count the times when they were overconfident, and it led to disaster, and they use this information as a tool to confirm their need to worry.

They are resourceful and resilient and overcome any difficulty. However, Dog spends a great deal of time visualizing potential problems, and they look for the storm clouds and never the silver lining.

Dog: Predictions for 2020

January 2020: *There is a Lunar Eclipse on January 10. Uranus moves forward again on January 11. The Lunar New Year begins on January 25. Your Lucky Days this month are 5, 11, 17, 23, and 29. [How to use your Lucky Days: On these days, plan to take decisive actions, make essential phone calls, and send emails. These are days when your energy levels and luck are high.]*

You feel the new energy of the Year of the Metal Rat already, even though we don't officially enter the new Lunar year until later this month. It's already giving you a positive boost. This year will be rewarding for Dog natives who have a firm plan for what they want to do and where they want to go. If you're vacillating between multiple ideas and projects, it's time to pick something and give it your time, energy and love.

You have access to power and negotiating skills now. You're worthy of more (money, time, consideration, etc.), but you need to let others know what you expect. Dog natives are naturally hardworking, and you are an asset wherever you put your efforts. This month, and as you go into the New Lunar Year, you will have the resources and support to make meaningful changes in your life.

Love is strong this month. If you're already in a love relationship, you have reason to celebrate. Even though not every day is rainbows and roses, it's still great to have someone in your life. This month take a look at what irritates you about your partner and turn it around. See if you can change anything about yourself in your relationship with your partner, and/or relating with others. A small change in yourself seems to quite magically change your partner (and everyone you relate with!).

If you're looking for love, you are very visible this month. Don't waste this opportunity trying to hide. Lift your eyes from your phone once in a while and smile at the world. You will find someone there waiting to talk to you.

February: *Mercury goes retrograde from February 16 to March 9. Your Lucky Days are 4, 10, 16, 22, 28. [How to use your Lucky Days: On these days, plan to take significant actions, make vital phone calls, send emails. These are days when your energy and luck are high.]*

The spotlight is on you this month. You may be launching a business, leading a team at work, or interviewing for a new position. You can shine now. All the work you've been doing behind the scenes is now coming to light. Others may be surprised at all you've accomplished. Dog natives can suddenly spring into action after much thought and preparation. You are ready to take center stage. Show your confidence and expertise. You've got this.

As Mercury goes retrograde towards the middle of the month, your finances need some attention. It may be time to gather the family and review the budget. You may wish this obligation was off your shoulders, but when you ignore the accounting part, everything starts to unravel. You can manifest more money this year by keeping track of what's coming in and what's going out. It may be something you do with a supportive family member or by yourself with a helpful app on your phone.

There are changes at home. You may be moving, redecorating, or doing some repairs. There is a disruption in your routines, but it's all good. Change brings out all your best instincts.

A new friendship is possible with someone who is quite interesting. And for those Dog natives looking for love, this one could become more than a friend at some point. Take it slow and build a quality relationship with this person. They can be quite a benefit to your life if you will let them in.

March: *Mercury goes direct on March 9. The Sun enters Aries on March 20. Saturn enters Aquarius on March 21. Your Lucky Days are 5, 11, 17, 23, 29. [How to use your Lucky Days: On these days, plan to take significant actions, make vital phone calls, send emails. These are days when your energy and luck are high.]*

It's abundantly clear a lot of positive financial energy is all around you this month. You may receive a pay increase, expand your business, or have a windfall from an unexpected source. At the same time, there are possibly some additional expenses with regards to the home, or it's possible a member of your extended family needs a helping hand. You are known for your loyalty to family, and this may be a request you find it hard to say "No!" to. But at least get the terms in writing so there can be an understanding on both sides.

Mercury goes direct around March 9, and a contract or agreement you've been waiting for can now be finalized. Even though you've been waiting for the right time to sign it, don't rush to get out your pen. Take your time and review the details before moving forward.

You're quite intuitive this month, and you may receive a psychic message. You may be following a spiritual practice such as meditation or yoga and start to find your flow. Dreams may be vivid and provocative now (though they should not be taken literally for the most part, as you are dreaming in symbols and metaphors).

Your partnership grows stronger as your sweetheart makes it clear how much you are valued in their life. Now is a time for romance, and you may want to carve out a couple of nights for love-making. If you're quite busy, at least give each other five minutes of undivided attention whenever you can.

April: *Pluto goes retrograde on April 25. Your Lucky Days are 4, 10, 16, 22, 28. [How to use your Lucky Days: On these days, plan to take significant actions, make vital phone calls, send emails. These are days when your energy and luck are high.]*

Everything is different this month. You have opportunities popping up all over the place. When it comes to love, you may have more than one interesting person to consider. You have several new possibilities in the friendship department, too. Be sociable and reach out to people you've wanted to make a connection with. The stars are lining up in your favor.

Changes are happening for you in your career as well. Dog natives may experience a burst of confidence, along with the sudden realization you're going to be okay. You trust yourself and know you are capable of handling the shifts and changes your company is going through. If you work for someone else, you may learn the company has been acquired, or there is a major management change. Visualize what role you want to have in these changes, and you'll start to see the seeds of possibility sprout as early as in just a couple of weeks. If you own a business, you may have a promising opportunity to collaborate with an influencer or to get some unexpected free publicity. You may get a boost in your social media numbers.

It's possible you feel more settled at home even before you've fully completed repairs or redecorating. That's okay. You don't have to have every duck in a row to feel good about the direction you're going. Dog natives are known for their resourcefulness. You can succeed even in imperfect circumstances.

While this is a busy period, try to get enough sleep. Turn off the devices and turn in early at least a few nights a week. The extra time resting will help you a lot this month.

May: *Saturn goes retrograde on May 10. Venus goes retrograde on May 12. Jupiter goes retrograde on May 14. Your Lucky Days are 4, 10, 16, 22, 28. [How to use your Lucky Days: On these days, plan to take significant actions, make vital phone calls, send emails. These are days when your energy and luck are high.]*

May is another high energy month for you, Dog native. You're fielding offers, and ideas projects are swirling through your head. Creative plans fill your mind. Added protection is available to you this month, and indicates you can take more risks than usual. You can put your art out into the world, or stand at the podium to share your thoughts with others.

This is a romance month, and your powers of attraction are enhanced now. Do not doubt yourself. Bold action (like asking out the person you like) is what's called for now. You are meeting new people. Let your friends know you're looking for love, and allow them to make suggestions or even set you up. This could be a very intense time if you get into a situation with more than one lover. Use caution when dating several people, or you may be found out.

Romance may be happening behind closed doors. If you desire to have more intimate encounters with your sweetheart, your wish comes true this month. You can do some exploring in this area by being open to new adventures.

It's good to put the house in order this month. If you have boxes to unpack, consider getting everything where it should be, then get rid of the stuff that doesn't fit in this home. You may host a house guest this month, filling your home with fun and laughter. Consider having a party and gathering together friends and friends of friends. Invite neighbors and people you know from work. Expand your circle.

June: Lunar Eclipse on June 5. Mercury is retrograde from June 17 to July 12. There is a Solar Eclipse on June 20. Venus goes direct June 24. Your Lucky Days are 3, 9, 15, 21, 27. [How to use your Lucky Days: On these days, plan to take significant actions, make vital phone calls, send emails. These are days when your energy and luck are high.]

This month it's essential to be supportive of yourself. Those around you may be putting a great deal of pressure on you, being less helpful than they could be. It is especially true around the time of the Lunar and Solar Eclipses. You're okay with a challenge, but when you're also hard on yourself, there's a comforting place to go. Give yourself space to rest and recover by being compassionate with yourself.

A strong presence of your guardian angel surrounds you with protection now. When unforeseen things happen, the outcome will be better than you might expect. This angel doesn't protect you from life teaching you lessons, but it can keep you from falling on your face. Take advantage of all of this extra energy—seek out your lessons, and work on them. Then you'll be entitled to the benefits when they drop from heaven and land at your feet.

Travel is on your mind this month. Keep in mind that Mercury goes retrograde around June 17, so be sure to remember to keep the important things you need on your person when you travel. Mercury retrograde can separate you from your luggage.

There is strong romance energy now. Arrange a date night with your partner. Don't miss opportunities to spend quality time together. However, if you're looking for love, you will have several opportunities to meet new people—if you can get out of the house and into some new groups of people.

July: Retrograde Saturn backs up into Capricorn. There is a Lunar Eclipse is on July 4. Mercury goes direct on July 12. Your Lucky

Days are 3, 9, 15, 21, 27. How to use your Lucky Days: On these days, plan to take significant actions, make vital phone calls, send emails. These are days when your energy and luck are high.]

Many of the impediments of previous months seem to now disappear like magic. You feel confident and sure of the way forward. Challenges from the past have helped build your endurance, and now you can climb to your destination swiftly, whether this is in your own business, or if you're part of a team in a company. If you work contract jobs, you have an opportunity to secure a second contract if you want it.

There is a lot of activity around neighbors and/or siblings. You may have more communication even from those you haven't talked to in a long while. This is an opportunity to do something together. Perhaps dinner, a neighborhood barbeque, or game night at your house. You'll make some good memories.

The Lunar Eclipse early in the month signals a disruption in your routine. This can indicate you're changing some basic habits, perhaps adding in exercise or a new way of eating. There can be changes with your partner as well. Adopt some new good habits together like yoga, meditation, or maybe something really out of the box like a bicycle trip on some mountain trails.

Love energy continues to elevate. If you're looking for love, it's good to do things this month that are slightly outside your comfort zone. Look at new Meetups to attend, consider going to a nightclub or happy hour by yourself, or find a local social club to try out.

August: Uranus goes retrograde on August 15. Your Lucky Days are 2, 8, 14, 20, 26. [How to use your Lucky Days: On these days, plan to take significant actions, make vital phone calls, send emails. These are days when your energy and luck are high.]

There is much going on behind the scenes now. You may be working on a project for work, a new product to offer in your own business, but you may not be ready to launch or present it to the world as of yet. This is the time to be patient—check and make sure you're finding extra things to do and not procrastinating. Leave any perfectionistic tendencies behind and just plow through the work. You're doing a better job than you think.

There are changes at home. Because of this moving/shifting energy, someone in your household may be moving in or moving out. Or you may get a request from a friend or relative asking to stay with you for a little while. This change at home is actually good for you, so try to roll with it even though you may not prefer the timing right now.

Finances benefit from a spiritual touch. Do a little magic to make more money. Consider prayer, meditation, or lighting candles. Follow the phases of the moon and reach out to gather more income during the waxing moon and then see if you can figure out where you to save money and reduce expenses during the waning moon.

Expect a lot of communication with children or younger relatives. Perhaps they are entering school and need a pep talk. Or you may be helping them navigate through their first efforts at job hunting and being hired.

Avoid fighting with loved ones, especially your sweetheart. There are sometimes differences of opinion, but this is a time when you should let your partner "win" the argument.

September: *Mars goes retrograde on September 9. Jupiter goes direct on September 12. The Sun goes into Libra on September 22. Saturn goes direct on September 28. Your Lucky Days are 1, 7, 13, 19, 25. [How to use your Lucky Days: On these days, plan to take significant actions, make vital phone calls, send emails. These are days when your energy and luck are high.]*

You may be rethinking your career at this time. It doesn't mean you're going to make some radical change, but it may be time for a course correction, one could land you in a different profession in a few months. It begins by thinking of what you might like to do differently in your life. Dog natives can be very good at assessing what they don't like, but finding what they do like can be more elusive. Think small right now. Design what a great day would look like for you instead of trying to think of a different job title or a new industry to work in.

Form a united front with your partner or a close friend now, it just feels like the right things to do. When challenges come up, it's good to have someone loyal to you and your cause beside you. This month, you can see this loyalty in action. At first, you may have doubts the support you want is there, but in the end, you're quite happy with the aid and assistance available to you.

As Jupiter goes direct around September 12, review your investments and debt repayment plans. You can negotiate for better terms. It's also good to put your finances in order in terms of a budget. Look at where you can reduce monthly spending on services you don't really use.

There continues to be a lot of activity in and around your home. You may be redecorating, or there may be some construction going on in the neighborhood. If you haven't completely unpacked from your last move, this is a good time to empty those remaining boxes.

You may connect with an old friend or past lover. Attending a reunion of some kind could be beneficial.

October: *Pluto goes direct on October 4. Mercury goes retrograde from October 13 to November 3. Your Lucky Days are 1, 7, 13, 19, 25, 31. [How to use your Lucky Days: On these days, plan to take significant actions, make vital phone calls, send emails. These are days when your energy and luck are high.]*

Mercury goes retrograde around mid-month, and an opportunity you've been working towards in your career comes suddenly to a halt. This is a temporary delay and may be due to a decision-maker being out of the office. Try to be patient. Soon things will be moving forward again. If you own a business, this interrupted energy may be around a recent hire. You may have thought you'd bring in someone to help you, but now the plan seems to be held up. If you don't want to wait, consider some creative solutions to your problem that don't involve this new person.

The energy of romance is around you, Dog native, and you may have an opportunity to travel to or with someone you care about. Dog natives in a long-distance relationship find you may be getting the chance to get together after not having seen each other for a while. This meeting can go a long way to help strengthen the relationship.

There is a lot of energy around communication now, as well. You may be considering getting a new phone, but soon Mercury will be retrograde—a time when there can be disruptions in relation to electronics. Better to wait until after the retrograde period ends next month.

Paperwork needs your attention. This issue could have come up as a result of some past medical or insurance requirements. It's not something you particularly like to deal with, but you can do it if you set your mind to it. Don't procrastinate. You'll feel better once it's done.

November: *Mercury goes direct on November 3. Mars goes direct on November 13. Neptune goes direct on November 28. There is a Lunar Eclipse on November 30. Your Lucky Days are 6, 12, 18, 24, 30. [How to use your Lucky Days: On these days, plan to take significant actions, make vital phone calls, send emails. These are days when your energy and luck are high.]*

Things are going well at home. Loved ones may be visiting for the holidays. Your family seems to be getting along. There is laughter and enjoyment within the walls of your family home. At the same time, there is a lot of energy around travel. It's possible people are traveling to visit you, but it's also likely you're getting in the car or on a plane to travel to visit those you care about. This can be a joyful meeting and bring about some fond memories.

There is fertility energy for you, Dog native. Perhaps you're working on a creative project or possibly (more literally) you're working on adding a baby to your family and your life (this may be the result of a pregnancy or an adoption; it could also prove to be a new pet to share your household). If you're seeking to add to the family right now, it would be a good idea to take precautions.

Finances improve. You can begin to see money coming in from several sources. Your hard work is paying off. If you have a business, you notice customers are finding you. A side job or hobby may start paying you some money. You may also be paid back a sum of money owed to you.

Work is going well, and you may receive some well-deserved recognition from a superior or a person in upper management. You are close to finding your niche. Meditate on what you're doing in your current job that could be parlayed into a better position for yourself in the future.

December: *Solar Eclipse on December 14. Saturn goes into Aquarius on December 16. Jupiter goes into Aquarius on December 19. Sun goes into Capricorn on December 21. Your Lucky Days are 6, 12, 18, 24, 30. [How to use your Lucky Days: On these days, plan to take significant actions, make vital phone calls, send emails. These are days when your energy and luck are high.]*

The Solar Eclipse in the middle of December brings you insight into something you may be doing in the future. A friend may open a door for you, or point out a skill you don't even realize is important and useful, and one you've discounted all these years.

It's good to now get up to speed in some area of technology. This may not be your favorite thing, but it's beneficial to you in the long run. Figure out what you need to learn when it comes to your phone, laptop, or tablet. Ask the question. Google will answer.

There's some romance ahead. Snuggling on the sofa together is a very likely activity. You may be watching your favorite holiday movies together or decorating the house in the style of your family tradition. For those Dog natives, who are looking for love, time to participate in doing good, attend charity functions, work holiday parties, and social get-togethers. Don't miss an opportunity to be social.

Romance may, in some way, connect to your job or career. A person from your past may seek you out. Maybe you used to work together, and now this person is working somewhere else and free from their past relationship. Possibilities lie before you. However, consider what you want before jumping in.

January 2021: *Uranus goes direct on January 14. Mercury goes retrograde from January 30 to February 20. Your Lucky Days are 5, 11, 17, 23, 29. [How to use your Lucky Days: On these days, plan to take significant actions, make vital phone calls, send emails. These are days when your energy and luck are high.]*

You feel more determined and disciplined now. It's easier to get up on time, get your exercise done, even eat a healthy breakfast. You are more productive than you have been in a long time. This is a great time to work on a pet-project. Perhaps this is a side business or a hobby you want to turn into a business.

If you're in school, use this highly motivated time to finish school projects or prep for exams. Find a study partner and hit the books. Schedule tests outside of the Mercury retrograde period if possible, so you don't have any unforeseen difficulties or delays. Mercury will go retrograde at the end of this month.

Friendships abound. People want to see you, and you may receive several invitations to parties and events. A new friend feels very familiar—maybe because of a deeper spiritual connection with this person. Possibly this is a new best friend.

There is movement at home. You may be considering changing residences, but there also may be people moving around you. Neighbors may be changing houses, renovating, or carrying out major construction. You may also be shifting rooms and furniture around. As the Metal Rat year comes to an end, you can get rid of what you don't need and bring in some fresh updates for the home.

You enjoy a great deal of positive interaction with children or younger relatives. One or more ask to spend time with you. You can consider a day trip or a gathering for a special occasion.

February 2021: Lunar New Year begins on February 12. Happy Year of the Metal Ox.

Attract New Love

You are a great catch. The problem right now is you don't like anyone who wants to catch you. That's okay because this year you'll have more opportunities to find someone worthy of you. Your charisma is high this year. Your smile lights up the room. People are attracted to your light, and among these people, love can be discovered.

Your friends are surprised you've remained single this long. You have a long list of qualities they admire, and they are proud to be your friend. You have an idea of your perfect love, and you don't want to settle. But this year, love may come in a surprising package. Accept invitations and see if there's a friendship there and maybe, by the end of the evening, you will be hearing love bells.

Power Dog native needs an equal, someone they can respect. So when you are looking for new love, you need to attract someone you consider worthy. A good Feng Shui cure for you this year is the Yin/Yang symbol.

The Yin/Yang symbolism depicts a balance of energies, the talents of one partner support a quality the other needs. To attract a new love, Dog natives can wear a Yin/Yang symbol (as jewelry, printed on a T-shirt, a patch on a jacket, etc.), or place the symbol in the bedroom.

Enhance Existing Love

Have you been experiencing some challenges in communication with your special someone? Perhaps this is due to a crazy work schedule or both working and going to school is making it hard for you to stay awake long enough to talk. It would be good to leave love notes for your beloved. This will open the doors to great talks and lots of support.

You may be moving this year. It's possible you'll take this relationship to the next level and move in together. This can be a stressful time, so it's good to be patient now. Moves hardly ever go smoothly, but if you keep your sense of humor, it can be an enjoyable experience.

You need a lifestyle change, such as adding exercise or healthy eating to your daily routine. You might think it would be better if you do it together, but this is one time when you're better off doing it yourself and seeing if your partner chooses to follow along. If they do, great. But if not, let them do their own thing for now.

The sweet, soft sounds of a flute have been used in Feng Shui for ages to bring harmony to the energy in a home. This year create harmony in your existing love relationship by hanging flutes. Simply take a pair of wooden flutes and hang them in the bedroom. Use a piece of red ribbon or string and tie the ends around each end of the flute. This will give you an easy way to hang the flute. See the diagram for hanging flutes below.

Looking to Conceive?

As well as being a symbol of money and abundance, fish are a Feng Shui symbol of fertility because fish have been so abundant in our waterways, lakes, and the sea. You could choose to have a fish tank in the bedroom (keep brightly-colored fish, or a school of fish, not fighting fish). Or, if live fish sounds like too much work, consider hanging pictures of fish (such as koi or goldfish in a pond), or brightly colored fish swimming through a clear sea. You could also place colorful glass fish figurines in a group on a surface in the room, or find some cute fish-motif pillows to put on the bed.

(From Donna Stellhorn's book, *A Path to Pregnancy: Ancient Secrets for the Modern Woman*)

Family and Kids

There is a lot of energy around you for changing your residence. If you don't want to move this year, it would help to make significant changes to the structure or decor of the current house to use up this energy. Otherwise, a move would be good at this time. It will bring you a better dwelling, more agreeable neighbors, and stimulate prosperity energy in your chart.

Your family relations are unpredictable this year. You may be separated from your family for some reason, or feel like family members are coming and going. This can cause some unrest, but it's just temporary. Most of the year, fun and laughter will be filling your home.

If you have children or younger relatives, you will highly value your interactions with them. You are a good influence on them, and you can feel the relationship growing stronger. Children living in the home will be independent and rebellious, but these can be good qualities later in life, so only focus on rules you really need them to keep. If you've tried to have children in the past but have had issues, this year you can find the fertility or adoption help you've been looking for.

Succulents are a type of plant that store water and can thrive in arid conditions. This is about using resources wisely and being able to handle whatever circumstances are thrown at you. It's also said succulents represent an enduring love. For this Feng Shui cure, find succulents without spikes or thorns. Place small succulent plants around the house, near the entry, in the kitchen, and in the family room. If you have a yard, you can plant succulents in areas close to your front and back door. This will help bring this positive, resourceful energy to your family.

Money

Financial success comes when you unite your vision of success with practical action. Focus your energies on getting yourself out of debt and making more money. When you combine this focus with action, you can get some spectacular results. You can make serious money this year, but you need to prioritize your goals so the money coming in goes where it's most needed.

There's a spiritual component to your income flow now. Doing money magic such as prayer, meditation, candle lighting, etc. is very helpful for you this year. Consider lighting a green candle each morning. Green is the color of growth. Say a money affirmation such as, "I easily see money opportunities and take action on them." Or write your affirmation on a sticky note and attach it to your credit card to remind you of your goal to find money opportunities, not just spend money.

The year starts strong for you with income and possible side income coming in. You can keep the money flowing by paying some attention to your accounting or bookkeeping. If you send everything out to a service, make sure you check the statements monthly. Visualize bank balances going up and up. Picture your savings and investments increasing. You can be a money magnet this year if you focus your attention on your accounts.

To stimulate monetary flow this year, add a picture of moving water to your home office or entryway. Position the picture, so the water seems to be flowing into the house. The picture can be large or small, it can be a photo or a painting, and it can be of the ocean, a river, or a waterfall.

Job or Career

This is a very positive career year for you. You have the potential to make more money than you have ever before. That said, you will find little time for socializing and rest. The more hours you put in, the more money you make—until you learn to work smarter and add in the spiritual component. You need to call in help from the Universe for the specific parts of your job that need support.

If you're coming home after a long day and just flopping down, exhausted, in front of the TV, then it's time to get some spiritual help. Start your day by thinking about what you want to accomplish, and then ask for support from your angels, guides, and/or muses to get everything done quickly with a minimum of energy expended. When on the job, minimize distractions and schedule in necessary breaks so you can be the most productive. This year it's possible for you to rise to a position that gives you more money and more flexibility in your schedule. If an opportunity doesn't come up at your current company, use the extra time to work a side project or even hunt for another job.

As you look at your options, you may find you're in a real growth industry. But if you see the industry your company is part of will decline as the technologies of the future take over, it's time for you to make a leap. The more computer skills you have, the better. You don't need to go back to school. Consider how much free information is on YouTube. If you're planning to start your own business, you can get all the info you need online. Avoid signing up for expensive video courses. Instead, figure out your questions. Once you know the question, the answer, or the way to find the answer, will come to you.

Bees represent community and helping one another. This is a good symbol for Dog natives this year. The bee reminds you to network and connect with helpful people.

You are quite helpful yourself. It's good to receive as well as give. This year, add the symbol of a bee to your home office, workplace, or living room. This could be a bee made of glass hanging from a plant. Or you can use the picture of a bee and hang it where you see it when you come into the room.

If you are allergic to bees or just not comfortable with this symbol, choose honey as a symbol instead. Have a small figurine of a honey pot or a picture of delicious honey and place this picture in your kitchen.

Education

Adding to your education is quite beneficial for Dog natives this year, but it may be hard to find the time in your busy schedule. An employer may ask you to learn a new computer system or take some management classes. Trust the Universe has a plan for you, and there's some reason this door is opening up for you. If you want to complete a school program started long ago, it's a fine year for that. Get help to determine what credits or classes you still need and finish the degree you've wanted for so long.

If you're already in school, this is a year to heal issues that may have come up with a teacher, administrator, or a whole institution. This could be done through communication, or you may get a mediator or advocate involved. Shifts in your own thinking and ideas about who you are will also aid greatly in dissolving past issues. You may consider changing schools this year. This could be due to a move, or because you have finished one program and are moving on to another. Your grades will improve if you prioritize sleep, and try not to complete projects or take tests when you're too tired.

Legal Matters

Agreements and contracts you were promised seem to evaporate before they even can be signed. You would do better with a handshake deal to start off with. Even when the agreement does cross your desk, it may be so convoluted and vague it's not enforceable. Trust your intuition, and deal with people who you have a good connection with. Lawsuits are unlikely this year. People can talk about them, doing their best to try to scare you, but you have no reason to fear. Legal matters begun in other years continue on. It will be difficult to bring these to a close this year with this hazy energy.

Health and Well-Being

Your health is a priority this year. Past issues can clear up as you let go of the emotional or mental hangups connected to the physical issue. You can find helpful doctors and practitioners. Friends and relatives may suggest good contacts for you.

July can mark a turning point in your healing process. You may begin a healthy eating plan and/or exercise routine. But most important will be making sure you get enough restful sleep. A lot of advancements have taken place in sleep science, and you would benefit by doing some research in this area. Dog natives are often night owls, staying up to "guard" the family or the home. Find a way this can work with your schedule rather than trying to force yourself to be up at sunrise.

To protect your health this year, consider getting a piece of petrified wood. Make it a part of the jewelry you wear or find a piece of polished stone to display in the home. Petrified wood is from ancient trees and represents a long life filled with joy and peace. It's been used for centuries as a barrier to protect against negative energy.

Find a piece of petrified wood you can display in your kitchen or family room. If it's a small, smooth stone, you can carry it with you in your pocket or handbag. If it's large and flat, you can set it on the coffee table where it's easy to see. Or you can display it near family photos to protect everyone in the house.

Pɪɢ/Bᴏᴀʀ

January 30, 1911 -- February 17, 1912: Yin Metal Pig/Boar
February 16, 1923 -- February 4, 1924: Yin Water Pig/Boar
February 4, 1935 -- January 23, 1936: Yin Wood Pig/Boar
January 22, 1947 -- February 9, 1948: Yin Fire Pig/Boar
February 8, 1959 -- January 27, 1960: Yin Earth Pig/Boar
January 27, 1971 -- January 15, 1972: Yin Metal Pig/Boar
February 13, 1983 -- February 1, 1984: Yin Water Pig/Boar
January 31, 1995 -- February 18, 1996: Yin Wood Pig/Boar
February 18, 2007 -- February 6, 2008: Yin Fire Pig/Boar
February 5, 2019 -- January 24, 2020: Yin Earth Pig/Boar

Pig Personality

There are two signs of the Chinese Zodiac that nobody ever wants to be, and one of them is Pig (or Boar) (in case you haven't guessed it already, the other is Rat). You should understand Pig is one of the best signs to be! Pig is the symbol of the prosperity and good fortune of the family.

When considering the qualities of a Chinese Zodiac creature, it's a good idea to examine the traits, behaviors, and personality of the animal and associate our traditional knowledge about the animal with the metaphorical creature who is part of the zodiac. Throughout history and in many cultures, there are traditions and stories about the pig.

The ancestor of the domesticated pig is the wild boar. While the male wild boar is solitary, the females and piglets live in groups and welcome the males at breeding season. The Chinese zodiac sign of Pig (or Boar), therefore, represents one of the most sociable signs, known for being community-minded and gregarious.

The animal pig is an omnivore, consuming both plants and animals. Pig/Boar natives are known for their culinary abilities (or at least their love of great food). They are delightful hosts who provide their guests with lots of comforts and splendid meals.

The animal pig is renowned for his acute sense of smell. People born under this sign are very discerning and able to suss out what's really going on. Scientists tell us that in social situations when we are connecting with others whom we may not know (or not know well), we often use our sense of smell to determine friend or foe. People born in the Year of the Pig (or Boar) are better able to access this ability in their daily lives.

At home, Pig loves a social gathering. The kitchen is always filled with ingredients should they be needed for an impromptu party. At the sound of the doorbell, Pig is ready to greet guests. The people who come to the party are lucky; Pig does whatever he or she can to make their guests feel welcome and comfortable. This doesn't necessarily mean that the house is spotless. Some Pig natives keep a very messy house, but they still welcome guests with open arms.

In the business world, Pig is often underestimated. On the outside, they seem "sweet," gullible, and rarely able to say "No!" However, Pig is quite smart and is ready to take on a leadership role whenever called upon to do so.

Pigs do not like confrontation and are always looking for a win-win situation; they dismiss insults and easily shrug off negativity. Should you hire a Pig to work for you in your struggling business, they will devote their time and energy to building your success.

Pigs are generous. They like to see a smile on someone else's face. They love the good things in life: gourmet food, designer clothing, the upscale exotic car. They are looking for a life of luxury, comfort, and ease, and they are willing to put effort into your being comfortable, too.

On the other hand, Pigs can trip themselves up with the excessive rules and limitations they put upon themselves. When others cross them, they can respond very aggressively, which can be quite a shock to the person on the receiving end.

Pig natives are susceptible to lawsuits and can become entangled for years. Because they want to see the best in people, they can be swindled, and need to watch out for con-men. Pig has a warm heart, and when things don't go well in their lives, they can be subject to depression. Their desire for perfection can overwhelm them, resulting in increased stress.

Pig: Predictions for 2020

January 2020: *There is a Lunar Eclipse on January 10. Uranus moves forward again on January 11. The Lunar New Year begins on January 25. Your Lucky Days this month are 6, 12, 18, 24, and 30. [How to use your Lucky Days: On these days, plan to take essential actions, make necessary phone calls, or send emails. These are days when your energy level and luck are high.]*

As the first year of your 12-year cycle comes to a close, you look back, knowing this wasn't an easy year. Now sit down and write out two lists, one a list of the things that seem to be working, and the other a list of what needs to be dropped or discarded. When you have the two lists, start setting the energy for your coming year in motion with a little ritual. Place the positive list in an area of the house where you'll see it, and decorate it with effective Feng Shui cures. This will give you a sense of direction and energy going forward. Burn the other list.

If you count up the valuable skills you gained this year, the money and better investment choices you made, you can truly assess this year as a success. Sometimes you are too hard on yourself, and this can zap your motivation. Make a point to be kind to yourself, and you will have more energy to do the right thing when choices (especially purchasing choices) arise.

Commit to reducing the amount of stuff you own to things that truly bring you happiness (or at least are regularly very useful). Get rid of duplicates and excess. You can sell off unneeded items now and bring in a little additional money.

If you're in a love relationship, this may be a superb start to your year. You have the opportunity to cement your connection with your beloved through open and deep conversation.

If you're looking for love, notice if you keep attracting the same type of person. If you're attracted to a personality type that has not been good for you previously, it's time to make a change. Date someone who's not like anyone you've ever dated before. Be curious about someone entirely new to you.

February: *Mercury goes retrograde from February 16 to March 9. Your Lucky Days are 5, 11, 17, 23, 29. [How to use your Lucky Days: On these days, plan to take significant actions, make vital phone calls, send emails. These are days when your energy and luck are high.]*

There is a lot of activity around friendships. You may be adding some new friends as a result of attending an event, convention, or joining a new group and attending the regular meetings. At the same time, a friendship may be leaving now. Possibly, a friend is moving somewhere else, but the separation may also happen as a result of a difference of opinion. You may love this person but not feel it's good for either of you to spend so much time together. It may be a sign you are growing apart.

The monetary circumstances in your life are beginning to show signs of improvement, especially concerning your income from a job or contract work. You can pay off a debt or add to your savings this month. A bonus is possible. If you own a business, you may get a boost in income from an online source or from new customers who have found you through social media.

This is a good sign during Mercury retrograde, which tends to double things, including windfalls.

There are opportunities for love. When you're looking for love, Pig natives should consider online sites for match-making. It may not be your usual way of connecting with new people, but it will certainly speed things up. Update your online profile and have a friend take some pictures of you. Light a candle or say a prayer to let the Universe know the qualities you're looking for in a partner, and to remind yourself of all of the good things you can bring to a relationship. Then step back and let the Universe set you up.

For those Pig natives already in a love relationship, it's a good idea to spend some quiet time together away from extended family and the kids. You don't have to go far. Consider making up the bedroom as your sanctuary and institute a "knock first" policy for the others who live in the house.

March: *Mercury goes direct on March 9. The Sun enters Aries on March 20. Saturn enters Aquarius on March 21. Your Lucky Days are 6, 12, 18, 24, 30. [How to use your Lucky Days: On these days, plan to take significant actions, make vital phone calls, send emails. These are days when your energy and luck are high.]*

Lots of luck and energy are with you this month. You may be called upon to stand before a group to propose a toast or make a short speech. While you may hesitate about stepping out on stage, you do wonderfully. Your words are heartfelt and warmly received. Pig natives have a strong empathetic nature. This month you will receive several missives of appreciation from those you know.

Something you've wanted to acquire is now within reach. Perhaps the price has been lowered, or you may find someone willing to help you fund the purchase. Consider holding back on this decision until after Mercury goes direct on March 9. Overall, you are being shown your ability to manifest what you want. Take it as a good sign.

A connection with a sibling or a neighbor is important during this period. If you've faced challenges, you may find a sudden shift of power—now it's your turn to call the shots. You're never one to hold grudges, and you readily accept apologies. Give them space to make it up to you.

If you're looking for love, let your friends know, and they will have suggestions for you. Also, accept a few invitations this month. It's not easy to meet new people when you only hang out in the same old places or never leave your own dwelling. Wear navy on your first date, as this color helps bring worthwhile conversations.

April: *Pluto goes retrograde on April 25. Your Lucky Days are 5, 11, 17, 23, 29. [How to use your Lucky Days: On these days, plan to take significant actions, make vital phone calls, send emails. These are days when your energy and luck are high.]*

Pig natives are highly intuitive this month. You may see symbols and signs in ordinary things; multiple instances of the same number or intriguing sayings will pop up all over the place. You'll find a special message for you in the lyrics of a song or in a line from an old movie. To read these signs clearly, have a question in mind such as, "Should I stay in my current career?" or "Is this the right house for me?" The signs answering these direct questions will be easy for you to read.

You may not be getting out very much this month. It's possible a pile of work keeping you chained to your desk. Or, you may feel like being a homebody, and so you're nesting for the next few weeks. If you can find the time, have a few friends over to bring positive energy into the house.

Finances improve as you lean into your real talent. It may be the time you get a promotion with an increase. If you're not sure which direction to go, focus on what you like to do, rather than what you think will bring you money. Pig natives are hard workers, but success comes when you focus on what you love to do.

Your love life is improving as well. If you're already in a love relationship, you show some happy times this month. You are getting along great and finding common ground on issues you may previously have bristled about. It can be fun to take a short trip together over a weekend to visit.

If you're considering getting a new vehicle, you can strike a good deal this month. Take your partner or a friend with you as they will help you get the best price.

May: *Saturn goes retrograde on May 10. Venus goes retrograde on May 12. Jupiter goes retrograde on May 14. Your Lucky Days are 5, 11, 17, 23, 29. [How to use your Lucky Days: On these days, plan to take significant actions, make vital phone calls, send emails. These are days when your energy and luck are high.]*

While this is a powerful time for you, it's likely you feel more than a little irritation about the many obligations you have. You may need a break. Look around to see if someone can help by picking up some of the tasks you have on your list. These tasks are not meant to be entirely yours to complete. You are surrounded now by helpful people, but you must ask to activate this energy.

Work is busy as well. You may have a new person in the office who needs training, or you may be short-handed while someone is away on maternity leave. Meet with your supervisor to revise expectations in the light of the shifts within your team or in the groups who rely on you.

You may meet someone of importance this month. It could be a celebrity or someone in your industry you admire. This is a great connection for you. Don't be shy but speak up, get their contact info or take a selfie with them. It's okay to ask for their autograph if they are quite famous.

A new topic has you diving deep in research mode. Pig natives love to learn and have a true thirst for knowledge. You may be buying and devouring books, but it would benefit you to find a group or organization where you can get a first-hand understanding of these concepts or processes.

You meet someone new who could turn into a romantic opportunity. The chemistry is as strong as it is unexpected. This one may surprise you, Pig native and your friends.

June: *Lunar Eclipse on June 5. Mercury is retrograde from June 17 to July 12. There is a Solar Eclipse on June 20. Venus goes direct June 24. Your Lucky Days are 4, 10, 16, 22, 28. [How to use your Lucky Days: On these days, plan to take significant actions, make vital phone calls, send emails. These are days when your energy and luck are high.]*

The Lunar Eclipse may have an impact on a planned trip. Be flexible about travel arrangements. Check luggage twice to make sure you don't forget something crucial. Once you're on the road, things will be fine, actually quite enjoyable. But the prep does seem to be fraught with errors if you're not careful.

Take advantage of all of this activity to revive a past spiritual practice such as yoga, tai chi, meditation, or dance. You can consider reconnecting with the ocean or nature. Doing magic now, especially around the time of the Solar Eclipse, can bring you benefits all through the year.

Things are going well at home. A friend or relative may come to visit and to spend the night. Tasty food will be shared, and memories will be made.

If you're in a new love relationship, you may find this connection intensifies now. You may talk about moving in together or getting engaged. Introduce your sweetheart to your family, though preferably not on June 20, the exact day of the Solar eclipse. The energy is a little too intense at the time of an Eclipse for this purpose.

The things changing at work may not affect you directly, but you will see ripples spreading out through the company over the next few months. New teams are formed, or you hear new procedures are being drawn up. You may be tempted to join co-workers in complaining, but supervisors are listening.

You would do well to begin an earnest dialog with managers instead of belly-aching.

July: *Retrograde Saturn backs up into Capricorn. There is a Lunar Eclipse is on July 4. Mercury goes direct on July 12. Your Lucky Days are 4, 10, 16, 22, 28. [How to use your Lucky Days: On these days, plan to take significant actions, make vital phone calls, send emails. These are days when your energy and luck are high.]*

This is a powerfully creative and fertile month for Pig natives. If you are involved in creative projects, you can make real headway now, especially in writing, painting, jewelry making, or photography. But a piece of art may not be the only thing you are creating. If you're planning to add to the family, you can make significant progress now. If you have been looking for the right connection to help you secure fertility treatments, finding a way through towards adoption, or perhaps just wondering about getting a family pet—now is the time. You have a big heart and love to share. Look for opportunities to present themselves all month long, pointing the way towards your fertility.

Your love relationship really works this month. You enjoy better communication, ideas, and feelings flow between the two of you. And you may have a dream where you receive information about the connection with your sweetheart. Insights and epiphanies bring you closer.

Teaching and learning are highlighted. Pig natives are always learning and growing. You may be going back to school or taking a class at your church or community center. Find a way to add to your computer or technical skills now. Wait to take certification exams until later in the month after Mercury goes direct.

Finances greatly improve as money you've been waiting for finally shows up. You can find some additional sources of funding at this time. This may be a side hustle or a source of passive income now showing itself to be growing from a trickle to a stream.

August: *Uranus goes retrograde on August 15. Your Lucky Days are 3, 9, 15, 21, 27. [How to use your Lucky Days: On these days, plan to take significant actions, make vital phone calls, send emails. These are days when your energy and luck are high.]*

Things are going well at home. In fact, home is where you seem to want to be. If others are trying to draw you out with promises of trips and parties, they need to make the offers extra tempting this month. You may have some guests over and be showing them the sights of your home town. But most of your energy and activity is centered around home and family at this time.

You may have an opportunity to change your health and wellness plan for the better. It could have something to do with health insurance coverage, or it maybe you've found a new system of exercise you truly enjoy. Group exercises are especially helpful for you now.

Excellent opportunities seem to be lining up for you. However, It might be a good idea to give the Universe a tip about what you're looking for. Set up a vision board or write a goal list. Place it somewhere you will see it daily and keep your vision at the forefront of your mind.

Finances indicate money flow in from more than one source. You may be selling off some old stuff or have an investment begin to pay off. If you own a business, your luck is particularly strong for increasing sales or landing an important client.

A potential romance begins with a call or text. Once communication begins, anything can happen. Suggest getting together. If this is a long-distance relationship, it would be good to make plans to get together soon. This will help build this relationship into something solid.

September: *Mars goes retrograde on September 9. Jupiter goes direct on September 12. The Sun goes into Libra on September 22. Saturn goes direct on September 28. Your Lucky Days are 2, 8, 14, 20, 26. [How to use your Lucky Days: On these days, plan to take significant actions,* *make vital phone calls, send emails. These are days when your energy and luck are high.]*

You are lucky this month, and you may feel the guiding hand of the Universe. The Full Moon will highlight a harmonious time for you. Something you've been waiting for now appears at your door, but it's not quite time yet to jump in. Allow this opportunity to unfold naturally. Pig natives are known to be thoughtful and patient. Wait now, and things will be even better in a week or two.

You are a little more emotional than usual. It's good to express yourself through writing, art, or movement. You may feel some stress over things happening in the world. While it's good to be informed, it's not beneficial to spend too much energy on circumstances you can't change. Say a prayer, meditate or light a candle and send positive energy. Then let it go and return to your own path.

There is a lot of activity around money and finances this month. You may be working on paperwork, accounting, or even taxes. Investments are possible, but give yourself time to review the prospective carefully. You may be asked to join a company where you both sell a product and recruit other salespeople. Think carefully before signing, especially if there's a sizable upfront investment. Pig natives have a lot of talent and a good work ethic. You can start something on your own if you want to have your own business.

This month highlights relationships. You will receive support and encouragement from close loved ones now. A true partnership is forming.

October: *Pluto goes direct on October 4. Mercury goes retrograde from October 13 to November 3. Your Lucky Days are 2, 8, 14, 20, 26. [How to use your Lucky Days: On these days, plan to take significant actions, make vital phone calls, send emails. These are days when your energy and luck are high.]*

This month, a new job with a new company or a promotion to a new position at your current firm is possible. You are valued, but it may still take some negotiation to get a package that works. Consider asking for more money or more flexibility in your schedule. You may want to suggest more vacation time for you as well.

While the changeover is good, you seem to be a little short on cash this month. You may have made a sizable investment last month, or perhaps you're just back from vacation. Pull out your written budget and try to stick to it. Keep spending in check, and you'll be fine, but if you go on a spree, you may find yourself a little short at the end of the month.

Mercury goes retrograde in the middle of the month, and this could change some plans related to travel for work or pleasure. If you're traveling at the end of the month, consider picking up some travel insurance or at the very least, stay flexible.

Love is very strong this month. You are admired by another, and they are not shy about letting you know. This could be a very interesting connection for you. If you're already in a love relationship, look out. You don't want to complicate your home life with someone outside of your current relationship.

There is a lot of energy around intimacy and fun things happening behind closed doors. If you're in a new relationship, things may be developing quite quickly. Dinner could turn into breakfast, and what was thought to be casual may become serious.

November: *Mercury goes direct on November 3. Mars goes direct on November 13. Neptune goes direct on November 28. There is a Lunar Eclipse on November 30. Your Lucky Days are 7, 13, 19, 25. [How to use your Lucky Days: On these days, plan to take significant actions, make vital phone calls, send emails. These are days when your energy and luck are high.]*

This is a power-infused month where you are singled out for your talent or expertise. You may receive an award or at least a verbal mention by someone you respect. The trouble is, you are being rewarded for something you don't want to do—like you being an artist, but being congratulated for being great at accounting. It's an honor for sure, but you may feel people don't know who you are. Try not to reject this out of hand—this can be a stepping stone to what you do want. Or, if you're still uncertain of your path forward, this can connect you with helpful people who may show you the way.

That being said, there are lots of periods of happiness this month. Your level of overall satisfaction with what's going on in your life is high. As challenges come up, you find the inner confidence to handle them and the external support system to support your efforts.

There are possible changes at home or the home of a family member. You may be moving or doing some renovations to the home. A family member may be moving, and you are helping them get settled.

Your intimate life continues with a lot of activity behind closed doors. Someone you've known for a long time may become an exclusive relationship, soon giving you a reason to celebrate.

December: *Solar Eclipse on December 14. Saturn goes into Aquarius on December 16. Jupiter goes into Aquarius on December 19. Sun goes into Capricorn on December 21. Your Lucky Days are 1, 7, 13, 19, 25, 31. [How to use your Lucky Days: On these days, plan to take significant actions, make vital phone calls, send emails. These are days when your energy and luck are high.]*

You are quite disciplined now, and you want to put your life in order. You may start exercising regularly and keeping your space extra tidy. You may not always be like this, but it's beneficial for you right now. Try to add other healthful habits such as eating your veggies, watching less TV, and reading good books.

The Solar Eclipse towards the middle of the month brings a change pertaining to an adult child or younger relative. There may be an addition to the family through marriage, engagement, or pregnancy. It may also indicate a pet is being added to the family.

A friend from your past returns into your life. They may be visiting or actually moving back into your area. There is a reason to celebrate even though it will take a little while to reestablish the relationship.

Job prospects look good. If you hope to sign a new contract, all indicators are pointing to "Yes." You may want to negotiate some smaller points, but for the most part, it's good to accept the offer and get started. Once in the organization, you will be able to gain a better perspective of where you want to go with this company. In a year or two, you may find an even better fit as the result of an opening in another department or team. The seeds for that move are planted this month.

January 2021: *Uranus goes direct on January 14. Mercury goes retrograde from January 30 to February 20. Your Lucky Days are 6, 12, 18, 24, 30. [How to use your Lucky Days: On these days, plan to take significant actions, make vital phone calls, send emails. These are days when your energy and luck are high.]*

Your popularity is on the rise. At work and in social situations, you are commanding attention as well as admiration. While Pig natives naturally accept these compliments with grace, you're still in a Metal Rat year for another few weeks, and. Keep your eyes open to see how these contacts and connections may open some doors for you.

You're busy at work, and the office seems a little short-handed. Ask for help and delegate what you can from your long list of things to do. Working overtime and skipping your workout is not a good idea, and definitely don't skimp on sleep. Take care of yourself and allow others to step up and help you.

Finances remain strong. A second or additional source of income likely comes through this month. Even small gains are a sign that a larger flow will happen in the future. It's a good idea to reinvest any unexpected gains in the business or pay down debt. You might have been eyeing a new pair of boots, but there are wiser places for your money now.

Expect to spend time and share a lot of activities with friends. You may be receiving more invitations than usual. You may travel to a wedding or host friends who are visiting your town. This is generally all good, as you love a social occasion.

You may have some difficulty with a device like a phone or small computer towards the end of the month as Mercury slows to go retrograde on January 30. If you need to replace this item, try to do it before then.

February 2021: Lunar New Year begins on February 12. Happy Year of the Metal Ox.

Attract New Love

You enter this year wondering if you're ready for love. That's usually when love shows up. This year, a new love may spot you from across the room and come to find you. You don't need to go much out of your way. But it would be good for you to smile back and say hello.

If you want a great love relationship in your life, use your powers of attraction and visualize how you want y our great love to begin. Write the story like you're writing a movie. Picture the awkward beginning, followed by the "getting to know" you period. And fast forward the view to the two of you happily established in a love union. This will attract a wonderful relationship for you.

The peony, especially the pink peony, is a flower used in Feng Shui to represent love and romance. It has a splendid sweet scent and beautiful appearance. It's said to inspire beauty in life. Hang a picture of a peony near the entrance of your bedroom, either inside the bedroom or in the hallway leading to the bedroom. This Feng Shui cure is best used to attract new love. Once you're in a happy relationship, remove the picture and give it to someone who's looking for love.

Enhance Existing Love

You're really in sync this year. You and your partner seem to be clones of each other. Your friends watch you fall into step like you've planned and rehearsed it together. While this is how things appear outwardly, on the inside, you may not feel as close as you would like.

You had a big growth year last year, and you are a different person now during this year of the Metal Rat. Even if your partner is also born in the Year of the Pig, it's possible you're both growing in different directions. It doesn't mean the end of the relationship. No. It simply means it's time for a chat. You need to talk about what interests you now. What are your goals? Where do you want to go from here?

To grow closer again, consider doing something with a bigger purpose together. Find a charity you can support together. Or get involved in a community organization where you can both play a part. Take your relationship to the next level by together doing something more for others than yourselves.

If your relationship is something you want to improve and to be stronger than ever, choose the crane as your symbol for love this year. The crane is a symbol of fidelity and marital bliss in many cultures. To bring greater happiness to your relationship, find or make some paper cranes. The origami bird is simple to make, and these symbols are said to bring love and longevity to the partnership. You can also hang a painting of actual cranes. Place the picture or the paper cranes in the bedroom where you can see them from the bed.

Looking to Conceive?

Pine cones are a great fertility symbol. Think of how a little seed grows between the hard petals of the cone. You can display a basket of scented pine cones in your family room or bedroom to promote conception energy. Eating pine nuts is also said to bring on good sexual relations, leading to a future happy event. You can add the nuts to a salad or create a decadent dessert with honey and increase your odds of getting pregnant.

(From Donna Stellhorn's book, *A Path to Pregnancy: Ancient Secrets for the Modern Woman*)

Family and Kids

If you moved last year, you can breathe a happy sigh of relief. You can spend this year settling in, getting to know your neighbors, dealing with some parking issues (no place is perfect,) and getting the last boxes unpacked. If you're still in the process of moving, you may have had to make some adjustments in what you wanted to spend for a home and your vision of the home itself. But Pig natives know how to make any situation comfortable and peaceful. You will be fine.

You may be too busy this year to see much of your extended family, but you know they are there for you. If visits can't happen, stay in touch by phone and video. The family may be coming together for a large celebration or an important holiday. Grow your get together larger as you invite close friends to join you.

For Pig natives who have kids, you will see them going in every direction possible. It's hard to keep up with them. Each one seems to have a large number of friends, and you're shuffling kids to parties, events, and sports nearly constantly. Older children may be traveling to distant lands this year. If you want a child, it is quite possible this year. You may also add a pet or two.

The Peace Lily is a favorite, easy-to-grow house plant. This plant is quite adaptable and can even grow in rooms where there are no windows at all. Of course, the Peace Lily is a symbol of peace in the home as well as promoting calm and balance. This plant helps clean the air, and it's pretty white flowers are a joy to see.

Find a good, healthy Peace Lily to have in your dining room, family room, or living room. This will bring positive energy to the home and family.

Money

Income from your career is healthy this year. This will most likely be the backbone of your finances, though money can come from other sources as well. Income from a job or your own business will be the lion's share of your funds. It's good to take additional income and put it towards debt repayment and investments.

If you're retired and live on passive income, it would be a good idea this year to manage your finances like a business. It would be risky just to put your money in someone else's hands and walk away. Consider playing an active role in your finances, and you will do well.

When it comes to your money, in general, this year you will breakthrough a money block you've had for some time. Perhaps, you've had a ceiling on how much you've been able to make thus far in your life, and this year you crash through that ceiling. Or it may be you overcome the block of asking for money from others. You may find the money you've been trying to get for a long time suddenly comes to you without effort. The more you actively work on money blocks, the quicker you will find a stream of money flowing to you.

Money also comes to you when you make your plans or project known to others. This may be through some organized system like GoFundMe.com, or you just let your followers on social media know what's going on in your life. Step out of your office or lab and show the world what you can do. This brings opportunities, as well as rewards.

This year hang chili peppers to stimulate the flow of money. You can use pictures of chili peppers, chili pepper lights, chili peppers made out of fabric, or real dried chilies strung together. Hang them in your entryway to bring luck with money. If you use dried chilies, however, hang them outside; otherwise, the smell can be overwhelming.

Job or Career

This will be a much better year for you career-wise than last year. You feel you're in a better position to ask for what you want. You like your boss, and you may feel like you can allow yourself to be comfortable. Unfortunately, it's likely the industry you are in will be going through changes (and if you're hoping these changes are going to take place after you retire, you may be just adding stress to your life).

Even if you changed jobs last year, you may not be done with the changing energy. This is just the second of your three seed planting years. You may find yourself even going back to a previous job or industry because the changes you made last year didn't work out. That's okay. There are really good career opportunities coming.

Financially your career energy is strengthened. You may be making changes directly related to increasing income. You also may have a side business that starts to take off. Marketing and networking really pay off. You can make important connections that directly bring you opportunities.

It may be useful to get involved in professional organizations, including taking a board position. You may also get into local politics and make connections with other business people through a shared political vision. Also, you can get with a friend and start a business, one you may have been talking about for many years.

The company you work for maybe expanding or perhaps it is acquired by a larger company. Keeping your current job may require a move on your part. If you have wanted to have some adventure, you can apply to work at companies around the world and see what opens up. Most Pig natives are homebodies for sure, but they also are adept at adjusting to a new home in a strange and foreign land. Those Pig natives who are thinking about retiring will do best if they involve themselves in community activities or local charities.

In the West, when we think of gold, we think of a gold bar, but in the East, a gold ingot is shaped like a little boat. This is called the *yuan bao*. These ingots were used as a form of currency. Now you can find replica gold ingots in painted metal used as symbols of wealth. They often have embossed Chinese characters of "wealth" and "fortune." Place your ingot on your desk or in your family room on a shelf near a picture of your family to attract a great job opportunity or a raise from your current employer.

Education

You may find you suddenly want to attend school. This is great if you're studying some aspect of technology, finance, or construction. But use caution about signing up for a long, expensive program. It would be better to focus on short programs or incremental programs where you can choose your focus. It's also a good idea to have a clear reason for going to school. Much of what you want to learn (outside of medicine or law) is available for free on the internet. You can especially gain technology skills of different types easily online.

If you're already in school and are in the middle or near the end of a long program, you may feel your attention waning. Find some friends and relatives who can give you a pep talk to help you finish. You may want to change up your class schedule for a semester by switching to some electives to renew your interest in school. Finance classes are very beneficial to you now. There are funding options for school for you and people who can help you make sense of the paperwork and options. Ask for help, and you will receive it. Use school now to expand your social circles. Try to meet more people.

Legal Matters

Contracts regarding employment are likely this year. You may also set up an agreement to start a business or secure financing for a business venture. You are quick to find what needs to be changed in the contract, and negotiations can go smoothly as the other side never seems as prepared as you are. You may be tempted to sue a past employer for some grievous wrongdoing. Seek out competent legal counsel before moving forward. While you could win a suit, seek to settle if possible to save yourself time and energy. Or find other victims and band together to strengthen your position.

Health and Well-Being

This is a year of improved health and general happiness. You worked hard last year, and so this year of the Metal Rat brings much relief as you see the seeds you've planted sprout into very viable options for yourself. Pig natives love the good life, and you recognize how occasionally indulging in what you love is beneficial for your health and happiness. What's important is to be mindful and stay in the present moment. This way, you experience the height of pleasure from these small indulgences.

The last year helped you know yourself better, and this year you benefit from continuing to follow that path. You easily release anger and disappointment now. This helps you sleep well at night and wake refreshed. June and November may bring some disruption at home. But after a quick flareup, everything settles back down to a peaceful pace. As you care compassionately for yourself, you will strengthen your relationships at home and help everyone find happiness.

The Feng Shui the gourd is a symbol related to health, longevity, and well-being. The gourd can be made of wood, metal, glass, or stone. It can also be a natural gourd that's been painted or otherwise decorated. Gourds like these are found in Asian markets and art & crafts festivals.

Place the gourd in the bedroom or family room. You can tie a red ribbon around the center of the gourd to increase the energy. But do this only if no one living in the house is ill. If someone in the house is recovering from illness, place the gourd in the family room and not a bedroom.

Compatibility Between Signs

In this section of Chinese Astrology: 2020, Year of the Metal Rat, I will explain a little about compatibility between the Chinese Zodiac signs concerning love and friendship. Sometimes a pairing of two signs isn't the most promising. We can often improve the energy by placing a Feng Shui Crystal cure to support the relationship.

Feng Shui Crystals are round, cut glass crystals which have a prismatic effect. When light hits the crystal, a rainbow of glittering, shiny light prisms twinkle around the ceiling, walls, or floor. Shiny things attract energy, so the sparkling crystal attracts energy to balance the relationship.

Cut glass crystals come in many shapes, but round is the most balanced and harmonious shape, so it's used to balance relationship energy. Whenever a Feng Shui Crystal is called for, you can use a clear one (clear crystals are the easiest to find). Or you can use colored crystals to bring in the energy of one of the five elements.

Use green to represent the Wood element if you want to increase growth and prosperity.

Use blue to represent the Water element, to activate good communication, flow, and harmony.

Use amber or yellow to represent the Earth element, to bring stability and longevity.

Use red to represent the Fire element, to stimulate energy and passion.

Use clear to represent the Metal element, to attract resources and business success.

Along with the compatibility listings below, you will find suggestions about where to place the crystal if your relationship needs some help. Choose a green crystal if troubles in the relationship are because of finances. Choose a blue crystal if the problems in the relationship center around communication.

Choose an amber or yellow crystal if there has been infidelity, and you want to try to heal the relationship. Choose a red crystal if there's been a lack of passion, romance, and sex. Choose a clear crystal to come closer together, and to receive help and support from your partner.

To find the correct direction for placing the crystal, think of your home and the rising sun. The sun always rises in the east. The sun sets in the west. If you know where the sun rises and sets in relation to your home, you will be able to identify the other cardinal directions, north and south, very easily. (Hint: Google Maps aerial view can make this task very easy, as it always shows north as up, south is down, to the left is west and to the right is east.).

To find the inner directions such as North by Northwest, find north and find west. Halfway between these two is northwest. North by Northwest is halfway between north and northwest.

Here's a diagram Place this diagram on the floor, east pointing towards the rising sun. The diagram will help you find the right direction for placing appropriate crystal.

If you can place the crystal in a window, it will catch the most light. If there is no window in that direction, hang the crystal on a lamp, a plant, a drawer pull, or simply from a wall hook.

To see all the different ways to use Feng Shui Crystals and how to hang them, go to WWW.FENGSHUIFORM.COM.

We can divide the 12 animals of the Chinese Zodiac into four groups. Each group has some key personality traits:

Rat, Dragon, Monkey are the action-oriented ones. The Rat takes care of the details; the Dragon has the big ideas, and the Monkey can improve the skills of others.

Ox, Snake, and Rooster are the deep thinkers. The Ox is methodical, thinking things through thoroughly. The Snake is wise and sees things from various perspectives. The Rooster is alert and aware of everything going on around him.

Tiger, Horse, and Dog are the freedom lovers. The Tiger is impulsive: he sees what he wants and pounces. The Horse runs across the prairies and lands with power and grace. The Dog can work alone or within a group, and still retain his independence

Rabbit, Sheep/Goat, and Pig/Boar are the peace lovers. The Rabbit is diplomatic and can bring opposing forces together. The Sheep/Goat is the humanitarian, wanting to bring peace to the world. The Pig/Boar is the homebody, wanting to create comfort and peace for the family.

Chinese Zodiac Signs and Compatibility

Rat Compatibility

Rat with Rat: Well suited and lots of fun. Always busy, doing things, making deals, and making money. You'll need to respect each others' time and secrets. Occasionally you'll need time apart as much as you need to be together. If you find one of you is too bossy, or you both need to focus a little more on the big picture and the future, hang a Feng Shui Crystal in the North side of the house.

Rat with Ox: A happy and long-lasting relationship. You will benefit from Ox's stability and strength. You are both optimistic and enjoy the little things in life. You can start the job and know that Ox will be there to help you finish it. If you find your partner is stubborn and not open to your ideas, hang a Feng Shui Crystal in the North by Northeast part of the house.

Rat with Tiger: Hot and cold, with lots of energy and excitement in this relationship. Sometimes the Tiger will ignore the little Rat, and sometimes the Tiger will be surprised at how loud a Rat can squeak. If Tiger's unpredictable ways get on your nerves, you can steady this relationship by hanging a Feng Shui Crystal in the East by Northeast part of the house.

Rat with Rabbit: Arguments after the fling is what we have here. You are both clever, but a little too clever. One wants commitment, and the other wants freedom, and neither wants the same thing at the same time. If you find Rabbit too passive and you're looking for more dedication to this relationship, hang a Feng Shui Crystal in the East side of the house.

Rat with Dragon: Happiness abounds when the Rat joins with the powerful Dragon. The relationship can be very intense. But use caution (and flattery) because if you break the spell, there is no putting the broken relationship back together again. If you find Dragon's head in the clouds and need a more grounded partner to help you with the day to day parts of the relationship, hang a Feng Shui Crystal in the East by Southeast side of the house.

Rat with Snake: Volatile pair that sometimes can be a good relationship… at least until the Snake gets hungry. Avoid being on the menu. This is more of a learning experience than a love match. If you find Snake too secretive and a little on the manipulative side, hang a Feng Shui Crystal in the South by Southeast part of the house.

Rat with Horse: Unhappy pair that can't see eye to eye. You find Horse's needs exhausting. If you get into this relationship, keep a life raft handy. You'll be paddling to shore in no time. If you insist that this is the relationship of your dreams and you want Horse to settle down and be not so restless, hang a Feng Shui Crystal in the South part of the house.

Rat with Sheep: Poor match because the sensitivity of the Sheep is no match for your quick tongue. Communication starts well, but there will be problems with words, and that will be the end of the relationship. You would think with horns; he wouldn't have such thin skin. If you only see eye to eye when pampering your Sheep partner and want to have things be a little more equal, hang a Feng Shui Crystal in the South by Southwest part of the house.

Rat with Monkey: Very lively meeting of people from different worlds. Monkey can take Rat on the trip of a lifetime and open new worlds. It's the unlikely pair in love. You will give each other new perspectives on life and living. But if all the excitement and Monkey's high energy starts to wear on you, hang a Feng Shui Crystal in the West by Southwest part of the house.

Rat with Rooster: Need to work hard at this to make it work at all. You are natural barnyard enemies, both hunting for the same big prize—and not just chicken feed. So you're better off avoiding this cage-match. If you find yourself with an overly critical Rooster on your hands, hang a Feng Shui Crystal in the West part of the house.

Rat with Dog: Lots of energy and togetherness; this is good for you, you both enjoy being out and about, enjoying others and each other. However, you may find you have trouble finding personal space. Dog will tag along wherever you go, and keep trying to pull you back home. If you feel your life restricted by Dog's constant bark, hang a Feng Shui Crystal in the West by Northwest part of the house.

Rat with Pig: Picture this charming pair of homebodies, both taking care of the other. There is optimum togetherness when you want it, and alone time when you need it. Pig keeps the house cozy and warm. If you find all this happiness and optimism is maxing out your credit cards, hang a Feng Shui Crystal in the North by Northwest part of the house.

Ox Compatibility

Ox with Rat: You are a happy, practical pair that compliment each other. You have the potential here for a very stable relationship with benefits for both partners. Rat sees the details, and your tireless energy can envision what will become of them. If you find Rat is too picky about the small things and can't get the big picture, hang a Feng Shui Crystal in the North part of the house.

Ox with Ox: A caring pair where each is interested in the comfort and security of the other. Not exciting to others, perhaps, but you can be quite content. You can enjoy decades of holding hands and feeling safe, as the cold winters blow outside. While you can remain content for long periods, should you want to add some fun (or at least a break from the constant work), hang a Feng Shui Crystal in the North by Northeast part of the house.

Ox with Tiger: Your goals in life are entirely different, as are your methods of pursuing outcome. This cat doesn't come when he's called (what cat does). There are quarrels that lead to nowhere. Build a stable home, and Tiger looks for the door. If you want this temperamental kitty with claws to be your lifelong partner, you have some work ahead. Hang a Feng Shui Crystal in the East by Northeast part of the house.

Ox with Rabbit: A so-so match. You want stability and clear rules, and Rabbit wants some pampering and kindness. It takes a while to get this one to work, but when it does, it lasts. He can be your lucky Rabbit in the end. But if you honey-bunny spends his or her time sulking in the corner and being overly sensitive, hang a Feng Shui Crystal in the East part of the house.

Ox with Dragon: Tricky pair; expect battles to start from day one. These are two powerful forces with two different ideas of what a relationship is and should be. Ding goes the bell, and the fight begins. If you can see the strong qualities in each of you, there's hope. Hang a Feng Shui Crystal in the East by Southeast part of the house.

Ox with Snake: Supportive, though there can be some conflicts. This is the strong Yin and Yang: together, opposite sides of the same coin. You need each other, and over time with Snake's clever thinking and your perseverance, you both can prosper. While Snake can make an attractive partner, if they are draining your bank account on clothes and toys, hang a Feng Shui Crystal in the South by Southeast part of the house.

Ox with Horse: Difficult match for you. The Horse is fast and careless, compared to your slow and thoughtful ways. There is little Horse can give you that you really want, and so you're more likely to send him on his way. If you want to stable this pony and try to make this restless soul settle down, hang a Feng Shui Crystal in the South part of the house.

Ox with Sheep: Steer clear, this one is trouble from beginning to end. You will have to be exceptionally patient to ride this one out. After butting heads for a while, heartbreak is the most likely ending. You can make this work if you have deep pockets, but it's more likely he/she will spend the money when they're feeling hurt or insecure. To balance the energy, hang a Feng Shui Crystal in the South by Southwest part of the house.

Ox with Monkey: Love and joy can abound with this combo. Monkey will bring you fun times and surprises every day. That will make your steady life more interesting. Once the Monkey settles down, the match can be good for both. If you find Monkey is only interested in him or herself, and too independent for your peaceful dream of a relationship, hang a Feng Shui Crystal in the West by Southwest part of the house.

Ox with Rooster: Good match for these barnyard pals. You both understand the need for hard work, and Rooster appreciates your patience and understanding. You like having someone around who can mind the details. Together you're the soul of productivity, if you would like to have a bit more romance or at least the occasional cuddle, hang a Feng Shui Crystal in the West part of the house.

Ox with Dog: Possibly good, but too many compromises will be required. This is too much Yin energy together; communication will suffer. Both of you are hesitant to lead. Let the Dog go and see if he comes back of his own accord. If you are tired of coming home and always finding a house full of people, or your partner is always on the phone, you can hang a Feng Shui Crystal in the West by Northwest part of the house.

Ox with Pig: This needs effort and adjustments on both sides. If there is chemistry (and good cooking), the relationship may last. But most likely, the Pig won't respect your goals and effort. You get frustrated with his/her play-all-the-time attitude. There can be harmony if there is an understanding of the work and sacrifice it takes to create a financially stable home. If overspending is a problem, hang a Feng Shui Crystal in the North by Northwest part of the house.

Tiger Compatibility

Tiger with Rat: Hot during the chase, and cold when caught, Rat is not a great match for you. Rat is too cynical to see your splendid qualities, and it will need to be taught how to behave. This is more work than you want to do. If you think this is a mouse you want to keep, but the pettiness and demands are hurting the relationship, hang a Feng Shui Crystal in the North part of the house.

Tiger with Ox: Needs effort to keep from being a boring relationship. You might think that Ox will help you settle down and get serious, but in the end, you are just bitter from having all the fun taken out of your life. But if you long for an established relationship that will withstand a bitter winter or a wild party, hang a Feng Shui Crystal in the North by Northeast part of the house.

Tiger with Tiger: Happiness… with claws. As long as you both retain your thick skins, this will be a happy, fun relationship. But arguments can get nasty, so be ready to forgive each other later—and keep bandages on hand. Of course, making up can be the most fun, and what's life about but having fun? So hang a Feng Shui Crystal in the East by Northeast part of the house.

Tiger with Rabbit: Can be good, but Rabbits are not known for their decisive action. You'll have to be patient with this one and prepared to leap into the fray of this relationship without waiting for the careful Rabbit to make the first move. If this Rabbit keeps sprinting away and you want to lure him/her back, hang a Feng Shui Crystal in the East part of the house.

Tiger with Dragon: The explosive power of you and the Dragon is legendary, making for either the most exciting relationship ever, or you'll both knock the world off its axis. If you want to be looked up to, this is not your match, but if you can work things out and share the leadership roles, giving credit where credit's due, this can work. Hang a Feng Shui Crystal in the East by Southeast part of the house.

Tiger with Snake: Steer clear no matter how attracted you are! You are not going to get the Snake's attention easily, and as soon as your back is turned, he's moved on. You can chase again, but after a while, it just gets tiresome. When you leave, Snake chases you; and when you are available, Snake is off without a care. To get this match together, hang a Feng Shui Crystal in the South by Southeast part of the house.

Tiger with Horse: Good ally out in the world, but there may be a conflict about who has to stay home and do the dishes. If you can accept and be happy with an unstable relationship, then grab an apron and give this one a try. Or, better still, pool your creative minds and social nature and make enough money to hire a maid. Stimulate this energy by hanging a Feng Shui Crystal in the South part of the house.

Tiger with Sheep: Can work it out over time, but the Sheep will be cautious. You will have to follow the rules given to you by the Sheep, and this can bring conflicts into the relationship. Mr./Ms Planner will not appreciate your impetuous nature. If you find Sheep too clingy (which surprises you, you thought you were the one with claws), and you wish he or she had more confidence, hang a Feng Shui Crystal in the South by Southwest part of the house.

Tiger with Monkey: It's very difficult to catch a Monkey who's swinging from tree to tree. You might be attracted to one playing hard to get, but after a while, it's no fun always being the one who has to chase... even for a Tiger. If you want to make this work, but Monkey's loud, know-it-all behavior is grating on your nerves, hang a Feng Shui Crystal in the West by Southwest part of the house.

Tiger with Rooster: You come from different worlds, so once at home, there's not much to talk about. You feel bossed around by the nagging Rooster who's frustrated that you don't seem to fall in line like the other chickens. If you find he or she is always on you about your spending and your inability to do the laundry right, smooth things over by hanging a Feng Shui Crystal in the West part of the house.

Tiger with Dog: Strong ally and a good match for you. The Dog can keep the home fires burning while you prowl the world for wealth to acquire. There are a few differences of opinion, but the good definitely outweighs the bad. Sometimes it's hard to get Dog to agree to a quick vacation or a last-minute party, but you can bring some energy to this partnership by hanging a Feng Shui Crystal in the West by Northwest part of the house.

Tiger with Pig: Good match if you take it slow. Pigs can be a little nervous facing Tiger's mandibles of death (actually that's just your smile). But if you approach Pig with gentle understanding, Pig will comfort and take care of you. You both have a tendency to help others before yourselves. If you find you're giving away too many resources to hapless friends, hang a Feng Shui Crystal in the North by Northwest part of the house.

Rabbit Compatibility

Rabbit with Rat: You may argue and fight, and this doesn't make your peace-loving nature euphoric. Rat will have too many demands on you, so a long-term relationship will be very challenging. You may seem similar, but your differences are huge. If your Rat partner is running you ragged with work and social plans, temper the energy by hanging a Feng Shui Crystal in the North part of the house.

Rabbit with Ox: If you want a long term relationship, this one can work—after you get past the boredom of the stable Ox. However, if you are looking for a fling, look elsewhere. Be in this one for the long haul, or not at all. If you find your Ox partner is not the one to sit down and have a good discussion about feelings and the relationship, hang a Feng Shui Crystal in the North by Northeast part of the house.

Rabbit with Tiger: Can be good if you like being pursued and what Rabbit doesn't? If the Tiger catches you, you can have a happy relationship… after you teach him to behave. Tip: Play hard to get even after you've been got. If you find this energetic Tiger keeps you up all hours discussing life and relationships and you just want a peaceful time to hold hands, hang a Feng Shui Crystal in the East by Northeast part of the house.

Rabbit with Rabbit: The pair of you are truly loving and having endless fun. You will play and laugh and bring each other tokens of your affection. You can cuddle in front of a fire or talk until you fall asleep in each other's arms. If you find, however, your bunny-buddy is not doing his or her share of the home duties, hang a Feng Shui Crystal in the East part of the house.

Rabbit with Dragon: Hard going at first, but things get easier over time. The Dragon is a bit of a show-off and hogs your stage. He may think you're small, but you're packed with power and easily a match for any Dragon. Your Dragon has big ideas for both home and business, and if you want to bring him or her back down to earth, hang a Feng Shui Crystal in the East by Southeast part of the house.

Rabbit with Snake: It'll take hard work to get this to be a happy match. The Snake may want you for a relationship, or just for dinner. Once you're in this relationship, you will be looking for a way out of it. You both have good taste and a desire for a good life, but if you're keeping secrets from each other, trouble is ahead. Hang a Feng Shui Crystal in the South by Southeast part of the house.

Rabbit with Horse: Can work it out as friends, even if it doesn't work out as lovers. There are a few conflicts here and there, but in the long run, there are many possibilities with this match. Just don't try to possess this one. Horse may want to run free, but he'll keep coming back. Trouble can arise when your Horse partner does everything by intuition rather than as a result of a discussion between the two of you. If more sharing is needed, hang a Feng Shui Crystal in the South part of the house.

Rabbit with Sheep: Great fun at times, because you'll always win against a Sheep. The Sheep will love you and keep trying. If you give a little to this relationship, the Sheep will give a lot. This could be the peace and happiness you've been waiting for. Your Sheep partner will be quick to depend on you, and this can make you feel great, but if the dependence becomes a burden, hang a Feng Shui Crystal in the South by Southwest part of the house.

Rabbit with Monkey: You'll need effort to understand the changeable and tricky Monkey. This is not a match that happens easily. You could be in danger of getting your heart broken by bad Monkey if you're not careful. If he or she is not understanding your feelings and is glossing over your anxieties, you may feel this Monkey's mocking you. Balance this relationship by hanging a Feng Shui Crystal in the West by Southwest part of the house.

Rabbit with Rooster: Many conflicts with this noisy bird who's constantly pecking and prodding you. Rabbits are the silent ones, and these Roosters are constantly making noises at you—too much so to make you happy. If your Rooster partner is telling all the friends and neighbors the intimate details of what works and doesn't work in your relationship, you can create a tighter bond between you by hanging a Feng Shui Crystal in the West part of the house.

Rabbit with Dog: More chasing than actually having fun. The Dog will make lots of demands on you, and you may find this relationship quite tiring in the beginning. If it lasts, it can grow into a real loving relationship, but it will take quite a bit of work. The loyalty of this partner can make this match worth it, but if you find the communication just not flowing, hang a Feng Shui Crystal in the West by Northwest part of the house.

Rabbit with Pig: Superb match; both of you can have a lot of fun. But if you get bored, you may try to create a little drama in the relationship just to stir things up. That could backfire big time! Once Pig's feelings are hurt, it will hard to tempt him back. Count your blessings, as your Pig partner can be devoted to you. If you find his or her attention on you is not strong enough, hang a Feng Shui Crystal in the North by Northwest part of the house.

Dragon Compatibility

Dragon with Rat: Suitable match where both feel compatibility and interested in one another. You can explore the world together. You will have secrets, and so will Rat, but the secrets won't hurt the relationship. Learn to trust, and Rat will take your grand ideas and turn them into reality. There is much the two of you can accomplish, although sometimes Rat will keep a tight hold on the purse strings. If you need to balance this energy, hang a Feng Shui Crystal in the North part of the house.

Dragon with Ox: Tricky times with the stubborn Ox will make the relationship rather exhausting. If you hold on, you can smooth things out and have a good long term relationship. This can happen because Dragons are said to live a thousand years. You love to dream up new ideas, but your Ox partner could be unsympathetic if he or she doesn't see immediate results. To temper this energy, hang a Feng Shui Crystal in the North by Northeast part of the house.

Dragon with Tiger: Requires patience and understanding, as together you represent two powerful Yang forces. Those around you might not believe the relationship will work out, but if you don't make too many demands on each other, you have a chance at a happy time with the Tiger. With two leaders and no followers, there can be some fights, even out the "eventful" energy by hanging a Feng Shui Crystal in the East by Northeast part of the house.

Dragon with Rabbit: Hard going at first, but you will soon find the Rabbit admires your good qualities. Rabbit also helps you strengthen some areas where you are weak: like being calm and quiet. You can help Rabbit be more detached and able to deal with the world. If you can let Rabbit have a soft place to land, you two will get along just fine, in the meantime, hang a Feng Shui Crystal in the East part of the house.

Dragon with Dragon: The best or the worst relationship for you. You love to be the center of attention, and so does your partner. This [airing will work if the two of you can share the stage. It can be glorious, or it can be a battle. You could make an enviable couple and rule the social scene. Agree now that you, together, will hang a Feng Shui in the East by Southeast part of the house to make this happen.

Dragon with Snake: Can be good as friends, but as lovers, things tend to break down. Snake wants you to try harder in the relationship, but your attitude is, "It will work if it's meant to be." This causes the Snake to slither away eventually. If you feel that holding on to this relationship is going to benefit you both, you can hang a Feng Shui Crystal in the South by Southeast part of the house.

Dragon with Horse: Lively pair; this combination can bring both fun and fights. You may become irritated that the Horse always thinks you're up to something. There will be more physical compatibility than intellectual or emotional. You both have a lot of energy but no patience for mundane tasks; create enough income to hire help by hanging a Feng Shui Crystal in the South part of the house.

Dragon with Sheep: Sheep thought he was on top of the world until he saw you flying overhead. You may want this relationship to work, but Sheep may get frightened by your power and energy. Coax him in slowly before you reveal all your greatness to him. If you feel strongly about this relationship, you can put in the effort to help temper your Sheep partner's moods by hanging a Feng Shui Crystal in the South by Southwest part of the house.

Dragon with Monkey: Good pair because you admire Monkey's cleverness. You have the inner strength to get Monkey to behave; this can be a good match. Monkey will amuse you every day! Take this act on the road, and you can be stars, or keep it close to home and be the toast of the neighborhood. Adding a Feng Shui Crystal to the West by Southwest part of the house will bring you some exciting opportunities.

Dragon with Rooster: The legendary Dragon and Rooster (okay, Phoenix). This pair feels a lot of attraction to one another. You can have a long term happy relationship as long as the Rooster doesn't look for reasons to be suspicious of all the happiness. If your Rooster partner starts snapping at you, hang a Feng Shui Crystal in the West part of the house.

Dragon with Dog: Not suitable, unless you like putting oil and fire together. This is a battle waiting to happen! Dog doesn't care how powerful you are; he's willing to take you down a notch. If your Dog partner wants to curtail your freedom and put you on a leash, hang a Feng Shui Crystal in the West by Northwest part of the house.

Dragon with Pig: It's hard not to like being at home with your Pig partner, nothing but comfort and good food abounds. But to keep Pig happy, you'll have to pitch in and do your share of the chores. Ever the peacemaker, your Pig partner will support you on your goals. Attract what you both want by hanging a Feng Shui Crystal in the North by Northwest area of the home.

Snake Compatibility

Snake with Rat: Is it love you're feeling? Or, is it just casual amusement? You may feel common interests at first, but unless you want to commit, Rat will flee the first chance he gets. You can have a very profitable relationship if you set the right tone from the beginning. Keep things moving upward by hanging a Feng Shui Crystal in the North part of the house.

Snake with Ox: Can be so supportive of each other, but someone has to make the first move. If you two get together, you are likely to enjoy a long and happy relationship. Set your boundaries and then take a chance. You both have the drive and interest in making this work. To keep the lines of communication open, hang a Feng Shui Crystal in the North by Northeast part of the house.

Snake with Tiger: Steer clear, this is a battle waiting to happen. The Tiger is seductive, and you might be tempted, but it's you who should be doing the tempting. This is a match destined for a breakup. If you're determined to stay together, and yet you're both suspicious of the other's actions and intentions, hang a Feng Shui Crystal in the East by Northeast part of the house.

Snake with Rabbit: It's hard work to find the balance here. Rabbit will bring out your deeper qualities, but his thin skin won't stand up to your assessments. There could be pain on both sides. On the other hand, if you can see the best in the other, you will both benefit from your refined sense and mental acuity. Hang a Feng Shui Crystal in the East part of the house to stimulate this positive energy.

Snake with Dragon: Can make a good couple—from dating to a long term relationship. There is fun to be had by both. Keep your demands light, and you and the Dragon will fare very well. Keep in mind how much you admire the qualities of the other and communicate this often. To bring more harmony, hang a Feng Shui Crystal in the East by Southeast part of the house.

Snake with Snake: Wonderful pair that can balance each other. If you share leadership with your partner, you can expect a long and happy relationship. You can work together to bring yourselves power and success. Hang a Feng Shui Crystal in the South by Southeast part of the house to increase success energy.

Snake with Horse: This combo is difficult. You might be afraid of being stepped on, but you should be more worried about being forgotten or left behind by the popular Horse. Keep your eyes open because Horse may not be all that faithful. If Horse's impulsive nature starts to drive you around the bend, hang a Feng Shui Crystal in the South part of the house to calm that energy.

Snake with Sheep: Needs concentrated effort, but by taking a thoughtful approach, you can find happiness together. Be considerate of the Sheep's feelings, and you will have to tread lightly at times, but you can work this out. This relationship may start out with you both in a constant embrace, but after a while, Sheep's clingy behavior may put you off. To ease this energy, hang a Feng Shui Crystal in the South by Southwest part of the house.

Snake with Monkey: Long-lasting match, once you get past the game-playing. You are both very clever, and you can learn much from each other. There is fun and romance for both here. But if this relationship is punctuated with fights and competition, temper that energy by hanging a Feng Shui Crystal in the West by Southwest part of the house.

Snake with Rooster: What seems impossible at first turns into a wonderful pair. Rooster may be lots of talk and fussy behavior, but deep down, he truly cares for you. Try not to get irritated, don't take things too seriously, and things will work out. Turn your attention to business, and you two will be the dynamic duo. For wealth energy, hang a Feng Shui Crystal in the West part of the house.

Snake with Dog: Quite charming match with you being both friends and lovers. But try not to be too possessive—Dogs need to run and play sometimes. (Know that Dog always comes home afterward.) On the other hand, when Dog is out of sight, you can do some of the things you may not be able to do under Dog's keen nose. Hang a Feng Shui Crystal in the West by Northwest part of the house for harmony in this relationship.

Snake with Pig: Not a good match, as your temperaments are entirely different. You are a deep thinker, and the Pig is looking for a comfortable, non-drama home. You might appreciate all that Pig can do for you, but the conflicts will be challenging. If you find your Pig partner being loving and supportive, not just to you, but the whole neighborhood and every charity they can find, you can bring Pig's attention back to you by hanging a Feng Shui Crystal in the North by Northwest part of the house.

Horse Compatibility

Horse with Rat: Poor match, because neither wants to compromise. Things may start out fun, but they will, for the most part, end badly as you exert your desire for freedom, and Rat extends his desire for control. Your Rat partner may be a big help to you at home, but often you will find you're not on the same level. Balance the energy by hanging a Feng Shui Crystal in the North part of the house.

Horse with Ox: Difficult to balance this relationship. You are impressed with Ox's stability, yet also bored by it. You wish Ox would not be so demanding, and pretty soon, you break out of the paddock to run free. If you're trying to get your Ox partner to drop the workload and live a little, you can try hanging a Feng Shui Crystal in the North by Northwest part of the house.

Horse with Tiger: Both enjoy good times! You and Tiger are the life of the party; you are always where the action is. As long as neither of you thinks the other should sit at home, you will have a great time. Instead of fighting about who does the housework, attract more money to pay for the help by hanging a Feng Shui Crystal in the East by Northeast part of the house.

Horse with Rabbit: Given time, this can be a good relationship. At first, you will enjoy a lot of passionate fun with Rabbit; this can easily grow into trust and companionship. But keeping up the romance will take some planning. If Rabbit feels lonely at your wanderings and starts to kick up a fuss, you can balance the energy by hanging a Feng Shui Crystal in the East part of the house.

Horse with Dragon: Lively discussions and dates for these two. You are likely to be involved in the best fun together, or the biggest fights. Both of you are powerful and energetic beings, and together you are unstoppable. Try to base your relationship on what you have in common. Look for the partnership to extend to business as well as personal, and you can attract much success. Hang a Feng Shui Crystal in the East by Southeast part of the house to attract opportunities.

Horse with Snake: This is a tough match. There's a lot of finger-pointing (at each other), yet both are guilty of something. Too much complaining leads to more fights. You might win, but that just results in a squished Snake. If you're Snake partner just seems like a stick in the mud, you can loosen up the energy by hanging a Feng Shui Crystal in the South by Southeast part of the house.

Horse with Horse: Caring and sharing and having a great time, frolicking through the pastures without a care in the world. You are beautiful together, and the world is your happy playground. Sometimes you're so alike it's uncanny... and a little boring. Spice things up by hanging a Feng Shui Crystal in the South part of the house.

Horse with Sheep: If you get past the first couple of months, this can work out just fine, but Sheep's sensitive nature may take offense when you try to be honest and straightforward. Give him time to cool off, then try again. If you find your Sheep partner glum and lifeless at times, you can stimulate the positive energy by hanging a Feng Shui Crystal in the South by Southwest part of the house.

Horse with Monkey: Quite a painful duel can result from your mixing with the tricky Monkey. But if the Monkey cares about you, he will make an effort, and things may work out over the long run. You're both smart enough to understand each other. Sometimes that makes things better, but sometimes it breeds contempt. Bring in the positive energy by hanging a Feng Shui Crystal in the West by Southwest part of the house.

Horse with Rooster: There are some pluses and minuses to this pair. You may feel that Rooster is leading you around by the nose, then dropping you without a moment's notice. Guard your heart if you're interested in this chicken. If you're feeling a little hen-pecked, hang a Feng Shui Crystal in the West part of the house.

Horse with Dog: Running and playing, two hearts beating fast, this is a great match. Dog is faithful and forgiving and looks up to your power and grace. You feel gratitude and dedication in this positive puppy. But if you feel your Dog partner snapping critically at your heels, you can hang a Feng Shui Crystal in the West by Northwest part of the house.

Horse with Pig: You can't help kicking up a fuss with the fussy Pig. Pig doesn't want to do battle, but an argument usually ensues. This can be a long term relationship if you don't mind a knock-down-drag-out every few months. If your Pig partner's clingy-ness is starting to bore you, spice things up by hanging a Feng Shui Crystal in the North by Northwest part of the house.

Sheep/Goat Compatibility

Sheep with Rat: Always starts well and ends badly, as both are under the impression they have a lot in common. But it doesn't take long to figure out that Rat is not a Sheep, and you just don't see eye to eye. If Rat seems nicer over time, you might take a chance—but don't put too much money on the bet. If you are determined to make a go at this, hang a Feng Shui Crystal in the North part of the house.

Sheep with Ox: Steer clear of this steer. You're both too stubborn to compromise, and butting heads with this giant will only give you a headache. Ox is too clingy, and you want balance; this just won't work. On the other hand, Ox will get a lot of the work done before you have even stirred, so if you want to smooth out the bumps in this relationship, hang a Feng Shui Crystal in the North by Northeast part of the house.

Sheep with Tiger: Can work it out—if you can house-train this kitty. Tiger wants worship, and you usually have more sense than that. But if you can stomach giving out all that flattery, this relationship will work just fine. If you need a little something to balance out the Tiger temper, hang a Feng Shui Crystal in the East by Northeast part of the house.

Sheep with Rabbit: Hot romance is possible with this pair. Rabbit wants to go have fun, and you are more than willing. It may be a hot date night after night. If you're a Sheep who likes to stay home, you may have a little trouble convincing this bunny, but everything will work out if you exercise some patience. To ensure this positive energy, hang a Feng Shui Crystal in the East part of the house.

Sheep with Dragon: Be prepared to be completely over-whelmed by Dragon's power and enthusiasm. Later, you may feel claustrophobic in this relationship. You will have to reach a compromise to make this work, and it will have to start with you. If you want to have Dragon share in some of the relationship responsibilities, hang a Feng Shui Crystal in the East by Southeast part of the house.

Sheep with Snake: Requires a good grip to hold onto slippery Snake. You might be a little shocked at the verbal matches you are drawn into with this forked-tongued lover. If Snake cares about you, he will tone it down, and you'll work it out in the end. The solution here will be a joint effort and a real understanding of the other's position. To facilitate compromise, hang a Feng Shui Crystal in the South by Southeast part of the house.

Sheep with Horse: A fabulous time filled with banter and playful kicks at each other. This can be a wild ride if you don't take things said too personally. You both want to run; try not to run in different directions. To have the thrill of running off into the sunset together, hang a Feng Shui Crystal in the South part of the house.

Sheep with Sheep: Your friends might think this is the dullest match ever, but you feel delight as both of you do kind and thoughtful things for the other. You're happy, dancing on cloud nine. Combine your strengths and learn you can rely on each other by hanging a Feng Shui Crystal in the South by Southwest part of the house.

Sheep with Monkey: You can work anything out if you can forgive some of Monkey's antics in the beginning. Let the past be the past, and you will find that you have a lot in common. Love will bloom after a time. To encourage the love and romance, hang a Feng Shui Crystal in the West by Southwest part of the house.

Sheep with Rooster: No one is as confusing as a Rooster. You seem to have similar beliefs, and yet you go about doing things so differently. You can become a depressed little lamb if you think that Rooster will ever see your point of view. If you find the energy of your Rooster mate a bit too dizzying, hang a Feng Shui Crystal in the West part of the house.

Sheep with Dog: It's a tough life with a Dog nipping at your heels. You're not sure you want to be herded. Dog is trying to show you loyalty and love, but sometimes it feels like you are penned in at the farm just when you want to climb mountains and be free. Soon you'll be looking to unlatch the gate. If you want to stay in this energetic match, hang a Feng Shui Crystal in the West by Southwest part of the house.

Sheep with Pig: What a pretty couple you make, and you're both so nice. Sometimes Pig is too casual, and you have to do all the heavy lifting in the relationship. But if you can let it slide, this could be a very nice romance. However, if you're finding that Pig has overbooked your social calendar and you just want a break, then hang a Feng Shui Crystal in the North by Northwest part of the house.

Monkey Compatibility

Monkey with Rat: If you've got your eye on a Rat it's because you're intrigued by his clever, money-making skills. Rat is easily flattered and impressed by your ability to take chances and fly through the trees. You can find yourself in a happy relationship with no effort at all. Boost your financial prospects by hanging a Feng Shui Crystal in the North part of the house.

Monkey with Ox: This can be a great match as long as you understand that an Ox can't climb trees. Come down to share Ox's domain every once in a while, and things will be just fine between you. Ox will give you the stability you crave while not curtailing any of the fun. But if this ends up being a contest of wills, you can balance the energy by hanging a Feng Shui Crystal in the North by Northeast part of the house.

Monkey with Tiger: Very rocky, so stay out of Tiger's reach. Tiger's impulsive nature and desire to be respected above all else rubs your fur the wrong way. Consider swinging past this potential disaster. If you've already been snared by this fellow jungle creature, you can bring more love to the relationship by hanging a Feng Shui Crystal in the East by Northeast part of the house.

Monkey with Rabbit: You can have a good time if you hold back on the tricks and teasing until Rabbit is in a happy mood. An unhappy bunny will take out their pain on you, so don't push. This can be a good combination, so save your witty remarks for someone else. If you're trying to coax this Rabbit out of the house for social occasions, you can hang a Feng Shui Crystal in the East part of the house to increase the energy of fun.

Monkey with Dragon: The perfect balance between power and intelligence, even your fights are fun. Dragon will show you the big ideas, and you will show him how it can all be done. There is so much potential for this relationship. There is also the potential to extend this partnership into money-making activities. Attract wealth energy by hanging a Feng Shui Crystal in the East by Southeast part of the house.

Monkey with Snake: A long-lasting match filled with intimacy and strong feelings. Emotionally, as time goes on, you bond more and more with the wise Snake. Anytime you want, he will wrap himself around you and gently squeeze. But although there are tumultuous times due to jealousy on either side, you can temper this energy by hanging a Feng Shui Crystal in the South by Southeast part of the house.

Monkey with Horse: Is this a relationship or a competition? Sometimes you're supportive of each other, but the inflexibility of Horse means that you have to do all the compromising and understanding. After a while, this rodeo is less and less fun. If you feel like you're always coming in second place, you can hang a Feng Shui Crystal in the South part of the house to brighten up the energy.

Monkey with Sheep: This may be fun in the beginning, but Sheep has a whole bunch of rules and regulations for you to follow to stay in this relationship—rules that are sure to drain the fun right out of it. But if you can stay, it could become a happy, loving, long-lasting relationship. Balance this uncertain energy by hanging a Feng Shui Crystal in the South by Southwest part of the house.

Monkey with Monkey: Full of fun and play; this is an easy, happy relationship. There may be times when you don't see eye to eye, but keep those times brief, or one of you may find someone else to chase. Work out some boundaries, and you will be laughing together for a long time. To bond you two into a strong partnership, hang a Feng Shui Crystal in the West by Southwest part of the house.

Monkey with Rooster: Like magnets, you feel pulled magically together, but at any moment, the poles can shift, and you will find yourself repelled by each other. This is a pair born to fight, and yet should the two of you have a long relationship, it will at least be interesting. More prosperity would help you both be happy in this match, so hang a Feng Shui Crystal in the West part of the house to attract more money.

Monkey with Dog: At first, it just doesn't seem to work. You swinging in the trees, and the Dog barking and dancing around on the ground—but if you both persist, suddenly, one day everything falls into place. If you get to that point, this can be an excellent match. Remember, it's a partnership, not a competition. To blend the skills of you both, hang a Feng Shui Crystal in the West by Northwest part of the house.

Monkey with Pig: This may be the easiest relationship you'll ever find: no hassles, no commitments, just comfort, and joy. Pig would love a commitment, but he's too much in love to ask, afraid you'll run for the hills. Consider settling down with this one; this could be one you cherish. To balance and harmonize this energy, hang a Feng Shui Crystal in the North by Northwest part of the house.

Rooster Compatibility

Rooster with Rat: You might work well together with Rat, but avoid getting into a relationship with this little mouse. He discovers all your weak spots, and he'll take you down a peg or three. If you're serious about your future happiness, kiss the Rat goodbye. But if you're committed to staying, temper the little mouse's petty complaints by hanging a Feng Shui Crystal in the North part of the house.

Rooster with Ox: Potentially a very good match, because even though you're both stubborn by nature, you are stubborn about different things. There's strength in unity, and as a united front, you can have a very happy relationship. Even your fights turn out okay. Strengthen this relationship further by hanging a Feng Shui Crystal in the North by Northeast part of the house.

Rooster with Tiger: This relationship will take a lot of effort because you both have different values. You have strength, but so does Tiger—and there will be communication issues. Your friends will try to help you stay together until they get tired of trying, and then they'll suggest you part. If you want to stay together and have fun instead of fights, hang a Feng Shui Crystal in the East by Northeast part of the house.

Rooster with Rabbit: A relationship between you and Rabbit just makes for one angry bunny. You try to use logic and reason, but you just make him madder. Even though initially you felt a kinship, you're just too different to have any harmony. To get your Rabbit partner to pitch in and pull half the weight of this relationship, hang a Feng Shui Crystal in the East part of the house.

Rooster with Dragon: The perfect pair, representing the Dragon and the Phoenix, this relationship is liberating and strengthening for both. With this winged creature, you revel in feeling on top of the world. Dragon feels like he's finally got his feet on the ground. Great times ahead. Hang a Feng Shui Crystal in the East by Southeast part of the house to capitalize on this successful union.

Rooster with Snake: You may have some differences in your daily routines, but that can be to your benefit as you will enjoy the times you are together all the more. Snake may like to argue with you, but you can hold your own. In the long run, this could work. Balance the extremes in this relationship, and you can make some serious money. Hang a Feng Shui Crystal in the South by Southeast part of the house to help.

Rooster with Horse: You are probably more interested in making this work than Horse is. When you fight, it will be you who has to say, "Sorry," first. This may be fine in the beginning, but after a while of eating crow, you may just give this one up. If you insist that this is the one for you, hang a Feng Shui Crystal in the South part of the house to soothe your differences and create harmony.

Rooster with Sheep: You are probably the more impatient one, so Sheep can outlast you anytime. This will cause conflicts at home and with raising children. Sometimes you're both playing a game to see if you can get what you want, but neither of you shares your rules with the other. If you find that Goat/Sheep has a hard head and way too soft feelings, you can hang a Feng Shui Crystal in the South by Southwest part of the house to balance the energies.

Rooster with Monkey: Hard going at first, but things can be smoothed over. You may be fascinated with Monkey's clever antics, and so you keep working on it. Over time there can be progress; it depends on how much you want to sacrifice to get this to work. If you start to think that Monkey is just in it for what he or she can get, you can hang a Feng Shui Crystal in the West by Southwest part of the house to bring the scales into balance.

Rooster with Rooster: Intense passion and intense fights will typify this relationship. Feathers will fly, and lots of words will be exchanged—but what you dish out you can receive. In the end, you will stick it out because you have put so much effort into it. If you both are too focused on being right rather than being happy, hang a Feng Shui Crystal in the West area of the house to remedy this.

Rooster with Dog: A Dog around the barnyard chases the chickens rather than being guided by one, so this relationship may be about who gets to be in charge. This power struggle will continue, and getting out may be your best bet. This is not an easy time for either of you. If all this relationship has become is two people snapping at each other, hang a Feng Shui Crystal in the West by Northwest part of the house to bring in loving, harmonious energy.

Rooster with Pig: You have a true admirer in this relationship, yet you doubt, thinking this is too easy. Pig wants to make you feel comfortable and happy, and yet your eye is ever wandering. Learn to respect the Pig, and this could be a dream match. Or, toss it all away and get chicken-scratch in return. Things can be good here if you can welcome in the positive energy. Hang a Feng Shui Crystal in the North by Northwest part of the house and be prepared to be happy.

Dog Compatibility

Dog with Rat: It will take cool nerves to make this match work. There's a lot of nervous energy between the two of you, and you may find Rat running for the door. Keep the lines of communication open to make progress long term. You may find you only fight over little things. Ease the disruptive energy by hanging a Feng Shui Crystal in the North part of the house.

Dog with Ox: You two can be great together because you're both stable and want to protect your partner. But power struggles can ensue. Your best bet is to lean back and allow Ox to drag the relationship forward. Ox can hold on to hurts from past fights for a long time. Heal the energy by hanging a Feng Shui Crystal in the North by Northeast part of the house.

Dog with Tiger: After a rough beginning, a relationship of mutual respect and admiration blossoms. The attraction to each other runs deep, and both can feel great happiness here.

There are good times ahead for this cat and Dog. Together you can do a lot a good out in the world. Hang a Feng Shui Crystal in the East by Northeast part of the house and bring in the opportunities you desire.

Dog with Rabbit: After an exhilarating chase, you could end up with a perfect match between you and the happy Rabbit. You both bring something to the relationship that the other lacks, and together you make a good team. It's the tiny things, like how he or she squeezes the toothpaste, that irritates you about your partner. Hang a Feng Shui Crystal in the East part of the house and find some peace.

Dog with Dragon: This is a star-crossed pair, intense love followed by severe pain. Dragon's power may tempt you, but he'll just fly away at some point. At some level, you know this, and so you may try to leave first. Save yourself the pain and avoid this match. If you insist on staying together, you must alternate with each other on who will lead. Hang a Feng Shui Crystal in the East by Southeast part of the house to find a truce.

Dog with Snake: If you do get together—which is not easy—you will need to work on your communication with each other. You are both smart but in different ways. You are much more loyal than Snake; don't give all your loyalty until you know it will be returned. If you stay realistic, this can work, so hang a Feng Shui Crystal in the South by Southeast to improve communication.

Dog with Horse: Dating will be an exciting chase, and if you do rope this Horse, you may end up with a very happy relationship. But Horse won't be caught easily. Be prepared for some work. Once you break this Horse of running, the romance will blossom. Hang a Feng Shui Crystal in the South part of the house to encourage cooperation.

Dog with Sheep: There is such strong attraction at first, but Sheep doesn't like being herded, and you are having trouble putting up with his not agreeing with anything you say. After quarreling constantly, you may not find anything to save in this relationship. If you find you're more irritated than in love, hang a Feng Shui Crystal in the South by Southwest part of the house and smooth over the differences.

Dog with Monkey: At first sight, you didn't think this was going to be a match... and you were right! Monkey's antics and different ideas can hurt your feelings deeply. Even when it seems to be working, the timing will be off, and the gestures you offer each other are misunderstood. But if you want to make a go of it, hang a Feng Shui Crystal in the West by Southwest part of the house to attract money, which will, in turn, attract a Monkey.

Dog with Rooster: Lots of chasing can make the beginning of this relationship a little rocky. Be patient, because there is more to this than meets the eye. There is a genuine compatibility here if you can get past some of the surface irritants. If you want to do more than just coexist, hang a Feng Shui Crystal in the West part of the house to bring out the best qualities in both of you.

Dog with Dog: You can run and play together, and you'll always be competing. You may even compete to show how much you'll sacrifice for the other. If you don't mind the constant quarreling, bickering, and barking, this will work out just fine. Hang a Feng Shui Crystal in the West by Northwest part of the house to promote mutual respect and material success.

Dog with Pig: You find that Pig is a blissful partner, and have never felt so happy. This makes you nervous, which in turn makes Pig nervous—and that could bring a breaking point. But in general this is a great match, just lie down and enjoy it. Celebrate and hang a Feng Shui Crystal in the North by Northwest part of the house to attract the resources for a comfortable and happy home.

Pig/Boar Compatibility

Pig with Rat: This is an interesting match, you share many interests. You see the world in a similar way and value similar things. The little mouse may need some puffing up sometimes, but flatter him, and together you will build a comfortable house, with lots of money in the cookie jar. Hang a Feng Shui Crystal in the North part of the house to bring abundance and happiness to the relationship.

Pig with Ox: This works at first, but if you think you will get your way, you're wrong here. You may be obstinate, but nothing beats an Ox for sheer stubbornness. The more you push, the more he will not budge. Save yourself the effort and pass on this match. If you plan to stay in this relationship, hang a Feng Shui Crystal in the North by Northeast part of the house to relieve some of the friction.

Pig with Tiger: You may think the hungry Tiger will have you for dinner on your first date, but after the initial nerves of a new relationship, you two can settle down and make a good match. Tiger's possessiveness will feel comforting and protective. Hang a Feng Shui Crystal in the East by Northeast part of the house to bring joy, laughter, and good times.

Pig with Rabbit: Once you get past the well-meaning criticism by this little bunny, you have a thoughtful, interested partner with whom you can share much. Rabbit may be slower to realize how good a match this is, so be patient. Rabbit will happily receive the outpouring of your affection, so to get some in return, hang a Feng Shui Crystal in the East part of the house.

Pig with Dragon: You are dazzled by the power and vision of your Dragon partner. He loves coming down to earth to be with you. While your friends may not understand this match, you are in heaven. You are sailing on the back of a Dragon. At times one or both of you will get carried away; balance out the energy by hanging a Feng Shui Crystal in the East by Southeast part of the house.

Pig with Snake: You have so many differences that you can't even begin to communicate. You are naturally nervous around the clever Snake, and so you become rigid and critical. It's not you; it's just a bad match. If you're staying in the partnership but can't stand all the secrets, hang a Feng Shui Crystal in the South by Southeast part of the house and let what's been hidden come out.

Pig with Horse: Horse feels this is a great relationship and that nothing needs to change. You, on the other hand, have a list of what needs to happen to start making this a happy relationship. But none of your subtle signals or overt signs will be a clue to over-confident Horse. To get your pony partner to pay attention, hang a Feng Shui Crystal in the South part of the house.

Pig with Sheep: Can work, but certainly not the most exciting relationship you'll ever have. This feels like the backup date for New Year's—maybe someone who might be a friend, but the passion's not there. If you want commitment, demand it; otherwise, let this one go. Stir up the romance here by hanging a Feng Shui Crystal in the South by Southwest part of the house and watch the magic happen.

Pig with Monkey: You and Monkey are so different, but somehow it works. This relationship is like a fine wine; it needs to age—and you both will occasionally need some time to breathe. Some irritations on both sides can make this relationship feel sour. Hang a Feng Shui Crystal in the West by Southwest part of the house to sweeten up your love life.

Pig with Rooster: As barnyard buddies, this is tough in the beginning as Rooster wants to be in charge. You will find it hard to get respect from this bossy boss as he is sure he rules the roost. But deep down, there is more love here than you may think. Give this a try before saying goodbye. Between the two of you, there is a solution to every problem. Hang a Feng Shui Crystal in the West part of the house to attract the solutions easily.

Pig with Dog: You feel secure and safe with Dog (and nipped at, and barked at, too). There are some strong positives in this relationship and a big helping of irritants. Give nervous Dog some time to settle into the relationship, and you will feel safe and loved in no time. If you find your lively pup too quick with the criticism, hang a Feng Shui Crystal in the West by Northwest part of the house to soften his or her words.

Pig with Pig: Hand in hand, here's a perfect match. You both share great depth of feeling and compassion for the other. Communication is fun and easy, and you spend many nights just staying up and talking. This may get to be a little routine after a while, but the deep feeling of happiness will last. Together you both give too much and may find others taking advantage of your kindness. Hang a Feng Shui Crystal in the North by Northwest part of the house to protect your finances.

Eclipses

Eclipses, both Solar and Lunar, happen six times between January 2020 and the end of January 2021. Eclipses signal times of change. Even for those who are unaware of an eclipse, its energy can throw a wrench into your plans. Fortunately, we often feel the energy of an eclipse up to a couple of weeks before the actual event.

It's always a good idea to find an astrologer to offer you some personal advice around the time of an upcoming series of eclipses. Or, if you can find a reliable resource for information about the effects of a specific eclipse, you may be able to determine what does need to change in your life. This gives you a chance to take action.

It makes a difference, believe me! It's as if you have a choice between being hit by a wave, versus being on your surfboard, ready to catch a wave and ride it all the way to the beach.

Eclipses are noted in most daily news websites and the weather section of a newspaper so you can see when one is about to happen. But it takes an Astrologer to tell you exactly where the eclipses hit in your chart, so you can be aware of the approaching energy, and keep an eye out for potential surfboards to grab hold of as you get ready to ride.

There will be a penumbral Lunar eclipse on January 10, 2020. This eclipse will be at 19 degrees of Capricorn. If you were born between January 5 and January 11, this eclipse will have a strong effect on your life.

There will be a penumbral Lunar eclipse on June 5, 2020. This eclipse will be at 15 degrees of Sagittarius. If you were born between December 3 and December 13, this eclipse will have a strong effect on your life.

There will be an annular Solar eclipse on June 20, 2020. This eclipse will be at 0 degrees of Cancer. If you were born between June 17 and June 27, this eclipse will have a strong effect on your life.

There will be a penumbral Lunar eclipse on July 4, 2020. This eclipse will be at 13 degrees of Capricorn. If you were born between December 1 and December 11, this eclipse will have a strong effect on your life.

There will be a penumbral Lunar eclipse on November 30, 2020. This eclipse will be at 8 degrees of Gemini. If you were born between May 24 and June 4, this eclipse will have a strong effect on your life.

There will be a total Solar eclipse on December 14, 2020. This eclipse will be at 23 degrees of Sagittarius. If you were born between December 11 and December 21, this eclipse will have a strong effect on your life.

Tip: It's a good idea to consider challenging areas of your life, and choose to make some changes. For instance, if you have been thinking about changing jobs for a time, it would be an excellent idea to get your resume ready. If you've been thinking that you're unhappy with your home, it's probably a good idea to start looking around for a new place. Or, if you've been thinking your relationship is unsatisfying, this may be the right time to sit down and have a chat with your partner (or consider packing your bags).

While eclipses may sound scary, you've actually been through many of them in your life. You've been through at least four eclipses each year since you were born. Every 8-9 years, the eclipse hits your chart with a bang like ringing a very loud bell. This is a signal that something in your life needs to change. The best course of action is to challenge yourself in whatever area of life you may feel "stuck." For more information on Eclipses, check out Diane Ronngren's book by the same name.

Mercury Retrograde

Each element of the five Chinese elements is ruled by a planet. The Chinese elements associated with the planets translate into the Western tradition as follows:

Wood is ruled by Jupiter, the largest planet in the solar system (named for the Roman king of the gods).

Fire is ruled by Mars, the red planet (named for the Roman god of war).

Earth is ruled by Saturn (named after the Roman god of agriculture).

Metal is ruled by Venus (named after the Roman goddess of prosperity).

Water is ruled by Mercury (named after the Roman winged messenger god).

2020 is a Metal year, so the energy of the planet Venus will figure prominently. Earth is necessary to create Metal, so Saturn is an important planet this year as well. Mercury is not directly involved with the main elements this year, so it will be somewhat easier to navigate through Mercury Retrograde periods.

Mercury Retrograde is an astronomical phenomenon that happens three or four times a year and has a very disruptive effect on those of us living on planet Earth. Things we rely on in our daily lives and work (such as our computers, cell phones, vehicles, email, snail mail, etc.) all seem to go a little haywire during Mercury Retrograde. Specifically, Mercury Retrograde can cause you to need to repeat something.

During this Rat year, the Mercury Retrograde periods will be:

February 16, 2020 to March 9, 2020

June 17, 2020 to July 12, 2020

October 13, 2020 to November 3, 2020

A few weeks before Mercury goes retrograde each time, it's a good idea to back up your computer. While you're at it, back up your cell phone contacts. If you're planning to have some work done on the car, try to get it finished before Mercury goes retrograde.

Anything you don't want to repeat—such as moving, lawsuits, root canals, surgery, expensive repairs, custody battles, breakups—you will be better off if you can avoid doing them during Mercury retrograde.

If at all possible, avoid purchasing electronics during the retrograde, especially ones you can't return. Make copies of important documents before you send them, as they may not reach their destination. If you are issued one traffic ticket, you're likely to get a second ticket during this period, so drive safely.

If you have to return your cable box, renew your driver's license, or make a doctor's appointment, take a book with you (something long, like one by Tolstoy). It's going to take a while.

During the retrograde, plan and do things you don't mind repeating. Take a vacation—but beware, sometimes Mercury Retrograde can send your luggage to Baltimore (even if you're going somewhere else). However, if you do carry-on, you'll probably be fine.

Visit a spa, have a massage, enjoy a romantic dinner with someone you love, or have a party with good friends. These are all things you might enjoy doing multiple times.

Start exercising. If you drop the program, you are very likely to be inspired to pick it up again at the next retrograde. Or, buy yourself some jewelry or a new pair of shoes, that's something none of us women mind repeating!

For more information on *Mercury Retrograde*, check out the booklet by Diane Ronngren.

What Is Feng Shui and How to Use Cures

This book is different than most Chinese Astrology books. It contains information on usable Feng Shui cures to turn bad luck into good and make stuck, negative energy flow and be positive.

Feng Shui is the ancient Chinese art of placement. Feng Shui is based on the concept that everything present in our environment affects us: the colors, shapes, symbols, building layout, furniture, and décor affect our energy, mood, and decision-making process.

Consider for a moment two buildings which both represent how we connect with money: a casino, and a bank. When you walk into a casino, your head spins with all there is to see. There are flashing lights in every direction, ringing bells signaling a win, the sounds of coins falling. You can feel the abundance of good fortune and money, money, money.

Looking down at your feet, you'll see the floor carpeted in a busy, colorful pattern. Look up, and you will see moving lights, curved ceiling soffits guiding us in different directions, and huge rooms filled with aisles of machines, tables, and open chairs inviting us to be seated. There is an overwhelming feeling originating from this décor; it tantalizes: "You'd be a fool not to sit down and try your luck," it tempts us.

Contrast this feeling with the one you have in a bank. The environment here is also a large room, but this room is nearly silent. People speak in lowered voices. A velvet rope guides us to a waiting teller who sits (or stands) behind a marble counter (perhaps even behind a plexiglass shield).

Behind her is a large round door made of shiny metal, a foot and half thick, standing open to reveal a few safe deposit boxes. Even though we know there are no stacks of money in the vault and it's mostly a prop, the image created by all of it still gives us the impression that our money is safe.

We're all affected by the décor of a place. We may not think so per se, but run-down areas in need of repairs cause us to feel less hopeful. We are more apt to believe it's not worth the effort to try something new.

When we see a neighborhood with flowers and manicured yards, we become more optimistic. We feel a sense of possibility, the desire and willingness to take on new things. When we face a desk topped with disorganized clutter, we'll likely avoid working on our finances, and instead, check out what's on the television (or on Facebook).

Thousands of years ago, it was found that if you set up a temple or a palace in a certain way, the people in these environments would make better decisions. They would become more prosperous and happy. Scholars of the time collected this information and created a system they called Feng Shui. In the West, we know this system as Environmental Psychology.

Feng Shui is much more complex than merely cleaning up the clutter in your home or office—this is what many Westerners think about when they hear the term. Clearing away clutter is almost always a beneficial activity to carry out when we want to improve our environment. But it's important to understand that to achieve the best effect from our Feng Shui efforts, we must learn to place certain objects in specific places with the intention of creating harmonious change in our lives.

There are many schools of Feng Shui. Different schools emerged at different times and in different areas of China and the Far East. Some schools were formed in mountainous regions and were based on the topography of mountains, rivers, and lakes. Some schools were more focused on Astrology and timing, and these practitioners would predict the future and change things around as the seasons changed. Some schools used a compass to measure the quality and quantity of energy from each direction.

All of the schools of Feng Shui are valid. They all work. For our purposes, we're going to focus on a school called Form

School, which has straightforward principles we can readily apply to a western way of thinking about traditional and environmental practices.

Your Front Door: The front door is where all new energy will enter the home, and therefore your life. Even if you never use your front door, this is the traditional area of a home where all new energy is welcomed into the lives of the people who reside in the home. (If you found stranger coming through your back door you'd call the police). If you invited the CEO of your company to dinner, you wouldn't say, "Just go through the garage, squeeze past my car, past my boxes of Christmas decorations, and old ski equipment, until you find the door into the kitchen."

Important people are greeted at the front door and invited to enter a home or place of business. Many deliveries are made to the front door of a home or apartment residence. Using this principle, when we want something new, such as a new job, new love, money from a new source, etc., we will concentrate on the area around the front door (inside and out).

Your Bedroom: Your bedroom is where love happens. If you want to attract a new relationship or you want to improve your existing relationship, your bedroom is the area of the home we are going to focus on. We also look at the bedroom when you want to conceive a child, to rest, or to recover from illness. So, if you have trouble sleeping, or if you are recovering from something, we want to focus our attention on your bedroom.

The Kitchen: Your kitchen is your source of health and weight loss. Kitchens tend to be the most powerful rooms in the house. You can confirm this by observing that when you have a party. Often your guests want to gather together in the kitchen. Kitchens are where we cook and prepare our food; food is the key to our health and well-being.

The Living Room: If you want to attract new friends, but not necessarily an intimate partner, focus on your living room. The living room represents a public area of the home where we can welcome and entertain people without revealing the private areas of the home (like a bedroom). Thus, when we entertain people in our living room, we can enjoy people, yet safeguard the private things in our lives.

The Family Room: If you have a separate Family Room, focus on this area to enhance family relations overall—both between members of the family who live with you and those who live elsewhere. So if your family fights (or is dysfunctional in some other way), or the teenagers are sullen and uncooperative, this is the area your Feng Shui practitioner will focus on. (If you only have a Living Room, then we would focus on that area for family relations.)

The Home Office: If you have a separate room where you take care of bills and investments, or a room from which you run your home business, focus on this room when we seek to increase prosperity. If you don't have a separate office, consider the area where you do pay your bills—whether at the kitchen table, in your bedroom, or in the dining room. (Or, we can focus on enhancing the area around your front door for bringing in money.)

The Dining Room: If you have a separate dining room, it affects not only family relations but also your weight and the weight of all who live in the home. If you are trying to lose (or to gain) weight, we will consider this area, even if meals are seldom served in this room.

The Bathroom: There are a lot of Feng Shui rules and misinterpretations around the bathroom. The bathroom is an area for health, but it can also be an area that affects the prosperity of everyone in the home. When things are not going well in your life, this is the first area we consider.

Other rooms like garages, media rooms, craft rooms, guest bedrooms, and more, all have energy linked to their use. In general, they are not as significant as the rooms previously mentioned.

There are, however, some exceptions. If you run a classic car business out of your garage, then the state of your garage will affect your success in your business. If you have a guest who is driving you crazy and won't leave your home, the state of your guest room will affect how your guest is treating you—even how long they'll stay. For tips on these and other more specific situations, contact me for a personal consultation, or see my book, Feng Shui Form.

Now that we have examined the energy of the various spaces in a home, let's define the concept of a Feng Shui cure. If you've ever experienced acupuncture, you know the doctor uses tiny needles, placed in specific areas of the body to stimulate your body's energy and natural healing ability.

Feng Shui cures are similar to these acupuncture needles—they are intended to stimulate your home's energy and help create benefit, good fortune, and natural harmony by working within the environment of your home, instead of your physical body. Cures are objects which represent a specific energy: such as love or money. For example, a heart-shaped pillow would be a representation, a cure, of love energy. (The heart shape is a universal symbol of love.)

Universal and cultural symbols make the most powerful cures in Feng Shui. This may all sound a little strange, But Feng Shui cures do work, just as the acupuncture needles stimulate specific body energy and facilitate our natural healing ability. If you want to know more about the science behind Feng Shui energy, keep reading; otherwise, you can skip to the next section.

Why Feng Shui Works

It may sound strange to you that placing a gold cat bank in the far left corner of your home would attract money, but it does. The Feng Shui cure is based on two principles. The first is the idea of collective consciousness.

Collective consciousness is a shared idea which creates a unifying force in the world.

One example might be the number of people who are afraid of spiders. Spiders shouldn't be scary; they're tiny, and they tend to mind their own business. But some people are so afraid of them that they are classified arachnophobic, even when they have not had personal, life-threatening encounters with spiders. In humankind's past, spiders have been perceived to be dangerous in many cultures. So today, many, many people have this innate fear.

Likewise, most people in the world for centuries have considered round metal discs to be money. Even currency from a foreign country is still seen as valuable, even when it cannot be spent at the neighborhood store. Many objects not only have a universal meaning but also evoke an emotion. They are potent symbols in our collective consciousness.

Besides universal symbols, there are also cultural symbols—particular to one culture, but not another. They also can be used very effectively (in fact, I have found using symbols from a different culture is particularly effective).

A symbol, such as a gold cat bank (a.k.a. Lucky Money Cat), is a popular symbol in Asia and works very well here in the U.S. If you have enjoyed a meal at a Chinese restaurant recently, you have probably seen one of these symbols next to the cash register, Lucky Money Cat waving his little golden arm, calling in money.

The reason cultural symbols work is there are enough people in the world who understand the symbol and connect to it emotionally; a mini "collective consciousness" is formed.

Our Reticular Activating System

The second reason Feng Shui cures work is our Reticular Activating System. This is a system within each of us, which allows us to filter the information reaching us through our five senses. If we were actually aware of all of the information bombarding us all the time, we would go mad.

For instance, just sitting here at my computer, if I were also listening to the computer hum, and the traffic outside, and the ticking clock, while watching the sun go down, observing the computer screen, not to mention all the things I'm touching, smelling, and tasting simultaneously, I would be completely overwhelmed. But fortunately, my Reticular Activating System allows me to focus only on the task at hand.

Your own Reticular Activating System activates when you place a Lucky Money Cat somewhere in your space. When you place your Lucky Money Cat in the far left corner of your home, also known as "the wealth corner," your subconscious awakens and begins to look for money opportunities.

When the money opportunity is detected, your ERAS-system alerts your brain. These opportunities were around you already, but you were unable to identify them specifically. Therefore, it was impossible for you to grasp them or focus on taking necessary action. But when your Reticular Activating System uncovered the opportunities around you, they became clear to your conscious mind, and now it is easy to welcome in the new money.

Because of these two reasons, Feng Shui cures work. It is essential to understand why we use universal or cultural symbols, rather than just any old item/personal symbol. For example, you might tell me that for you, the vulture is a symbol of love because your beloved had a vulture tattoo on his right shoulder.

But this symbol is only a love symbol for you (and this particular relationship). So all the energy behind this symbol must be generated by you alone. If you're interested in focusing on vulture-tattoo-guy, you can fill your house with vultures, and it will possibly attract his energy to your door.

But let's say you want to attract a new man—maybe one who is vulture-free. In that case, it will be much easier to attract the new love energy if you choose to use a universal or cultural symbol of love. Many other people recognize these symbols. When you choose to use one of them, the combined energy of all of these others who acknowledge this symbol as a sign of love combines with your energy to attract what you want.

The peony flower is a cultural symbol of love. In Chinese art, this symbol is used to represent love and beauty. So if you choose to use this symbol, your energy combines with a couple of billion other people who also use this symbol to attract love. By using the collective consciousness, and your Reticular Activating System, you can use specific objects to attract wealth, love, and other things you want into your life.

As we talk about the individual predictions for each sign, I will be suggesting specific Feng Shui cures for creating the most positive energy for your year. You can substitute these cultural symbols for universal symbols if you choose. If you have questions about these concepts or substituting cures, you can write to me at DONNASTELLHORN@GMAIL.COM

2020 Flying Star

8—Northwest	3—North	1—Northeast
Prosperity Star: very lucky	Conflict Star: unlucky	White Star: very lucky
To increase happiness, wealth, and family unity, add fire by burning white or gold candles.	If there are problems with career, lawsuits, or arguments, burn off excess energy by burning a blue or yellow candle.	To increase wealth and fame and improve career, add Earth by adding granite, marble, or citrine.
To balance career energy and have good relations with kids, add Earth by placing a clear quartz crystal.	If you need a job or lots of change, add a string or a pile of coins.	To balance spirituality and thinking, add metal in the form of a music box or iPad dock.
9—West	**7—Center**	**5—East**
Future Prosperity Star: lucky	Violent Star: unlucky	Misfortune Star: very unlucky
To increase achievement and growth, add wood such as green, healthy plants.	To decrease bad luck, add Water.	To protect from accidents,illness, or lawsuits, remove stone and heavy objects.
To have good luck, add Fire by burning purple or gold candles.	To protect from robbery, legal problems, injury, and health issues, burn off excess negative energy by burning black or dark blue candles. Add exterior lighting or keep the porch light on.	To balance mental energy and have happier children, place coins.
4—Southwest	**2—South**	**6—Southeast**
Romance Star: lucky	Illness Star: unlucky	Luck Star: lucky
To attract romance and have better career and education choices, add the color red and pairs of ducks.	To protect against illness or loneliness, reduce negative energy by adding plants, dried medicinal herbs, or pictures of flowers.	To increase success in career, military, science, or technology, add large crystals like citrine, amethyst, and smoky quartz.
	To balance health, pregnancy, or communication, add a six-rod metal wind chime.	To balance energy of health and wealth, add brass vases or bowls.

Flying Star for 2020

Each year the energy changes and "stars" fly into new locations. Some directions which may have indicated positive, lucky energy last year, become weaker and unlucky this year. Some, which vibrated with weak, unlucky energy in the past, have found strength and become more positive for us now.

In other forms of Feng Shui, we are concerned with the directions of our home, based on the position of the front door, but not with Flying Star. With Flying Star, we are concerned with compass directions.

The general principle of Flying Star is to increase energy in the directions of good stars and reduce energy in the direction of bad stars. If you live in a giant mansion and your bedroom is now on a negative star, you can choose a new bedroom to sleep in. But for the rest of us, we use "cures" to mitigate the negative energy and to increase the positive energy. Here's the forecast for 2020:

Flying Star 1—The White Star: Luck finds its way to the Northeast of the house with the 1-Star. This is a star whose energy has changed over the last few thousand years. It has become more lucky, although it's a good idea to keep its history in mind as you increase the energy of this star.

If, after placing the cures, you find things are not going as well as you hoped, switch from increasing the energy (by adding water or metal cures) to reducing the energy (by adding wood cures).

That being said, to increase wealth and fame and improve career, increase the earthy energy by adding granite, marble, or citrine (a gemstone) to your space. To balance spirituality and clear thinking, add metal in the form of a music box, or an iPod/radio.

Flying Star 2—The Illness Star: A somewhat unlucky star, the 2-Star, flies to the South. I say this star is somewhat unlucky because years ago in China, this was a lucky star for those people working in government. Therefore, if you have a government job, you can receive some benefit from this star.

But, for the rest of us, this Star can cause health problems, especially digestive and intestinal problems. To protect from illness and loneliness, reduce the effects of the negative energy by adding live plants, bundles of dried medicinal herbs, or pictures of flowers to the South part of your home.

If you are or become pregnant, you can support and protect the pregnancy by adding a six-rod metal wind chime outside of the South part of the house.

Flying Star 3—The Conflict Star: The somewhat unlucky 3-Star flies to the North this year. This is the star of quarreling and disputes, but its energy can be directed positively to help you keep a job and pay your bills. Balancing the energy of the 3-Star is important.

If you are having problems with career, lawsuits, or arguments, burn off the excess negative energy by burning a blue or yellow candle in this area once a month on the full moon. If you are in search of a job, need more work, or wish to preserve a source of income, set a small pile of coins (choose an odd number of coins) on a windowsill facing the North of the space.

Flying Star 4—The Romance Star: The 4-Star lands in the Southwest this year, and brings with it mixed luck. This star is both associated with positive romance and career opportunities, but it is also known as "The Six Curses." Like the 1-Star in the Northeast, as you enhance the energy in the Southwest, notice how your luck changes.

If you find that your experiences in the area of romance are not as positive as you would like, add fire (by burning candles or wood in a fireplace) to reduce the 4-Star energy. Also, be cautious about participating in games of speculation, or signing off on risky investments.

To enjoy more romance, add the color red, and pairs of Mandarin ducks as cures. To protect against bad investments, add silver or Chinese coins. For better education and career choices, add green plants with round-shaped leaves.

Flying Star 5—The Misfortune Star: Trouble comes as the 5-Star flies to the East this year. This star represents illness, potential disaster, and lack of knowledge. To protect from accidents, illness, and lawsuits, remove stone and heavy objects from the East area of the house.

If heavy objects are attached to the house (such as a stone fireplace), channel some of that energy away from the East of the house by adding objects made of wood, like a wood bowl, wood furniture, or a picture of trees. To balance stressful energy and to have happier children, place pictures of them in metal frames in this area.

Flying Star 6—The Heaven Luck Star: The 6-Star flies to the Southeast this year, and luck comes with it. To increase success in career, military service, science, or technology, add large crystals (over 2 inches) like citrine, amethyst, and smoky quartz to the Southeast part of the home.

To balance the energy of health and wealth, add brass vases or bowls. You can place messages and wishes for your family's health and prosperity in the bowls each New Moon.

Flying Star 7—The Violent Star: The unlucky 7-Star flies to the Center this year, and brings the very unlucky energy of robbery, legal troubles, fire, injury, and arguments. To decrease bad luck, add the Water element. Good Water element representations are fountains, fish tanks, pictures of moving water, or decorative objects made of glass.

To protect yourself from robbery, legal problems, injury, and health issues, it is best to 'burn off' excess negative energy by burning black or dark blue candles once a month. Because this is the Violent Star, adding protective symbols to the Center of your home is wise. These can be things from your ancestors, your religion, or your country.

Flying Star 8—The Prosperity Star: Luck moves to the Northwest as the 8-Star finds it's home there for the year. This is the area of your home or space to enhance and to experience increased happiness, wealth, and family unity. Do so by adding representations of fire. For instance, you can place red pillows or art that depicts a distinct triangular shape; or burn white or gold candles in this part of the home.

To balance career energy and enhance good relations with children and young people, add earth to the 8-Star area by placing clear quartz crystals on a table at the Northwest of the house.

Flying Star 9—The Future Prosperity Star: This star brings us more lucky energy. The very lucky 9-Star flies to the West this year. This is your success area for the year. Try to do things like goal setting, meditating, beginning new projects, or making important contacts by phone from this area of your home or office.

To increase achievement and growth, add wood energy to the space with things like green, healthy plants, pictures of forests and greenery, or add a new wood floor. To increase good luck and good fortune, add fire cures by burning purple or gold candles once a month.

For more information on the cures mentioned in this book, refer to the Feng Shui cure guide at the back of my book, "Feng Shui Form." In it, you will find an 80-page guide to how to use Feng Shui cures.

The Grand Duke (or Tai Sui) lives in the Northwest area this year between 352.5 degrees and 7.5 degrees. You can use a compass to find these exact degrees.

The Grand Duke doesn't like being disturbed. The Grand Duke is like the King of all the Kings. It's said that you cannot confront him, only show him deference and respect. This year, those born in the Year of the Snake should keep a protective Feng Shui cure by their bed. This could be a Pi Yao (winged lion) statue or a Tai Sui plaque.

This year you can plant a tree in the Grand Duke's section of your property to show your respect. But beware, you cannot cut down a tree in this direction, or there will be misfortune. Also, be cautious about doing construction or renovation in this area of your home or your property this year, as the process can be plagued with problems, and bring trouble to the household.

The Five Elements

Rat's natural element is Yang Water. With the active, fast-moving Rat energy this year, we feel the power and dynamic nature of this element. In 2020 we are in a Yang Metal year. With this combination, the desire to create and manifest will be strong. Quick actions combined with bold ideas will bring fruit. At the same time, we need to be aware of the others we care about who may not be moving so quickly. You may not need to wait for them or to carry them, but to allow them their journey at the speed they choose. Don't hurry them along, and don't hold yourself back.

Earth and Water are just two of the elements. The ancient Chinese philosophers looked at the world and categorized all they could see into five elements, five building blocks which are the basis of all things. The five elements and their representations are:

Wood—represents growth and all things that grow.

Fire—represents energy itself and all of the things energy creates or produces.

Earth—represents stability and things in a state of rest.

Metal—represents resources and things that make up the material of tools.

Water—symbolizes connectivity, things that help connect one thing to another.

As mentioned previously, each of the five elements can be either Yin or Yang. Yin represents the more subtle and flowing energy, and Yang represents the more "in-your-face," direct energy. The Yin/Yang symbol is probably familiar to you. The black part represents Yin, and the white part is Yang.

The dot in the opposing color in the Yin/Yang symbol represents the concept: "One cannot exist without the other." To understand the concept of larger, we must be familiar with smaller. For us to understand the essence of weaker, we must know stronger.

Each of the five elements exists in a state of Yin or Yang.

Yang Wood is like a forest of the tallest trees, growing in the wild. Or, energetically, it is expressed in the life of the student who studies all the time. It is like the feeling of being on a new job, where you have to learn everything as quickly as possible (and you love every moment of it.)

Yin Wood is like a seedling, just popping out of the dirt to see the sun for the first time. It's the realization that you've grown as a person and don't need as much help as you did when you were younger. It's the act of tweaking a favorite recipe with just one new ingredient, to see what it will taste like.

Yang Fire is a forest fire burning out of control. It's like celebrating a college spring break at a beachside resort, daddy's credit card in hand. Or, it's like driving in a NASCAR race, exhilarating, demanding your entire focus and all your attention, simply to keep from crashing.

Yin Fire can be represented with the image of a match or a single candle. Imagine the energy of taking a stroll down a beautiful path and having the time to enjoy nature. Or, think of the amount of energy our body uses to digest food: it happens automatically, without effort or thought.

Yang Earth is a tall mountain, majestic, and still. It's like a lazy retirement, one where you enjoy your time sitting on the porch, day after day, in a comfortable chair. There are no worries about finances. There are no obligations to create stress in your life.

Yin Earth is like a sandy beach, flat and smooth. It's like a Sunday afternoon in summer, nothing pulling at you, your list of chores is completed. You take a restful, peaceful nap.

Yang Metal is similar to the power of collecting gold bars, having them stacked, and representing greater abundance than you will ever need. It's a world filled with unlimited resources. You can present a Black Visa card and purchase anything you wish. Or, it's like becoming CEO and receiving or having access to all the perks.

Yin Metal is like possessing a stack of coins or receiving a regular paycheck: you have just enough to feel secure; you can count on support to arrive as expected, week after week. It's like having just the right amount of cash in your pocket to buy what you need at the store.

Yang Water is a springtime waterfall, rushing downhill and churning up the body of water below. It's water bursting from a dam and rushing towards the town. Or, it's like melted snow pouring down the mountainside to flood the fields below.

Yin Water is like a still pond on a summer's day, no movement on the surface, it appears to be as still as a sheet of glass in the sunlight. Or, it's like a peaceful lake in the quiet of a moonlit night, the reflection of the moon glimmering on the surface. It's a glass of water, the exact perfect amount you need to drink to quench your thirst.

When the ancient people who brought us Feng Shui looked at the world, they divided every existing thing into these Five Elements. They also observed how one element could interact with another. This interaction can be seen in a *Creative Cycle* or a *Destructive Cycle*.

The Creative Cycle is: Wood creates Fire, Fire creates Earth (by producing ash), Earth produces Metal (because when we dig into the earth we find metal), Metal produces Water (when metal becomes cold it pulls water from the air in the form of condensation) and Water produces Wood (when water is poured on the ground, things grow).

The Destructive Cycle is: Wood depletes Earth (Trees and plants take nutrients from the earth), Earth blocks Water (dams can be made of earth), Water puts out Fire, Fire melts Metal, and Metal chops Wood (when metal is formed into an ax or other sharp tool, it can cut wood).

In Feng Shui, we are always looking for the *larger* to support the *smaller*. For example, if you, as a single individual, need to feed and clothe your entire community, you would soon become depleted of energy and resources. But if the community helps feed and clothe you, food and clothing would be abundant for you.

This year is a Metal Year. Your individual element may be in harmony with this year's element being part of the Creative Cycle; or, your individual element may be in disharmony with this year's element by being part of the Destructive Cycle. Check the list at the beginning of the book and find your element.

If your element is Wood: Your element is Wood, and the element this year is Metal. You are on the destructive cycle as Metal chops Wood. The opportunities that come you may not be in a form you first recognize. You might think you're not qualified for the job, or this is not the type of person you normally date. But in the destructive cycle, if you allow it, the opportunities can remake you into something stronger and better. You may feel some fear, but fortunately, Wood element people are nearly fearless when they have the opportunity for growth.

At the same time, in this destructive cycle, there will be many who tell you who you should be. These might be teachers or advertisers, or it might be your parents or your partner. Some will mean well, some just want your money. It's imperative you stay on your path. Not sure what your path is? This year it will be the way that feels like a leap, where you have to do more than you thought you were capable of. And as you leap, fears will disappear, and things will work out better than you hoped.

If your element is Fire: Your element is Fire, and the element of this year is Metal; Fire melts Metal. You, the individual, are trying to melt the world, to form it into what you want, to hammer out the opportunities you've been looking for. This means you have an endless supply of materials (opportunities for career, for love, for creativity), but since you are only one person, your flame is much smaller than the world. You must work at building your flame through the practice of your craft and the understanding of what you want to create.

Many people will be coming to you with offers and opportunities, but you have limited resources and so, in the words of the old saying, "How do you eat an elephant? One bite at a time." It will be necessary for you to have patience in an impatient world. You will need to do homework ahead of time, not on the bus on your way to the test. But if you can get a clear picture of what you want to achieve and the type of people you want to connect with, this will be a great year because an abundance of choices is available to you.

If your element is Metal: Your element is Metal, and this year's element is Metal, so you are in harmony with the energy. You have an innate understanding of the energy of Metal and its desire to collect and organize resources. You are admired for your skill and efficiency this year. Cultivate your ability to see situations clearly, to make the list of steps, outline the action plan, find the support and resources so you can begin. Beginning will be the most important action this year. Without beginning it's just a plan on paper.

Your challenge this year is to avoid getting bogged down, doing so much planning and organizing that the real work doesn't begin. You can gain much insight brainstorming with friends and organizing your ideas on paper (or an app will work too). Don't hold back when you have a working plan. Don't wait for perfection. Take action and things will go well.

If your element is Water: Your element is Water, and this is a Metal year. You are on the creative cycle as Metal creates Water. This year the whole world is available to offer support and help with your ventures. This doesn't mean everyone will line up in perfect order. There will be many who come to you with an agenda. But in the context of what they are offering, it's possible to find some benefit for both of you.

Water takes no particular shape. It wants to flow from one place to another. The Metal element represents a container. This means many opportunities coming to you may seem limiting, even constricting. We all see how Metal creates Water as water drops gather on the outside of a cool metal container. Water is not contained. So when the opportunities come, it would be good for you to remake the job you have into what you want it to be; or shift the friendship in the direction that suits you. You are in a powerful position this year. Any limitations you perceive are based on your own fears. Release them, and you will find success.

If your element is Earth: Your element is Earth, and this year the element is Metal. You are on the creative cycle as Earth creates Metal, however you, the smaller, are trying to create the larger: the whole Earth. This means that nearly everyone you meet will believe you are vital to their success. You may be pulled in every direction. Many projects and opportunities will come to you, but many of these will be more work than what you are looking for, and certainly not all of them will be along the path you want to take.

This year you must consider what you want to accomplish and be choosy about where and when you get involved in other people's plans. As you begin to gather a team for yourself, others may say their projects are more important, and move yours to the bottom of the list. You are experiencing positive energy this year, so you can make sure this doesn't happen, but if you are not paying attention, you may end up doing the lion's share for little credit. Take the time to find the right fit, and you will achieve what you want.

Using and Clearing Feng Shui Cures

"Okay, I did what you said, and it worked for a little while, but now it's not working."

When we place an object to attract new energy—and we place it correctly—we will get results within the first week. But after that, the energy will start to dissipate. There are several reasons for this.

Mainly, we are very quick to adapt to the new energy, and so even though new energy is flowing in; we cease to notice it. Also, when we first place the Feng Shui cure, we see it every day, but after a time it becomes part of the background and therefore is no longer activating our subconscious.

Often, the solution is to move the cure, or if that's not possible, to take the cure down and dust it off and then replace it where it was. I had a client who was using my "double lucky money fish" cure to attract money. She placed a pair of fish by her front door, and business started to flow in effortlessly. However, after a week or two, she would become overwhelmed by so many new clients.

So she would take the "double lucky money fish" cure away from her front door, and place the cure in her home office instead. The result of this was she would receive quick and easy payment from her clients.

Then, after a couple of weeks, she would find she needed new clients again. So she would take the "double lucky money fish" cure and once again hang them by her front door. By moving the fish over and over, she was always attracting positive money energy.

How to Clear Gemstones and Crystals

After a few weeks, gemstones and crystals have been absorbing energy, and it can seem they are not as effective as they were when you first placed them. Here is an easy solution. The gemstone or crystal needs clearing. There are several methods you can use. Each is very effective, choose the method that is most convenient for you.

Clearing with Sage: you can smudge the gemstone or crystal using Sage. Take your smudge stick and light it, then pass the crystal through the smoke several times. Turn the crystal so the smoke touches all sides. The crystal is now clear, and you can hang it back up where it was. You should see a bump up in the energy levels during the next few days.

Clearing with Salt: you can clear gemstones and crystals using salt. Some gemstones and crystals are sensitive to salt, When clearing these with salt, place the crystal on a dish and draw a ring of salt around the crystal. (The salt should not touch the crystal.) Then place the dish where it will not be disturbed for 24 hours.

Once the 24-hour period is completed, remove the crystal from the plate and dispose of the salt in a trash can outside of your home. (Tossing the salt in the kitchen garbage will just release the energy back into the house.) Replace the crystal where it was. You'll see an increase in energy within the next few days.

Clearing with Sunlight: you can also clear gemstones and crystals in sunlight. Take the crystal down and wash it thoroughly in clear water and a gentle soap. Dry the crystal with a soft cloth. Place the crystal on a dish outside in the sunlight for a full day. In the evening bring the crystal back into the house and allow it to cool. Then re-hang the crystal where it was. If you don't see an increase in energy in the first week, use one of the other two methods to clear the crystal.

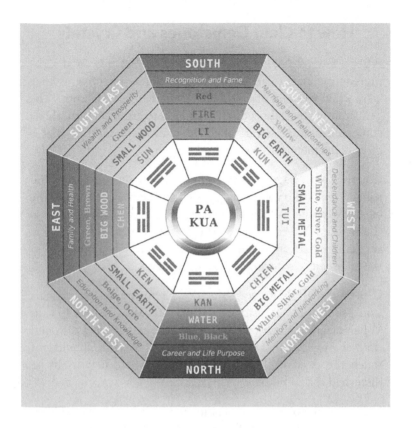

How to Identify the Wealth and Love Areas of Your House

To identify the Wealth areas of your home, stand inside the front door entrance to the house, take the above diagram, and place the side that says "career" up against your closed front door. The diagram will show you the location of the Wealth area.

In fact, you will quickly identify two Wealth areas: one is the far left corner of the entrance area (or, the far left corner of the room where the front door opens into the home). The other important Wealth area in your home is the far left corner of the whole house.

To identify your "love" areas, stand inside your home by your front door. Using the above diagram, place the side that says "career" against your front door.

Now the diagram shows you the location of the Love area in the far right corner of the entrance area (or, the far right corner of the room where the front door opens into the home). The other significant Love area in your home is the far right corner of the house.

Bibliography and Recommended Reading

Bartholomew, Sarah, "Feng Shui: It's Good for Business," ETC Publishing, Carlsbad, CA, 2005

Brown, Simon, "Practical Feng Shui," Wardlock, London, 1997

Carus, Paul, "Chinese Astrology," Open Court, LaSalle, IL, 1974

Chuen, Master Lam Kam, "Personal Feng Shui Manual: How to Develop a Healthy and Harmonious Lifestyle," Henry Holt & Co, New York, 1998

Craze, Richard, "Teach Yourself Chinese Astrology," Arbingdon, England, Bookpoint, 1997

Cunningham, Scott, "Cunningham's Encyclopedia of Crystal, Gem and Metal Magic,."Llewellyn Publications, St. Paul, MN 1988

Cunningham, Scott, "Cunningham's Encyclopedia of Magical Herbs,." Llewellyn Publications, St. Paul, MN 1997

Cunningham, Scott, "The Magic of Food," Llewellyn Publications, St. Paul, MN 1996

Eberhard, Wolfram, "A Dictionary of Chinese Symbols," Routledge, London, 1983

Gong, Rosemary, "Good Luck Life," New York, Harper Collins, 2005

Kwok, Man-Ho, "The Elements of Feng Shui," Elements Books Limited, Dorset, England, 1991

Lau, Kwan, ."Secrets of Chinese Astrology: Handbook for Self-Discovery,." Tengu Books, Trumbull, CT, 1994

Lau, Theodora, "The Handbook of Chinese Horoscopes," New York, Harper & Row, 1979

Lip, Evelyn, "Chinese Numbers," Heian International, Union City, California 1992

Lip, Evelyn, "Chinese Practices and Beliefs," Torrance, Heian International, 2000

Ronngren, Diane, "Color: A Secret Language Revealed," ETC Publishing, Carlsbad, CA, 1997

Ronngren, Diane, "Eclipses," ETC Publishing, Carlsbad, CA, 2001

Ronngren, Diane, "Mercury Retrograde," ETC Publishing, Carlsbad, CA, 2000

Ronngren, Diane, "Sage & Smudge: The Ultimate Guide," ETC Publishing, Carlsbad, CA, 2003

Ronngren, Diane, "Simple Feng Shui Secrets," ETC Publishing, Carlsbad, CA, 2005

Ronngren, Diane and Stellhorn, Donna, "Money and Prosperity Workbook," ETC Publishing, Carlsbad, CA, 1999

Rossbach, Sarah, "Interior Design with Feng Shui," Arkana, London, 1987

Skinner, Stephen, "Flying Star Feng Shui," Tuttle, Boston, MA, 2003

Stellhorn, Donna, "Feng Shui Form," ETC Publishing, Carlsbad, CA, 2006

Stellhorn, Donna, "How to Use Magical Oils," ETC Publishing, Carlsbad, CA, 2002

Stellhorn, Donna, "Sage & Smudge: Secrets to Clearing Your Personal Space," ETC Publishing, Carlsbad, CA, 1999

Sun, Ruth Q, "The Asian Animal Zodiac," Castle Books, Boston, MA, 1974

Tai, Sherman, "Principles of Feng Shui: An Illustrated Guide to Chinese Geomancy," Asiapac Books, Singapore, 1998

Too, Lillian, "Easy-To-Use Feng Shui: 168 Ways to Success," Collins & Brown, London, 1999

Too, Lillian, "Unlocking the Secrets of Chinese Fortune Telling," Metro Books, New York, 2006

Twicken, David, "Classical Five Element Chinese Astrology Made Easy," Writers Club Press, New York, 2000

Twicken, David, "Flying Star Feng Shui Made Easy," Writers Club Press, New York, 2002

Walters, Derek, "Chinese Astrology," Watkins Publishing London, 2002

Walters, Derek, "The Feng Shui Handbook," Aquarian Press, San Francisco, CA 1991

Williams, C.A.S., "Outlines of Chinese Symbolism & Art Motifs," Dover Publications, New York, 1976

Wydra, Nancilee, "Feng Shui: The Book of Cures," Contemporary Books, Lincolnwood, IL 1993

Acknowledgments

I want to thank Diane, Gary and Kelly at ETC Publishing for their support, patience and hard work on these books each year. I couldn't have done it without their help. All their names should be on the cover too.

About Donna Stellhorn

Author, Astrology and Feng Shui expert, Donna Stellhorn, is a speaker, a supportive personal coach, and a practical business consultant, with more than 25 years' experience. In addition to building three successful businesses of her own and logging more than 20,000 hours of consultations with clients, she teaches a variety of classes, offers apprenticeship programs, leads workshops, and continues to write on a variety of topics. She believes in encouraging others to achieve success in their careers and their personal lives.

Donna has written 16 books. Her Chinese Astrology series, of which this book is the latest one, *2020 Chinese Astrology Year of the Metal Rat*, is the most popular Chinese Astrology book series according to Amazon.

One of her earliest books is *Feng Shui Form*. First published in Germany, it is a collection of many of her best and most popular concepts to help her readers create a supportive and comfortable living and working environment.

Her best-selling booklet for more than ten years, *Sage and Smudge: Secrets of Clearing Your Personal Space*, shares the concept of how to cleanse and clear space, objects, or environments.

A recent book is a Feng Shui expert's look at the puzzle of fertility, entitled: *A Path to Pregnancy: Ancient Secrets for the Modern Woman.*

She is currently working on a book—a Feng Shui expert's guide to losing weight by changing how you eat, where you eat and how you store food in the home. This book is: *Plate Size Matters,* and it's coming soon.

Donna lectures on both Chinese Astrology and Western Astrology as well as Feng Shui. Recently, Donna has lectured at Western Digital, Warner Records, Room & Board, the Rancho Santa Fe Water District, Brion Jeannette Architecture, and the San Diego Airport Authority. She's been on Coast to Coast AM with George Noory. She spoke at the 2018 United Astrology Conference in Chicago and the 2019 NCGR conference in Baltimore. Donna writes for Horoscope. com, Astrology.com and Conscious Community magazine. She is on the board of the International Feng Shui Guild and National Council for Geocosmic Research—San Diego.

For fun, Donna does improv comedy with ImprovCity. She lives in Orange County, California with the magical cat, LaRue.

For more information check out Donna's blog, YouTube channel and her website:

Blog: https://fengshuiform.wordpress.com/

YouTube Channel: https://www.youtube.com/c/DonnaStellhorn

Website: http://www.fengshuiform.com/

or email her at donnastellhorn@gmail.com

One last thing...

Thank you so much for purchasing this book. I hope you found the information helpful, and if you did, please let your friends know about it. If you can take a moment and give it a review at your favorite retailer, I would be very grateful.

Made in the USA
Columbia, SC
21 January 2020